ALSO BY PETER BART

Fiction
Destinies
Thy Kingdom Come

Nonfiction
Fadeout: The Calamitious Final Days of MGM
The Gross

WHO KILLED HOLLYWOOD?

WHO KILLED HOLLYWOOD?

...and Put the Tarnish on Tinseltown

PETER BART

RENAISSANCE BOOKS

Los Angeles

Library of Congress Catalog Card Number: 99-068098
ISBN: 1-58063-116-9

10 9 8 7 6 5 4 3 2 1

Design by Jesus Arellano

Published by Renaissance Books
Distributed by St. Martin's Press
Manufactured in the United States of America
First Edition

ACKNOWLEDGMENTS

The columns in this book cover a span of several years during which I benefited from the insights and encouragement of many generous individuals. I am especially grateful to Art Cooper, editor of *GQ*, whose keen intelligence and nihilistic sense of humor steered me through seven years of columnizing for his excellent magazine. Special thanks also go to Lisa Henrickson, the executive editor of *GQ*, for her guidance in thinking through these pieces. I have frequently solicited advice from the reporters and editors of *Variety* during the ten years that I have written a weekly column and from its superbly knowledgeable publisher, Gerry Byrne; without their help, my task would have proved overwhelming. I thank them, both for their suggestions and for their forceful arguments which served to clarify my own thoughts. I owe thanks also to my wife, Blackie, for her encouragement; to my assistant, Bashirah Muttalib, for her diligence; and to my friend Michael Levine for proposing this book to begin with and helping to give it shape and substance. Lastly I owe a debt of gratitude to those many individuals within the world of show business—the artists and the executives and the workers who get the job done—for being informative and candid, even when their responses to my questions posed a danger to their own careers. Without their help this book would have been impossible.

CONTENTS

WHO KILLED HOLLYWOOD?

PREAMBLE

Hollywood is a boomtown—make no mistake about that. The dream factories are pounding out product. American-made movies and TV shows have established an unprecedented hegemony around the world. Show business will shortly become this country's number-one export.

In view of all this, it's no surprise that young people are streaming to Hollywood, seeking fame and fortune even more avidly than they sought out investment banking during the booming '80s. Show biz is suddenly "in." It's the place to be.

Why then do I ask, "Who Killed Hollywood?"

The answer is that Hollywood bears no relationship to the Hollywood that existed through the first eight decades of its development. The studios have lost their identities as seedbeds of pop culture. They've been relegated to a new role as mere appendages of vast multinational corporations grinding out "content" for their global distribution mills. Hollywood's assembly line has been scaled down and retooled, not only to feed the world's movie theaters and TV screens, but also to channel new product and ideas into theme-park rides, music, toys, videos, video game emporiums, and all the other ancillary goodies that enhance the revenue streams of their corporate parents.

The impact of all this is not hard to discern. Given the mania to develop new Disney Worlds, movies themselves have all too often become special-effects odysseys devoid of personal story or point of view. Studios have obsessed on creating "event pictures" and their sequels which can be merchandised in conjunction with McDonald's or other fast-food partners. Budgets of these "megapics," as *Variety* terms them, have soared well beyond the $100 million level, accompanied by marketing outlays of $50 million or more to launch the projects.

Fewer movies are being made. Fewer filmmakers are under contract to the studios. Fewer projects are being developed, and the ones that get the "green light" (that is, approval to start production) are as close to being "risk averse" as possible, tailored to whet the appetites of financing and marketing partners rather than audiences.

I can already hear voices out there protesting, "Hold on, the studios have always chased the Big Bucks. They've always been a dumbing-down force on our society."

While my purpose here is not to defend the Hollywood of Louis B. Mayer and David O. Selznick, I'd argue, however, that the studio system at its best created a diverse menu of shrewdly crafted commercial fare. Survey a list of the ten nominees for Best Picture in 1943: *Casablanca, For Whom the Bell Tolls, In Which We Serve, Heaven Can Wait, The Human Comedy, The More the Merrier, Madame Curie, The Ox-Bow Incident, The Song of Bernadette,* and *Watch on the Rhine.* There's true diversity here—even glints of artistry.

Even in the '60s and '70s, after TV stole much of Hollywood's "habit audience," the studios were turning out edgy movies like *Bonnie and Clyde, The Godfather, Taxi Driver,* and *Chinatown.*

I was right in the middle of the action when Hollywood first spun off its axis. Unexpected blockbusters like *Jaws, Star Wars,* and *ET: The Extraterrestrial* forever changed the way the film factories were regarded by the moneymen. Watching the lines wind around the block at theaters in the U.S. and overseas, the Michael Eisners and Rupert Murdochs of the world recognized that movies were not just a business but a downright bonanza. If a film could make $500 million almost inadvertently, why not build an assembly line that would systematically tap into these markets?

This strategy ignored the fact that nearly all of the early blockbusters were envisioned by their creators as personal films. George Lucas envisioned *Star Wars* not as a sci-fi "event" movie, but as a quirky moral parable. Global giants like Murdoch's News Corporation, Viacom, Seagram, Sony, and the like were not interested in these subtleties, however. Saddled with huge debt, they desperately needed product for their global distribution platforms. The new era of movies-as-merchandise had begun.

For insight into the impact of all this, one need only eavesdrop on the meetings of Hollywood's decision makers. In the late 1960s and 1970s, the debate on whether or not to green-light a picture involved a mere handful of studio executives. I was involved in hundreds of such meetings during stints at three different companies. One executive might comment on the script; another would assess the cast or director. In the end, the key questions usually were: Did the project stand a reasonable chance of finding a mainstream audience in the U.S.? Given the size of the budget, were the downside risks acceptable? Upon occasion, an executive would even be forgiven if he mumbled something inane like, "I think this will be a really good movie."

I vividly recall the abortive debate on whether or not to proceed with the idiosyncratic cult classic *Harold and Maude* starring Bud Cort and Ruth Gordon, a love story with a fifty-year age gap between the lovers. Despite the fact that the script was a hoot and the young director, Hal Ashby, was deemed a real "comer," several of my colleagues understandably didn't "get it." My argument in favor of the project was simple: I felt it was hilarious and unique. Skeptics at the studio finally surrendered mainly because they found the story too annoying to even discuss. "Besides, for $1.2 million, how embarrassed can you be?" proffered one of my colleagues with an air of resignation. Though the quirky comedy opened to empty theaters, it ultimately turned a handsome profit, running on a few screens for over a decade.

Today the decision as to whether to green-light a movie may involve scores of executives, with the debate hinging on questions like: Will the movie play well in Europe and Asia? How strong is the video and DVD aftermarket? Will the subject matter attract marketing partners like a McDonald's? Will there be tie-ins for toys and other merchandising opportunities? Could the story line inspire a theme-park ride? Could the narrative be captured in a brief TV commercial? Will the star be willing to travel to openings around the world? If the budget is north of $60 million, is cofinancing money available? Can the producers find a completion guarantor who will intercede if overages occur?

Welcome to the world of movies-as-merchandise. In the era of the event picture, no one has time to worry about anachronistic issues like whether the story works or the characters are believable. The process of starting a movie is more akin to introducing a new toothpaste, with one major difference: With toothpaste, the key lies in marketing prowess, not in the quality of the product. With a film, every moviegoer in America seems to know from day one whether it works or not. If the movie isn't entertaining, no amount of ad spending can make a difference.

Which steers us right back to the basic question: Who Killed Hollywood? Who's responsible for an environment in which the studios are hellbent on building an assembly line for "event" pictures? How did we find ourselves in a situation where production costs are so high that it's all but impossible to take artistic risks? Who decreed that the primary responsibility of filmmakers is to provide the equivalent of a theme-park ride rather than relating a personal story about believable characters?

Film historian David Thomson has argued that filmmakers like Lucas and Spielberg are principally responsible. As the architects of the modern blockbuster, they have spawned a movie culture bathed in fantasy, utterly reliant on "an intricate set of rigged effects." In the new lexicon of filmmaking, character and story, says Thomson, are reduced to a "cheerful incoherence."

While Thomson has a point, I would argue that their "crime," if indeed there was one, was a case of classic inadvertency. While spawning the modern blockbuster, Spielberg, in *Schindler's List* and *Saving Private Ryan*, and Lucas, in *American Graffiti*, have demonstrated their own genius in mastering "non-event" moviemaking.

I think a more persuasive case could be made that the multinational corporations are themselves the principal transgressors. It is these vast instrumentalities in the hands of Rupert Murdoch, Michael Eisner, Sumner Redstone, and Edgar Bronfman Jr. that, in transforming Hollywood into a "content" factory, have, albeit unintentionally, sapped its creative zeal. Again, these were not acts of corporate malevolence: Ironically, it would be hard to imagine any corporate owners who have admired and understood movies more than Redstone (who started as an exhibitor) or Bronfman (who is also a part-time songwriter). The "enemy," indeed, is not the corporate leadership, but rather the sheer economic weight of the empires they rule. Media leviathans like Time Warner or Disney or News Corp. or Viacom seem to spawn a disease of corporate gigantism. They've become media monsters whose cyberspace circuitry has somehow become perversely crossed. How else could one explain the bizarre and self-destructive escalation in production costs that has spawned movies with budgets of $150 million and beyond?

The problem with these megapics of course is that, like *Godzilla*, they crumble under their own weight. Because of the sheer magnitude of the investment, corporate committees intervene at every opportunity to offer "advice" about cast, story line, and other "creative issues." Deputations from Burger King, Pepsi, and the like also increasingly have their input. Soulless, by-the-numbers megapics like *Twister* or *Godzilla* are the inevitable result. Movies become "product," just as ideas become "content," and studio executives become mere corporate apparatchiks.

Will the studios be able to reverse this cycle? Reversals have happened before. I was a young studio executive in the 1970–71 movie recession when several production entities simply packed up and left the party. Movie stars went for months without offers and soundstages stood empty. At Paramount, a small band of executives quietly moved off the lot to reestablish a beachhead in a suite of offices on Canon Drive. The back lot itself was peddled to a maverick band of foreign investors loosely connected with the Vatican Bank—a deal which ultimately collapsed. From its tiny new headquarters, the "new Paramount" embarked on a production schedule that was in sharp contrast to the elephantine disasters that the studio had lately been turning out—no more *Darling Lili*s or *Paint Your Wagon*s. Instead what emerged was a string of modest-budget hits such as *The Godfather, Rosemary's Baby, Chinatown, Romeo and Juliet, The Longest Yard,* and *Harold and Maude*. All of which reminds us that Hollywood is a resilient place.

It would be hard to imagine this scenario ever repeating itself, however. In the early 1970s the studios were mostly small, single-product companies led by noncorporate types like Ted Ashley or Arthur Krim. These men could sit down with a star and honestly say, "We don't have twenty million bucks to pay you—we're tapped out." Under no circumstances could a Rupert Murdoch make that statement. Given the monumental resources of the multinational corporations, the demands of stars and star filmmakers will continue to escalate. Further, it's hard to imagine the vast production bureaucracies that rule the studios today agreeing to move to more modest quarters, as Paramount once did. The proposition that ten could do the work of two hundred would cause civil insurrection.

More likely Hollywood's future, in part, resides in the hands of what is loosely termed "the independent sector." These are companies like Miramax, October, Fine Line, Fox 2000, and the like—the very entities that have been stealing the thunder from the majors at recent Oscar races. In reality, of course, these companies are not independent at all, but are owned by the very studios they so frequently upstage.

Why have the majors been quietly buying up these maverick players? The reason is that the majors see in them the seeds of their own salvation.

Suddenly bigger isn't necessarily better. Decisions do not have to be made by corporate committees. It's permissible to factor in whether a filmmaker has a passion to risk a particular film, not just whether McDonald's wants to help sell it.

If they continue to prosper under their new corporate parents, the independents may help remind Hollywood of some valuable lessons. As stated earlier, the movie business has long since shown its talent for reinventing itself. The studios may some day emerge from their corporate cocoons and, phoenix-like, take on a fresh identity. After all, the old tycoons who founded them once called them "dream factories." All they require is a new dream.

PART I

SUITS

Occupying center stage in corporate Hollywood are a cluster of highly competitive megamoguls intent on global dominance in the media and entertainment industry. In December 1996, I sought to analyze the personalities and motivations of these movers and shakers. In so doing, to be sure, I had little inkling that it would be young Bronfman who would imminently run into the most serious thicket of difficulties. Further, I did not realize that Frank Biondi, the CEO that Sumner Redstone fired and Bronfman hired, would soon be axed by Bronfman as well.

THE NEW MOGULS

The first time I met Edgar Bronfman Jr., we took a short stroll across the Universal Studios lot, which he owns. No one took any particular notice of the slender billionaire heir to the Seagram fortune, which was OK with Bronfman. A soft-spoken, thoughtful man of 42, he has never especially liked reception committees. As we chatted about Universal's far-flung operations, his comments were astute but guarded. Finally, I said, "So here it is. It's all yours. What do you want to do with it?"

Bronfman peered at me. "As I explained earlier, there's a substantial list of strategic objectives. . . ."

"But I mean change. Quick change. Instant gratification. What would it be?"

Bronfman stopped walking and stared at the somber buildings that surrounded us. He made an expansive gesture. "I would change the way all this looks," he replied with a pained smile. "The whole lot . . . there is no plan, no style."

"It has been called the ugliest lot in Hollywood," I said.

Bronfman nodded. "It will change," he said simply.

The conversation took place several months ago, and already the face of the Universal lot is changing rapidly. The Black Tower presided over by the fabled Lew Wasserman is being renovated and redesigned, its antique furniture tossed onto the woodpile. Other ragtag structures are receiving a face-lift, and a new, fifteen-year master plan is being hammered out for the entire 440-acre Universal City lot, which is visited annually by some two million tourists. All this is happening not because some committee of corporate bureaucrats deemed it appropriate but because Edgar Jr. wanted it, and what Edgar wants, Edgar gets.

And why not? After all, it's his candy store. Indeed, Bronfman is one of a vanguard of new leaders who have taken command in Hollywood—men who don't simply work for huge global entertainment companies but actually own them. Because of this ownership, their power and standing is unique in the annals of Hollywood, a community that respects power and knows how to manipulate it. Even the moguls of old—the Louis B. Mayers and Harry Cohns—had to report to the moneymen in New York, who ultimately controlled their destinies. Not so the new moguls of '90s Hollywood. As the costs—and risks—of playing in the worldwide entertainment industry have grown exponentially, show biz has become a sport of kings, not kingmakers.

This new royalty can be divided into two tiers. On top are Bronfman; Sumner Redstone, who owns Viacom; and Rupert Murdoch, who controls the vast News Corporation. Michael Eisner of Disney is an honorary member of this group; even though he doesn't own enough stock to control the Disney empire directly, his domination of the board of directors is so complete that he might as well. Another honorary member is Ted Turner, who has been active in guiding his TV holdings, such as CNN, but has not chosen to be hands-on with his various movie entities, such as New Line and Turner Pictures.

In the second tier of owner-managers are such stalwarts as Harvey Weinstein of Miramax, Bob Shaye of New Line, and the team of Steven Spielberg, David Geffen, and Jeffrey Katzenberg of DreamWorks. None of these men preside over the sort of media leviathan controlled by Rupert Murdoch, but they nonetheless run powerful machines that manufacture "content," which in turn is devoured by the distribution arms of the media empires. And once again, they don't just manage companies—they, too, own the candy store.

Spending time with these men, one is struck by how little they have in common. They range in age from 42 (Bronfman) to 73 (Redstone). Harvey Weinstein is as thunderously extroverted as Murdoch is reserved. And as mind-bendingly wealthy and successful as Spielberg is, it would be hard to find anyone easier to talk to—he actually listens, asks questions, and makes eye contact. Michael Eisner, on the other hand, tells you what he thinks, and when he is done, he basically tells you to get the hell out of there. Sumner Redstone can be imperious, but he can also be the benevolent grandpa, gracious and patient with his visitors, often flashing a glint of sly humor. A discussion with David Geffen is like a running argument—he tells you where he stands and seems irked if you do not respond with equal fervor. Shaye is utterly mercurial: Get him in the right mood and he will be charming if not downright ingratiating, but touch the wrong button and you can expect to be conversationally nuked.

Though each approaches his job with a messianic zeal, their styles are, again, sharply divergent. Redstone says he's the most hands-on. When he dismissed Frank J. Biondi Jr. as his CEO, Redstone complained about Biondi's propensity to delegate key tasks, such as negotiating big output deals with European TV networks. While Biondi supposedly relied on his senior executives to make these billion-dollar deals, Redstone, the septuagenarian, climbed into his corporate jet to confront his European customers face-to-face.

By contrast, Bronfman, the man who promptly hired Biondi when Redstone fired him, is keen on delegating authority. Though he talks to his top executives at the studio every day and keeps up-to-date on deals, Bronfman spends more time in New York than in

Hollywood. An occasional songwriter, he also stays closer to the music industry than to the arcane details of movies or TV.

When a motion picture is completed at Miramax, it's all but impossible to keep rotund, roisterous Harvey Weinstein out of the editing room. But Rupert Murdoch would rather have a root canal than suggest cuts for one of Twentieth Century Fox's upcoming motion pictures. Indeed, some contend that Murdoch's attitude toward movies is fatalistic. I encountered him arriving at the first public screening of Fox's expensive Arnold Schwarzenegger action comedy *True Lies*. Another Schwarzenegger epic, *Last Action Hero*, had bombed for Columbia Pictures only a few months before, and Fox executives were fearful that *True Lies* might meet a similar fate. Their boss, however, seemed almost cavalier.

"Good luck," I said to him as I made my way to my seat.

"Let's just hope we haven't accidentally made *Last Action Hero*, Part II," Murdoch shot back with a grin.

This is not to suggest that Murdoch doesn't covet hits. Indeed, he demands them. Whatever their differences, the one trait that all the owner-managers have in common is their ferocious appetite not just for success but for megasuccess.

When the Redstones, Bronfmans, and Murdochs first took command of their ships, some showbiz experts predicted that they would exert a moderating influence in the Hollywood marketplace. It was candy-store logic: Since they were playing with their money, in their own stores, frugality would prevail.

Not exactly. This logic did not allow for the fact that the owners were even more zealously competitive than the previous generation of corporate managers. Bronfman is a vivid case in point. Under his aegis, Universal has committed to a wide range of deals with stars and filmmakers—Sylvester Stallone, Demi Moore, the Zucker brothers, Mike Nichols, and Danny DeVito, through the company he co-owns, Jersey Films. Bronfman also extended Imagine Entertainment's deal, keeping it on the lot until 2001, and bought fifty percent of Brillstein-Grey, the managers and producers who count Brad Pitt and Nicolas Cage among their clients. Bronfman's defenders insist that Universal was faced with a shortfall of talent at the time of the acquisition and that the new owner has simply been responding to that brain drain.

All of which raises the most interesting question: Why are these men willing to risk their money and their reputations in such a volatile business? What's driving them? The easy answer is glamour—the old seduction of Hollywood. But does this stand up? Rupert Murdoch is about as interested in movie stars as Boris Yeltsin was in AA meetings. Bob Shaye would sooner read a good novel than attend a Hollywood premiere, and Redstone, who started out as an exhibitor, would rather study a computer printout of theater grosses than read a new script.

A more likely explanation is that each of the players in Hollywood's neo-Napoleonic era is pursuing a private dream—one that is only partially visible even to intimates. The most obvious component is simply recognition. Edgar Bronfman could have remained in obscurity, steering the family's booze business, but understandably, he found that a boring prospect. The Bronfman family gave up its twenty-four-percent stake in DuPont by selling $8.8 billion in stock to finance the buyout of MCA-Universal. Similarly, Sumner Redstone, when he was 71, could have sat back and basked in the glory of his achievements. His Viacom empire consisted of such superb franchises as MTV and Nickelodeon, which were as hip as they were profitable. At an age when many men retire to Florida, Redstone embarked on an acquisition drive that brought him the Paramount studio, the huge Blockbuster Video chain, the publishing house Simon & Schuster, and other entities. Some Wall Street analysts think that the Viacom franchise is no better bet for investors now than it was before these mammoth acquisitions. Redstone disagrees. He's having the time of his life, racing around the world in his jet, locking up still more franchises.

Other motives are also driving the new moguls. Take DreamWorks. Why did three high-profile players like Spielberg, Geffen, and

Katzenberg decide to put their lives on hold in order to raise the staggering sum of $2.7 billion to start their enterprise? In the case of Spielberg, it was, in part, a question of finding a new toy. No filmmaker had ever designed his own soundstages and postproduction facilities. Indeed, no one had built a studio from scratch in the three generations since the so-called golden age of the studio system.

For Jeffrey Katzenberg, creating DreamWorks provided a delicious form of revenge. The hyperactive executive had been a virtual appendage of Michael Eisner, first at Paramount, then at Disney, for almost a quarter of a century, but their relationship ended in a nasty swirl of litigation in 1994, when Eisner declined to give him the number-two job at Disney. What could be sweeter for Katzenberg than to have the muscle to compete with his mentor?

Of all the new moguls, none remains as inscrutable as Rupert Murdoch, arguably the boldest and most innovative of the tribe. A 65-year-old billionaire who exerts enormous influence over the world's opinionmakers, Murdoch continues to astonish his competitors with his risk taking. "Rupert wants to rule the world, and he seems to be doing it," says his feisty rival Redstone, who regards Murdoch with a mixture of annoyance and admiration.

As one of Murdoch's top lieutenants points out, "Every year, just when you think that Rupert might start behaving like a senior citizen, he seems to ratchet up the energy level one more time. Look at him now—he's out there, way out there."

Six years ago, Murdoch almost lost control of his company as a result of rampant indebtedness. Was he chastened by the experience? If so, why is he coping with Star TV partners in Asia, Canal Fox associates in Latin America, and UTV allies in India while trying to realign the digital-TV future of Europe? Why is he closing a $3-billion buyout of Ronald Perelman's New World Communications Group while juggling executives at the Fox TV network and bankrolling huge films at Twentieth Century Fox?

The evidence would suggest that not only does Murdoch court controversy but he also seems to be energized by it. So far-reaching and complex is his empire, that almost wherever he turns trouble follows. The Chinese have expressed their extreme impatience with his expansionist philosophy in Asia. The Japanese government this fall took the extraordinary action of rejecting Murdoch's attempt to name his top representative in Japan to the board of a major broadcaster, Asahi, in which Murdoch owns a 21.4-percent stake. This spurred Murdoch to take to the Japanese airwaves to plead his case. And Europe's media community is irate over what it perceives to be Murdoch's effort to establish an oligarchy in global sportscasting.

Murdoch's company already approaches $10.4 billion in annual sales and encompasses everything from newspapers (the *New York Post*, *The Times of London*) to broadcast media (British Sky Broadcasting) to books (HarperCollins) to magazines (*TV Guide*)— what more is there to grab? And why would he want potentially to destabilize his existing empire to invest in satellites that beam TV directly into households around the world? Is it ideology? Some fret about the global reach of media oligarchs like Murdoch, fearing that he may use his power to force his politics on a huge audience. I do not share this fear. Murdoch leans to the extreme right, but he is basically a businessman, not an ideologue.

Wall Street, for one, refuses to buy Murdoch's act. While investment bankers admire his vision and are dazzled by some of his money moves, the stock of Murdoch's News Corp. still hovers around $22 a share, which he regards as something of an insult.

When you sit down and talk with Rupert Murdoch, you do not come away with the feeling that you are in the company of a megalomaniac, or any kind of maniac for that matter. He comes off as a thoroughly reasonable, rather sage man who is intellectually engaged, if not obsessed, with the revolution sweeping the global communications industry and who wishes to fill the power vacuum that it is creating. If he has correctly judged the course of this revolution, Murdoch will achieve a special kind of immortality: He will cast a shadow over the world's media for generations to come.

It is too early to assess the ultimate impact of the new breed of owner-managers. Since they are such a disparate lot, their influence may be too difficult to chart. Ironically, the basic commodity that attracted them to begin with—variously called "content" or "intellectual property"—may sow the seeds of their disarray. It is yet to be seen whether vast multinational corporations can truly manage creative output for their own growth and profit. Some seers in the entertainment business predict that to survive, the big companies will ultimately subdivide into smaller, autonomous units, responding to the whims of the artists and also those of the investors who are seeking "pure play" deals. This in turn will fragment the holdings of the moguls, who may opt to retire to the sidelines.

In the short term, however, all signals point in the other direction, as the new moguls continue to play chicken with one another, expanding the frontiers of their empires. Sumner Redstone may have been speaking facetiously when he said Rupert Murdoch wanted to rule the world, but he may also have been hinting that, were Murdoch to fail, he, Redstone, would like to take a shot at it himself.

—*GQ*, December 1996

.   .   .

By the summer of 1996, Rupert Murdoch's insatiable appetite for acquisitions increasingly troubled the entertainment community. How could one man make so many deals on so many continents? Following publication of this column in Variety *at that time, Murdoch the Marauder seemed to become even more hyperactive, divorcing his wife and plunging into a still more chaotic agenda of dealmaking.*

TALE OF MULTIPLE MURDOCHS

We are entering that part of the summer when denizens of the news business bemoan the absence of "hard news," so perhaps it's time to examine an oddball theory that's making the rounds of the media community. To wit: That there really is no Rupert Murdoch but that the vast empire known as News Corp. is run by a post-Murdochian junta of faceless apparatchiks who are making decisions in his name.

"Absurd!" you might say. Murdoch is a mainstay of the business. He is ubiquitous, at any given time closing immense deals in Buenos Aires, Berlin, and Beijing.

But that, of course, is exactly the point. How could any one man appear in all the places Murdoch is supposed to have been? the conspiracy theorists ask. How could a 65-year-old individual simultaneously be coping with Star TV partners in Asia, UTV allies in India, and Canal Fox associates in Latin America, while at the same time be realigning the digital-TV future of Europe and fervently celebrating the success of *Independence Day* in Hollywood?

By the way, this alleged Murdoch also managed earlier this month to sneak in a $2.5-billion buyout of Ronald Perelman's New World, thus sinking the shaft into King World, which thought it had also closed a Perelman deal.

Given this whirlwind, it's little wonder that conspiratorial types have propounded the theory that Rupert Murdoch had actually been overthrown in a silent coup amid his financial crunch six years ago, to be succeeded by a committee of fearsome activists. The apparent contradictions in the behavior of the "alleged Murdoch" represent a significant clue, they argue.

If there were actually one Rupert Murdoch, the argument goes, how could he be at once a rampant ideologue and a cool-headed pragmatist? How could he be such an ardent purveyor of tabloid trash, and also admire good art and music and pursue a personal lifestyle embodying good taste? If there were a single Rupert, how could associates laud him as being a gracious and supportive boss, but also fear him for turning on employees so coldly? How could he be so adept at piling on debt, yet so persuasive with bankers about wanting to reduce it?

Again, if Rupert were really one person, would he really give a damn about clinging to a paper like the *New York Post* at a time when he was redrawing the map of TV and sports all around the globe? Why would he care?

Now, I personally discount the multiple-Murdoch theory, but, on the other hand, I can also testify to having witnessed these oddly divergent traits. I remember running into him at the first public screening of Twentieth Century Fox's Arnold Schwarzenegger epic *True Lies*, which opened not all that long after Schwarzenegger's Sony debacle. Filing past his ashen, pinch-faced executives, Murdoch saw me and quipped, "Well, I sure hope this doesn't turn out to be '*The Last Action Hero*, Part II.'" Rupert enjoyed this mordant jest; a couple of his executives looked like they were about to have a seizure.

On the other hand, I have been with Murdoch when, in response to a question, his face would tighten and his eyes screw up as he recited from memory the most arcane data of some complex international co-venture.

The Rupert who enjoys gossiping about the foibles of rival megacompanies—a truly humorous and charming Rupert—can just as quickly become a somber, gray-faced analyst of how to cope with Chinese bureaucrats or European "left-wingers." I have rarely witnessed anyone so eminently reasonable transmogrify into someone so supremely doctrinaire.

Do I believe there are multiple Murdochs? No. Do I believe Rupert exhibits symptoms of a multiple-personality syndrome? Possibly. Do I believe that any 65-year-old man can single-handedly mobilize so many deals in so many places? Not quite.

One longtime associate of his put it this way: "As Rupert gets older, he keeps turning up the energy level, making more and more demands on himself. It's daunting."

Hearing this, I couldn't resist asking him, "Do you think there's really one Rupe or rather a Rupe Group?" Turning away, he snapped, "That's the stupidest thing I ever heard." Then he looked back at me for a beat and said, "Do you mind running that theory by me one more time?"

—*Variety*, July 29, 1996

.   .   .

Despite initial good impressions, Edgar Bronfman Jr., by spring 1998, seemed to have his hands full with a growing array of problems. After this column was published in April of that year, he completed a $10.2-billion acquisition of Polygram, a global giant in the music and film arena. Sensing that Polygram's movie division was redundant, he unsuccessfully tried to sell it off for $1 billion. His frustration only increased when Universal's own program of pricey movies, including Meet Joe Black *and the sequel to* Babe, *failed miserably at the box office in the fall and winter of '98.*

HOLLYWOOD MAKES ANOTHER U-TURN

MEMO TO: Edgar Bronfman Jr.

Have you noticed a whirring sound lately, Edgar? It may be unfamiliar to you, but those of us who have worked in Hollywood for a time know it all too well.

That whir is the sound of Hollywood collectively turning on someone, Edgar. In this case, turning on you. It's a remarkable phenomenon when you come right down to it. One moment someone is a hero of show biz, the next a bad guy.

Three years ago I remember talking to you in the Black Tower and you were brimming with optimism about your newly acquired company. Wherever you went in town, everyone applauded your gracious manner and your resolve to energize Universal.

So what's gone wrong? Magazines and newspapers are lining up to blast you. The revisionist thinking on your deal with Barry Diller is that Barry got the best of you. The sudden removal from Universal last week of the popular auteur-attorney Howard Weitzman set you up for still more barbs.

You can't even deliver a simple speech without everyone nattering at you—witness what happened last week at *Variety*'s Big Picture conference when you advocated more flexible ticket pricing. Others have made that proposal without getting zapped by both the trade and the press.

As one of the town's top agents told me last week, "We all understand where Rupert Murdoch wants to take his company. We understand Michael Eisner. We don't get Edgar."

That's certainly one of your key problems, Edgar—that old saw known as "the vision thing." We have all heard your complaints that Wall Street undervalues Universal relative to other showbiz megacompanies. Your much-advertised "re-engineering" program will save Universal some $150 million a year, you remind us, which in turn should help trigger a twenty-percent annual earnings growth over the next few years, before taxes, interest, and depreciation. Yet there's been no major bump in the stock price reflecting these optimistic forecasts.

I guess the problem is that "re-engineering" isn't equated with "vision," Edgar. People who follow Universal are still confused about too many things.

First and foremost, of course, there's the Diller issue. Your various spokesmen may keep emphasizing that you have deftly positioned yourself to ultimately take over Diller's empire several years down the road, should you opt to do so, but the fact remains that Hollywood is persuaded that you have let the fox into the henhouse—that Diller is positioned to take you over.

Part of your problem in conveying your point of view, Edgar, is that no one else at Universal has exercised an especially persuasive "voice." Your principal executives are very likable and respected professionals, but no one seems to want to take on the mantle of the spokesman. They are "inside" men, not "outside" men. Just like you.

Even apart from Diller, there's the movie conundrum. How can it be, the town asks, that Universal will have no major movies out there this summer? *Godzilla* may cast a long shadow, but surely the studio could muster up at least one big movie to give it a run for its money.

Again, Casey Silver, your production chief, is much admired by the creative community. But it's not unreasonable for outsiders to speculate that there must be something wrong with the corporate machinery above Silver—too many consultants or too many executive shifts—that may have partially immobilized the decision-making process.

Last year the studio generated such hits as *Liar Liar* and *Jurassic Park*: *The Lost World*. But it got saddled with the Bubble Factory deal—an arrangement that, sources say, might have cost Universal in excess of $150 million.

Primary Colors has only helped spread the malaise. That much-ballyhooed Mike Nichols movie, which cost north of $65 million, will generate only about $40 million in domestic B.O.

Meanwhile, the major deal-making announcements involving Universal seem to come from satellite companies like Imagine and Beacon. Silver's group has a bundle of interesting projects in the works as well, but they're following the Universal mantra—silence is golden.

In past conversations, Edgar, you have spoken enthusiastically about your plans for the theme park business, especially your vast expansion in Orlando. But inevitably all this will be overshadowed in the short term by the hoopla emanating from your Orlando neighbor, Disney. They're opening their billion-dollar Animal Kingdom, reminding everyone that their dinosaurs are sexier than your dinosaurs.

Then there's your real first love—music. Universal has made considerable strides in this sector, to be sure, but somehow that big announcement that everyone had expected has never been made.

None of this is intended to remotely suggest that all is lost, Edgar. Your reign at Universal is only starting, I realize, and it's not your nature to rush headlong into things. Moreover, you have all those people mumbling in your ear about the DuPont holdings—that Seagram shares are now worth twenty-five percent more since the Universal acquisition while DuPont shares have more than doubled in value (Seagram sold its 24.2-percent stake in DuPont in 1995 before buying eighty percent of Universal).

My principal message here is a simple reminder that you'll need a very strong stomach to keep moving ahead in the entertainment business. The combination of your gracious low-key nature and your behind-the-scenes management style inevitably will set you up to take a lot of guff.

Here's the reality: Today's vast entertainment megacompanies are more akin to nation-states. They need to have extroverted, communicative spokesmen at the helm. Investors and creative partners alike want to know their aims and objectives.

Universal has accomplished some admirable things over the past three years. It's also become something like a stealth missile, trying to fly beneath the radar.

That can't be done, Edgar. Bigness is both a blessing and a curse. That's why, like it nor not, it's your turn in the barrel.

—*Variety*, April 13, 1998

. . .

In firing his CEO, Frank Biondi, Edgar Bronfman Jr. helped increase the ranks of Hollywood's "golden parachute" club—executives who regularly seemed to benefit to the tune of tens of millions of dollars from their abrupt dismissals. Biondi's achievement inspired the following commentary in Variety *on November 23, 1998.*

FIRED UP OVER GETTING FIRED

A wave of firings always seems to hit Hollywood as the holidays draw near, reminding us of the industry's unique spin on the Christmas spirit. Not surprisingly, Frank Biondi was this wave's best-known victim.

I say not surprisingly because the 53-year-old Biondi has truly raised getting fired to an art form. The Harvard Business School should require careful study of his exit skills, his civility in accepting dismissal, his generous words for the boss who fired him, and, finally, the consistency with which he extracts extraordinary largess.

Biondi is surely the superstar of the golden-parachute set, a man who has turned two firings in three years into a $45 million windfall.

Always self-effacing, Biondi would be loath to boast of his skills, but were he to create a manual called "How to Get Rich by

Getting Canned," I think its guidelines would read something like this:

Always recruit your boss, don't let them find you.

Be sure you and your new boss are fundamentally incompatible in terms of style and temperament.

Work diligently in your initial months on the job to exacerbate these differences.

Encourage your new company to deal off that sector of the business that constitutes your principal specialty, thus rendering you irrelevant.

Create a public image through press interviews and industry speeches that is at once respected yet invisible.

Construct an exit strategy focusing on lavish perks that cannot possibly be withdrawn or rescinded upon termination.

Always speak well of your former bosses so that, if necessary, you can make the rounds yet again.

In implementing these stratagems, Biondi set about becoming CEO first of Viacom, then Universal, thus putting himself under the aegis of two hands-on, get-it-done bosses in Sumner Redstone and Edgar Bronfman Jr. Both Redstone and Bronfman are unique in that they essentially own as well as manage their corporate empires. As such, both manifest a need for instant gratification when it comes to achieving strategic objectives.

Even at age 75, Redstone always seems to be climbing aboard his jet, intent on negotiating a complex deal. To be sure, this impulse was inconsistent with Biondi's Harvard-bred philosophy whose central dictate was "don't do it if you can delegate it."

In his position at Universal, which entailed a move to Los Angeles, Biondi's low-key approach began to border on the laconic. No one was especially shocked, therefore, when Bronfman flew West last week to have a dialogue with his CEO. As disclosed by Biondi, Bronfman said, "Frank, I want to be more hands-on. Therefore, please resign."

"So I did," replied Biondi, flashing his customary eloquence.

This episode seemed inevitable as a result of Universal's move last year to deal off its cable TV assets to Barry Diller. In making this deal, Biondi was left managing such assets as theme parks, movies, and music, for which he had little firsthand experience.

I once had a vivid conversation with Biondi in which I asked him how he felt about running a music company. "It's a business," Biondi replied.

It was insights like this that had earned Biondi a heavy schedule of invitations to make speeches before industry groups and to dispense interviews to reporters. In his public addresses, he was at once statesmanlike and soporific, leaving audiences consistently puzzled as to what he had imparted.

In dealing with the press, Biondi mastered the technique of the quoteless interview. A *Variety* survey of journalists who had interviewed Biondi over the past year revealed that, while ninety percent approved of his graciousness, only five percent could remember a single point that he'd espoused or could quote a single epiphany.

It was Biondi's exit strategy that clearly made the most vivid impact on industry colleagues, however. In moving West for Universal, Biondi had secured a commitment from the studio to construct a $2.5-million screening room. His deal provided that Universal could reclaim the studio upon termination, though it was unclear why Universal would need a screening room in Brentwood.

The $2.5-million cost also raised a few eyebrows, even from those familiar with the construction of screening rooms. I consulted one expert who commented: "Even if the room had a sound system that put the Academy theater to shame, I'm frankly puzzled, unless he's installed velvet curtains with gold tassels, silk moiré–padded walls and leopardskin art deco seats with snakeskin piping."

One rumor had it that the studio also had built him a clay tennis court with underground sprinklers. But Biondi, with his customary modesty, consistently denied it, even though his tennis game has shown remarkable improvement over the past year.

Having superbly implemented his strategies, would Frank Biondi find a new corporate home?

I put this question to one distinguished headhunter and his reply was immediate. "Of course some company will seek him out," he assured me. "Any man who can negotiate parachutes like that could also negotiate mergers and acquisitions. There'll always be a market for his skills."

I asked Biondi to comment on this observation, and he had a good reply. For the life of me, I cannot recall what it was, however.

—*Variety*, November 23, 1998

. . .

Ted Turner became the wealthiest of the media hierarchs as the share price of Time Warner kept climbing throughout 1998. But, following the absorption of CNN and the other Turner networks into the vast Time Warner behemoth, it was increasingly difficult to figure out what Turner's role would be, if he wanted to have one at all, as I pointed out in this column late in 1996.

IS TED IN TURNER-ROUND?

MEMO TO: Ted Turner

FROM: Peter Bart

While no one has ever accused you of being an open book, Ted, the job of Turner-tracking these days has become increasingly demanding. Take your New York adventures of a week ago: All of us were greatly amused by your efforts to rattle Rupert's cage, but the precise objective of all this hyperbole remained somewhat obscure. Similarly, while we empathized with your impromptu exit in the middle of your Friars Club tribute, how many awards can anyone harvest in the course of a week? Arguably you could have decided that the Friars were expendable before the banquet, not during it.

Then there's all the shuffling of your movie assets. New Line is being shopped this week to potential buyers, Turner Pictures is slated to be absorbed into the Warner hierarchy, and Castle Rock is also up for grabs. Only a couple of years ago you lavished so much affection on these companies they became known as Ted's Toys. Suddenly they're toys in the attic.

When I first met you a decade ago you were in the midst of acquiring MGM/UA from Kirk Kerkorian and you told me in no uncertain terms that you loved the movie business and intended to make a major commitment to that studio. Somewhere in the middle of that process your passions shifted: You bought the library instead of the studio. There have been other sudden shifts along the way. Your people at TNT seem to feel that you put a production called "Strange Justice" on hold because of fears it would offend Justice Clarence Thomas at a time when the Supreme Court was deliberating over cable deregulation. Say it ain't so, Ted.

Your attitudes toward CNN also have been hard to track. Some months ago you seemed poised to implement significant changes at the all-news network in light of all the new competition. Whatever happened to those changes, Ted? CNN is still a terrific enterprise with new sports and financial offshoots, but aren't you worried about all those newsies nipping at your ankles?

Now, we realize you've had a lot on your mind lately, Ted. The astonishing corporate behemoth called Time Warner Turner has only recently come into existence, and there are myriad policy questions to be hammered out. During your award marathon last week, you chose to articulate some of your concerns in the context of vivid World War II metaphors. Before the merger, you said, "I'd thought of myself as Poland caught between Germany and the U.S.S.R." After the merger, you confided: "I'd shake all night like the German children did in 1944." German children?

Well, you may be shaky one moment, but you seem pretty unyielding whenever Rupert comes up. During one banquet, you ad-libbed: "Since Murdoch's newspapers keep saying I'm insane, doesn't that mean that if I shoot him I'll get off?"

These are vintage Turnerisms all right, but, again, they don't quite track. The metaphors change as quickly as the attitudes.

Which brings us back to the basic question many are asking, namely, what is your real attitude about your role in Time Warner Turner? Are you going to become Super-Suit, jousting for power in New York? Or will you be the Anti-Suit, safely ensconced at your Montana ranches? Some of your longtime associates say they still don't know the answer to this question and, more important, that you don't know either.

That, indeed, is why Turner-tracking has become such an inscrutable task. One moment you love the movie business, the next you're fleeing from it. One moment you covet awards, the next you're walking out on one.

Now, we realize you've always seen yourself as the Lone Ranger of the media landscape. Nonetheless, now that Time Warner Turner has become a reality, your constituencies are looking for clear lines, not dotted lines. They want direction, not hyperbole. They want you to stop accepting awards and start dictating policies.

That is a helluva spot to be in, isn't it?

—*Variety*, November 18, 1996

.   .   .

While the titans who run the worldwide entertainment industry are hardly an introspective lot, Michael Eisner, following his heart attack, decided to complete his memoir, entitled Work in Progress, *which conveyed more insights about the Disney empire than it did about its boss, as I discussed in the fall of 1998.*

MEMOIRS FROM THE MOUSE HOUSE

Of all the chieftains of the global entertainment companies that own Hollywood, Michael Eisner can be the most engaging. He has a sly wit, likes to gossip and to crack self-deprecating jokes, and, most important, actually shows a keen fascination for his company's product, not just its financial or distribution structure.

Indeed, in the forward to his newly published memoir, *Work in Progress,* he describes his role at Disney not just as CEO, but also as chief creative officer. What other corporate head would so describe himself?

And what other CEO would admit that he had no training in business and, midway in his career, couldn't even read a balance sheet? The prospect of taking an accounting course at UCLA was so painful that he begged his wife, Jane, to take it with him, and both were taunted by their three sons each night as they agonized over homework.

It is Eisner's engaging personality, not to mention his formidable achievements, that makes his curious memoir such a good read. I say "curious" because it is a book of almosts. It is almost an autobiography, almost a business book, almost even a "tell-all." Almost, but not quite. Eisner is too subtle, too self-protective, and involved in too much litigation to let his guard down and tell us what he really thinks about his competitors or his principal executives, past and present. As such, the chief of the Mouse House plays something of a cat-and-mouse game with the reader.

But there are plenty of goodies for those willing to plunge through the 434 pages.

On Jeffrey Katzenberg

Eisner was offended when, less than thirty-six hours after the death of Frank Wells, Katzenberg delivered an ultimatum that "either I get Frank's job as president or I'm going to leave the company."

When Katzenberg visited Eisner in the hospital after he awoke from surgery, "rather than being supportive and offering to do what he could to help, he seemed distant and uncomfortable."

Eisner felt it a conflict of interest for Katzenberg to launch with Steven Spielberg a restaurant chain called Dive. Though Wells gave it his OK, Eisner argued that it was competitive with Disney ventures, put Katzenberg in an impossible position to be in business with Spielberg at Disney, and was a foolish use of his time.

Katzenberg had his own version of these events, to be sure, and filed a lawsuit to reinforce them.

On Michael Ovitz

Though Ovitz had always been secretive and covert, Eisner was shocked at how Ovitz "became a moth to the media flame" after coming to Disney.

Ovitz was hellbent on making deals and acquisitions at Disney, even though Eisner says he kept lecturing him that "the deal is not the essence of Disney, operations are the thing."

Ovitz's aversion to operations was such that he continued to duck meetings with Steve Bollenbach, the chief financial officer, who wanted to familiarize him with the numbers.

All this runs counter to the contention of Ovitz supporters at the time who said he was never given operational responsibility and that no one reported to him.

Apart from these intrigues, however, Eisner's book presents in vivid detail the story of Disney's turnaround from a company with a market value of $2 billion in 1984 to one of $75 billion in 1997. It does not duck the difficulties of the Euro theme park near Paris nor the failed attempt to build a historical theme park in Virginia. "We failed to recognize how deeply people felt about maintaining their communities just as they are," said Eisner, a man who likes to change everything.

The timing of the memoir is ironic, to be sure. It is a book about astonishing growth that comes out at a moment in time when Disney stock has been taking a beating and analysts are questioning whether Disney can return to its annual twenty-percent growth rate.

Further, Disney and DreamWorks are about to go head-to-head on the animation front with two bug epics, not to mention Disney's competitive efforts to nullify the clout of *Prince of Egypt*, Katzenberg's centerpiece for DreamWorks.

So why would a man as busy and preoccupied as Eisner take the time to write a memoir at this hyperactive moment in his life?

Ask Eisner and he'll tell you he started the book five years ago in concert with Wells as an effort to refocus their thinking about Disney and where it was headed. Then everything turned topsy-turvy, Wells was killed, and Eisner decided to expand his book into what he hoped would be a "richer, multidimensional story."

Well, it is and it isn't. As innovative as he may be, Eisner is a creation of business, and this is, in the end, a business book. When he tries to summon up deeper perceptions, he tends to revisit his boyhood. Amid all the problems in melding Disney and ABC, he writes, "Our two companies shared a set of values that I first learned at Camp Keewaydin: Work hard, help the other fellow, tell the truth, and when you make a commitment, stand by it."

OK, but camp values can get you only so far in life. Ironically, Eisner's helpmate on his memoir is a writer named Tony Schwartz who, after making a lot of money co-writing *The Art of the Deal*, decided to take time off to tour the world to inquire into the meaning of life. The result was a bizarre but fascinating book called *What Really Matters: Searching for Wisdom in America*. I remember reading the book and, while admiring Schwartz's search, was even more perplexed as to which philosophy he ended up embracing, if any.

Work in Progress reflects no such journey, asks no hard questions, and leaves us with no such confusion.

On the other hand, Eisner was deeply affected by his emergency coronary artery surgery. "Something happened to me that is a big deal. My life has a finite sense to it and there is certainly a hollowness that comes with such realizations. I try not to think about it, but I think about it all the time."

And that, no doubt, will be the subject of his next memoir.

—*Variety*, September 28, 1998

.   .   .

Both of the Japanese megacompanies, Matsushita and Sony, that ended up controlling Hollywood studios, found the cultural barriers all but impossible to penetrate. Matsushita ended up selling its stake in MCA/Universal, but

Sony, despite massive write-offs, decided to stay the course. Following the dismissal of the Peter Guber/Mark Canton management team in 1996, however, Sony's chief, Nobuyuki Idei, seemed frozen about his next moves, as I pointed out in a memo to the Sony chief in summer 1996. Shortly after the column appeared, Idei appointed John Calley to lead his next management and also sent word to me that, exasperated by my prodding, he had acted more quickly than he had earlier planned.

SONY'S SOUNDS OF SILENCE

MEMO TO: Nobuyuki Idei

Since taking over the job of overseeing Sony Pictures Entertainment, Nobuyuki, you have been a frequent visitor to Hollywood. However, I wonder whether you are aware of the two conflicting theories that are circulating about you in town.

One theory is that you don't know. A second theory is that you don't care.

All this may sound rather harsh, so let me explain: Those who feel you "don't know" are referring to the urgency of the problems facing the studio. There's a pervasive feeling in town that Sony is essentially dead in the water, with few if any important projects getting the green light. Talk to the town's key agents and they'll tell you that Sony is their last stop; they'd prefer to take projects to other studios where they might get a "yes" from an executive who will still be holding his job a few months later. Are you aware of all this, Nobuyuki? Do you realize how long it takes to bring a studio back to life once its momentum has been lost and its production line shut down?

Maybe you know but don't care, consistent with the second theory. By "not caring," I am not suggesting that Sony denigrates the importance of the "content" business. Rather, I am propounding the theory that the hierarchies ruling the big Japanese companies tend to make decisions at a very slow, deliberate pace relative to their American counterparts. There is always a five-year plan or a grandiose generational design that comes into play. Hence, Nobuyuki, while you may realize that Sony has hit some bumps in the road, you and your colleagues may be pondering some more intricate long-term solutions that we impulsive Yanks may not comprehend. But if this is the case, why are there so many major players in Hollywood who claim they've been approached to take top positions at Sony? And why are they all replying, "Please, not me." Among those names that have been published or bandied about are Michael Fuchs, Bruce Ramer, Joe Roth, and, of course, Jeff Sagansky, the very respected and experienced executive who presently occupies a shadowy enclave in the Sony hierarchy.

Again, there are two theories about these meetings, Nobuyuki. Either you don't know or don't care.

That is, you may be unaware that intermediaries are making these approaches—in some cases because they want to come to you with a new management scheme, in others because they want to acquire all or part of your content business. Or perhaps you know all this is taking place and don't care to stop it, on the off chance that something interesting may turn up.

In either case, you must understand the negative impact that all this is having on the studio. On the film side alone, Mark Canton and his aides have been rocked by such recent disappointments as *The Cable Guy, Multiplicity, Striptease, City Hall,* and *Mrs. Winterbourne.* Three respected executives have recently departed the studio—Marc Platt, president of TriStar; Lisa Henson, president of Columbia; and Sid Ganis, Sony's marketing chief.

All this sends a message, Nobuyuki—a message of a company in distress. Now, there are two theories about how you read this message. One is that you don't know, the other is that you don't care. In other words, perhaps the distress signals have not reached your lofty perch in Tokyo. Or perhaps, having been reached, it's your feeling that the Americans deserve to wallow in their misery for a while. "Japanese companies like to watch their executives marinate," one veteran of the MCA-Matsushita wars told me recently.

To be sure, you could clear all this up with some swift moves or some sage pronouncements, Nobuyuki. You could indeed announce a new slate of managers to run Sony Pictures Entertainment. You could sell the company to Polygram or another suitor. Or you could issue a statement enunciating your support for current management and your confidence in the future—something a little more persuasive than the rather curious missive sent out August 8 under the name of a Sony deputy president named Ted Kawai, who is unknown to denizens of Hollywood.

Inevitably, some guess that you did not know about this statement while others speculate that you did not care. But then we've been through all this before, haven't we?

—*Variety*, August 12, 1996

.   .   .

When Edgar Bronfman Jr. took the reins at MCA and changed its name to Universal, one inevitable result was to send proud old Lew Wasserman to the sidelines after a fifty-year reign. Wasserman's exit left a huge hole not only at Universal but also in the industry as a whole, as I explained in March of 1993.

MCA'S NO. 1 "TOUGH GUY"
IS HARDLY THE RETIRING KIND

Though he turns 80 today, Lew Wasserman is not exactly the retiring type. Every morning at 8:00 A.M. he still materializes in his office, a tall, slender, imperious presence with a swath of silver hair.

Though he may walk a little slower and go home a little earlier, there is no doubt that Lew still stands tall as the boss of MCA, as he has for nearly fifty years. As such, his tenure far surpasses that of any other mogul—an amazing display of both continuity and durability.

As stubborn as always, Wasserman imposed constraints on today's birthday observance. There will be a luncheon involving principal officers of the company, a few short speeches, but nothing sentimental or flashy.

Wasserman predictably rejected any suggestion of press interviews to mark the occasion; he has not sat still for a reporter's questions for many decades.

None of his colleagues can explain this reticence. Wasserman is highly articulate—a superb raconteur who, when spinning a story about, say, some arcane negotiation with Irving Thalberg, can summon up the precise numbers and even the name of the project. He is indeed a living archive—an oral history of Hollywood who prefers to keep the history to himself.

One doesn't argue with Lew Wasserman about issues like this. At 80, when most mortals may waver or procrastinate, Wasserman still delivers decisions with a steely finality.

Around the austere corporate corridors of the Black Tower, it is still Wasserman who wears the black hat, who enunciates the tough decisions and wields the axe. "Sid Sheinberg has acquired this reputation as the MCA tough guy, but when it's time to get tough, it's still up to Lew," advises one MCA insider.

Wasserman's iron will makes itself felt far beyond the walls of the Black Tower. He still religiously attends every key meeting of the Motion Picture Association of America, for example, and on many occasions it's been Wasserman who has held together this often quarrelsome, mismatched group. When talk turns to labor negotiations, political relations, or similar topics, industry leaders still reflexively turn to Wasserman. There is often no formal vote, but rather a "sense of the meeting," which, as one MPAA veteran says, "usually comes down to Lew's view."

"The only way to describe him is to say he's the indispensable man," says Jack Valenti, president of the MPAA, who was personally recruited by Wasserman when he was still in the Johnson White House.

"Lew never goes back on his word. When I told him that I would accept the job, I laid down one condition. I said, 'Lew, when things are really on the line, you have to be there in the meeting.' He has never broken that pledge in a quarter of a century."

There is widespread concern about the ability of the MPAA to formulate coherent policy once Wasserman decides to take a backseat. "There was a time when the film companies were all in the same boat," says the CEO of a rival company. "Today you have conflicting agendas even within the same company."

If the film business worries about a potential power vacuum, so do some political figures. As with most of his activities, Wasserman's involvement in politics expanded in a cautious, calculating way over the years.

Initially, the young Wasserman resisted pressure from the moguls of an earlier generation to support their pet conservative candidates. Jack Warner tried to bully him into becoming a Nixon supporter, for example, but Wasserman declined.

As MCA continued to grow, however, Wasserman began to realize that neutrality was futile. The Justice Department's effort to block MCA's acquisition of Decca Records thirty years ago dramatized the need for greater political clout.

Before long, Wasserman had become a major Kennedy supporter and fundraiser for Democratic candidates. Only Arthur Krim of the old United Artists wielded as much muscle in American political circles.

As Wasserman's power continued to expand into politics, civic affairs, and philanthropy, he became increasingly rigid about personal style.

Though he was a classic Hollywood mogul, his manner and bearing were in sharp contrast to the moguls of old.

The Harry Cohns, Jack Warners, or Louis B. Mayers were boisterous and mercurial. Wasserman, with his dark suits and black building filled with antiques, registers austerity and restraint.

The old-timers regarded Hollywood as their playground. To Wasserman, it represented an industry in need of discipline and organization. "Lew was capable of being as cantankerous as the old moguls, but his tantrums were always behind closed doors and there was always an agenda behind the rage," observes one of the town's best-known agents.

Just as Jules Stein had anointed Wasserman as his successor almost half a century ago, so Wasserman two decades ago named

Sidney Sheinberg as his heir apparent and the chain of command has essentially remained in place.

Today the corridors of power at MCA are lined with Sheinberg appointees. While Wasserman still holds the ultimate authority, it's Sheinberg, a tough-minded onetime law professor, who has the mandate to plan MCA's future in an era of fast-changing technology.

Both men are aware that MCA has its list of persistent critics. Some argue that MCA has been slow to react to the changing environment in which the networks are becoming dinosaurs and the film business is being squeezed by ever-tightening margins.

There are those who question whether, under its new corporate parent, Matsushita, MCA will retain the flexibility to adapt and innovate.

The Matsushita deal brought vast wealth to MCA principals and vast resources to the company. But some wonder what effect Matsushita's critical problems with its own core business may ultimately have on MCA.

When Carl Laemmle strolled through the ragtag chicken farm in 1915 and envisioned building a studio, no one could have envisioned the worldwide business that would come into being in a relatively short span of time.

And no one would have imagined that one man—Lew Wasserman—would shape so much of that era.

Some of the black-clad execs at today's birthday luncheon will doubtless peer down the table at Lew Wasserman and wonder what this austere, inscrutable man must be thinking—whether he has come to terms with his own legend.

But, naturally, none of this will be articulated, not within the corporate corridors of the MCA of Lew Wasserman. It will all be terribly proper and understated, the way Lew likes it.

—*Variety*, March 15, 1993

.   .   .

Of all the Hollywood studios, none has been more accident-prone over the last generation than proud old MGM. Its saddest chapter was surely during the regime of a bizarre Italian wheeler-dealer named Giancarlo Parretti, who, financed principally by the giant Crédit Lyonnais bank, led the studio to virtual ruin before Kirk Kerkorian seized control yet again in the late '90s. In 1992 I described Parretti's curious modus operandi in the following words . . .

CIAO, GIANCARLO

It would seem churlish and ungrateful somehow to let 1991 slip into oblivion without a final goodbye to Giancarlo Parretti. The munchkin manipulator has been exiled to a Sicilian jail cell on charges of tax evasion, where he further learned that a Delaware court has finally stripped him of control of MGM-Pathé, but that doesn't mean that the Parretti legacy should be banished from memory.

Consider for a moment the positive attributes that Parretti contributed to the Hollywood scene during his brief moment in the sun:

- Lack of intellectual pretense, for one. Would-be moguls have always imposed their instant wisdom about scripts and casting decisions, but the Oracle from Orvieto, upon taking power, uttered these immortal words to his production chief, Alan Ladd Jr.: "Laddie, you make-a the pictures, I fucka the girls." Parretti held to his pledge on both counts.

- Resistance to bureaucracy. While some studios are all but strangled amid bureaucratic layers, Parretti adhered to the ultimate "lean-and-mean" management structure. Indeed, the only person empowered to write checks at MGM was his 22-year-old daughter, Valentina. When Valentina went shopping, production companies shooting on location would occasionally have to shut down for lack of pay, to be sure, but this was a minor price to pay for managerial efficiency.

• Respect for tradition. While Jim Aubrey once took Irving
Thalberg's name off MGM's administration building, Parretti so
revered MGM tradition that he even invited a living replica of Leo
the Lion to be present at the initial corporate closing (Parretti had
to hide behind the trainer when Leo starting gnawing on his arm).
The portly princeling even brought back the old MGM tradition
of signing starlets to exclusive contracts—girls with such exotic
names as Dimitra, Cinzia, and Marina who, alas, also required
English lessons and never appeared in any MGM movies.

Despite these positive traits, Parretti felt Hollywood misunderstood
him and he wasn't wrong. Parretti complained bitterly that the
Hollywood community accepted on face value a "phony quote"
attributed to him by the Italian newspaper *L'Unità* that "the Jews
have ganged up on me" in Hollywood. Once, in his office, Parretti
grabbed my sleeve and roared: "How can they believe I hate Jews?
I hate no one." He reconsidered for a beat. "Well . . . maybe the
Japanese, just a little . . ."

And now Parretti has vanished from the scene. Some believe he
might end up sitting on a beach in Majorca like yet another
former MGM owner, Christopher Skase. Others insist he is too
stubborn—that he will try to fight his way back.

Meanwhile, what of MGM, itself battered and bereft? The
once-regal studio has drifted into limbo, awaiting resolution of the
Delaware suit. Crédit Lyonnais has made no effort to conceal its
fervent desire to have MGM surgically removed from its client list.
Several possible scenarios present themselves:

Kirk Kerkorian may make yet another play for the studio.
Having picked such quality buyers as Skase and Parretti, he surely
has still other candidates in mind on whom to bestow the studio.
George Steinbrenner might be one candidate, based on his record
with the New York Yankees. Michael Milken may be another.
John Sununu has shown the skills of diplomacy needed to run a
studio—Kerkorian surely must consider him as well.

A new White Knight might appear from the ranks of former studio CEOs—men who may have lost their offices but not their appetites. Frank Mancuso, late of Paramount, is the subject of persistent rumors that he may mobilize a substantial group of investors. There are others as well: Remember Victor Kaufman of TriStar? Jerry Weintraub of UA? The once ubiquitous Marvin Davis might feel his management skills are not sufficiently challenged at the Carnegie Deli.

Despite myriad layers of tarnish, the MGM logo still burns brightly around the world—a miracle of staying power. And there are still giant puddles of money in Taiwan, South Korea, and Japan that could still spill over into the most mythic of all "growth industries"—global entertainment.

Some of the money sources Giancarlo Parretti tried to hit on may still be good for one more go-around. The King of Malta for example—he reportedly was keenly interested in MGM, except that no one could find him. Samuel Doe was a solid backer of Parretti and, even though he may not be around anymore, there must be a few other affluent Liberians prepared to take a flyer.

To be sure, none of this will do Parretti any good. Jail seems a poignant ending for a man who, despite a total absence of resources, was able to con a French bank out of a billion dollars; for a onetime waiter who ended up making deals with Sean Connery; for a small, inarticulate man who, in his own eyes, was qualified to walk among kings and presidents. Maybe Parretti was not cut out to own a movie studio, but he might yet provide grist for the next best thing—a very funny movie about his rise and fall.

—*Variety*, January 6, 1992

.   .   .

If Hollywood was puzzled by Parretti, it was even more perplexed as to why the biggest bank in France would want to finance his ill-starred endeavors. In November 1995, I put a series of questions to the chief of Crédit Lyonnais. Not surprisingly, he never responded. His bank, however, virtually withdrew from its activities in the movie business shortly thereafter.

HAVE FRENCH BANKERS LEARNED
TO LEAVE MOVIES TO MOVIEMAKERS?

MEMO TO: Guy-Etienne Dufour, Crédit Lyonnais

"Terminez . . .?"

Whenever I dine in Paris, that's the word I most frequently hear from those ever-disdainful French waiters as they hover at my shoulder. Loosely translated, it means another customer is waiting for my table, so the dishes will be cleared whether I'm finished or not.

I mention this, Monsieur, after learning of the comments you made to two reporters from *Variety*—comments indicating that your august bank has a revived appetite for the motion picture business.

You hinted to them that Crédit Lyonnais might be exploring the possibility of holding on to MGM/UA beyond the 1997 deadline; you also said your bank now had an inventory of about nine hundred "repossessed" films in its library and might even set up a division to sell rights in those projects.

If this is indeed the case, Monsieur, I would like to give you one word of advice: Terminez.

At the risk of sounding chauvinistic, I'd remind you that Crédit Lyonnais over the years has not been especially discriminating in its loans to filmmakers. I vividly recall one meeting I had with Giancarlo Parretti in which that porcine pillager spread an array of correspondence from your bank across his vast desk and screamed, "Crédit Lyonnais will back me to the grave." The erstwhile owner of MGM/UA didn't specify whose grave, to be sure.

Now I realize, Monsieur, that any bank can make a misjudgment. I also understand full well that Crédit Lyonnais is busily setting up a new entity called CDR that will focus on some $40 billion of the bank's bad loans, of which movies represent a mere ten percent. That mere ten percent, nonetheless, has been sufficient for the bank to build up what probably is the third largest film library in the world—an astonishing twenty-three hundred titles, including fourteen hundred from MGM/UA and nine hundred of your newly "repossessed" projects.

Companies have struggled for years to build film libraries, but only Crédit Lyonnais could do so inadvertently, simply by financing bad companies and bad movies. How could one bank, Monsieur, have cooked that many turkeys without coming up with an occasional soufflé?

Indeed, the list of companies contributing to the "nasty nine hundred" reads like a sort of rogues' gallery of moviedom—Hemdale, Epic, Gladden, Trans-World Entertainment, 21st Century, et cetera. None of these companies could have made movies without the unique philanthropy of Crédit Lyonnais, the bank that loves to lose.

I realize it must be a great temptation to cut your losses by trying to sell off the remaining rights of this potpourri of losers— that is, if any rights remain unexploited. However, I have a better suggestion. How about making a huge bonfire and simply burning the negatives?

Think of the statement this would make, Monsieur. You would be warning all the rascals of the movie world to find some other business to loot. It's hard enough for legitimate players these days to make and market their movies, without letting all the crooks in on the action.

I have a feeling that the people who manage your biggest movie asset, MGM/UA, might appreciate that gesture. They've struggled mightily to resurrect that once-proud studio. In spending more than $2 billion of your bank's money, they've actually accomplished the unthinkable: They've seen to it that your money has been channeled to worthy projects made by honorable filmmakers. But now we're entering a dangerous period, Monsieur. With the deadline for selling MGM/UA only eighteen months away, suddenly the fortunes of that studio are looking brighter. *Get Shorty* is a hit. I saw the new James Bond picture, *Goldeneye*, the other day, and it's the best Bond since the Connery days. I can picture the bankers at Crédit Lyonnais sitting around a table and saying, "Mon

Dieu, our movies are suddenly making money, so why are we selling so quickly?"

That's the time for you to stand tall, Monsieur, and urge your colleagues, "Terminez!" As they say in Las Vegas, if you finally get lucky, run, don't walk, from the tables.

My spies in Paris tell me that an array of representatives from various financial institutions already are lining up to handle the sale of MGM/UA—the usual suspects like Lazard Freres, Goldman Sachs, Merrill Lynch, and Banque Paribas. Take them up on their offers. Surely MGM/UA deserves to be under the auspices of a substantial entity that understands the business and is willing to nurture it back to health. If DreamWorks can afford to build a new studio from scratch, why shouldn't MGM/UA follow suit?

It was just seventy years ago when Louis B. Mayer's Dream Factory in Culver City was unveiled amid the hoopla of brass bands and political speeches. Perhaps it's time for a Second Coming.

—Variety, November 6, 1995

·   ·   ·

While the major studios continued to fight their way through both good times and bad, the independents, habitually undercapitalized, faced even more dire struggles. Some, like Miramax, were acquired by bigger entities such as Disney. Samuel Goldwyn Jr., however, tried to fight on alone and, as this summer 1995 column indicated, it seemed like a losing battle. Two years after this column, Goldwyn's company was absorbed by MGM and Samuel Goldwyn Jr., sadly, found himself on the sidelines, still later to return to the fray.

LATEST GOLDWYNISM:
FISCAL WOES FOR LAST TRUE INDIE

MEMO TO: Samuel Goldwyn Jr.

Say it ain't so, Sam!

Rumor has it that your company has hit some fiscal potholes and that you may be forced to sell. According to Hollywood lore, this town is supposed to rejoice when one of its players runs into tough times, but I think you'll be the exception to this rule, Sam.

The Samuel Goldwyn Co., after all, is not just your average company. Arguably, it's the last true indie. Miramax is part of Disney now and New Line belongs to Ted Turner, but your company, Sam, proudly has maintained its autonomy. Only three months ago, Kenneth Turan wrote in the *Los Angeles Times* that the release of *The Madness of King George* marked "the culmination of a career—proof that, at age 69, Sam Goldwyn has fully come into his own."

And now your company is on the block! What kind of "culmination" is that?

Which leads us to a more disturbing question: Is there really room any longer for a true "independent" in today's turbulent film business? Is it possible to subsist without a sugar daddy?

This question is especially germane given the transition of Miramax into a sort of supermarket for niche product. With forty-plus films on the release schedule, the brothers Weinstein have destabilized what was once a rather sedate industry.

The irony, of course, is that Harvey and Bob Weinstein, in some ways, are reminiscent of the stubbornness and ferocity of your father, Sam—the remarkable Samuel Goldwyn Sr. Old Sam "came from the street," as you like to put it, but he knew how to dream the big dream. He plied his trade the hard way, funding his own films and paying them off step-by-step, like a home mortgage. And what extraordinary movies they were—*The Best Years of Our Lives*, *Wuthering Heights*, *The Little Foxes* et al.

You chose to go it alone too, Sam. As early as 1964 you were trekking from college to college, plugging your movie, *The Young Lovers*. Even as a kid you were winning prizes for documentaries that you shot in Europe.

The Goldwyn Co. today can not only boast of some superb arthouse releases like *King George*, but also *Eat Drink Man Woman* and *Mystic Pizza*. There are TV ventures like *American Gladiators* and, of course, your circuit of 126 specialized screens.

So what went wrong?

An assortment of number-crunchers on Wall Street are even now trying to figure that out, since the asset value of your company apparently is somewhere in the area of $120 million to $140 million. Part of the problem, clearly, stemmed from some wrong guesses. While the Weinsteins rarely get into a pricey project unless their bets are covered by foreign pre-sales and other ancillary deals, you made a hefty $11-million bet on *The Perez Family*, and there were other write-downs too, on *Oleanna, To Live,* and TV shows like *Why Didn't I Think of That?* and *Wild West Showdown.* Again, no corporate sugar daddy was there to cushion the blow.

Then, too, the structure of your company is mind-bendingly complicated. Though you took a salary of only $155,833 in 1994, Sam, I'll be damned if I can figure out the ramifications of the Goldwyn Trust, which, through its ownership of the old Goldwyn library, paid you some $6.4 million in fees over the past five years (albeit some of it deferred). Nor do I understand the arrangement with your president, Meyer Gottlieb, whereby he, too, has an outside company, Nightlife Inc., that produces movies and TV shows and that, according to documents filed with the SEC, has been "reimbursed" or advanced as much as $14 million since 1990 to cover various expenses.

I'm not suggesting that there's anything mischievous about these dealings—just that your company, while publicly owned, still seemed to some investors to be an odd mixture of public and private.

I suppose the bottom line, Sam, is that you were never "street" like your father. You are, in fact, "the last Hollywood Brahmin," as one British friend put it. You live the regal life of the moguls of old, replete with fabled art collection and patrician habits. Still rangy and slim, with your splendid mane of silver hair, you are an elegant anachronism, trying to cope with the tough, mean-spirited commoners of a new epoch. Who else can spin stories over tea of sitting on Clark Gable's knee, or can recall when your mother went to see *The Jazz Singer* with Irving Thalberg and he told her, "Sound is a passing fancy that won't last." Your competitors only know about last weekend's grosses.

I remember once having lunch with your father in his declining years, Sam, and I found him very gracious and a superb raconteur. At that time I was a reporter with the *New York Times*, and, after lunch, old Sam Goldwyn looked at me and said, "Well, son, we've talked about many things, but the *Times* always likes to write about 'Goldwynisms' and I haven't given you any, have I?"

"No," I replied. "But we can make an exception."

"I don't think I really said most of those things anyway," he reflected. "But I always especially liked one of the 'Goldwynisms' attributed to me. I was looking back on my early days at MGM and supposedly said, 'Forget about all that, we've passed a lot of water since then.' I never said it, mind you, but that was a good one. The *Times* liked it too."

So that brings us back to your present dilemma, Sam. When you founded your movie distribution company fifteen years ago, it seemed like a great idea to go it alone. But, as the saying goes, we've passed a lot of water since then.

—*Variety*, July 10, 1995

. . .

Given the nature of their product, and the limitations of their marketing budgets, the independents have always been vastly more reliant on the critics and on awards than major studios. No company campaigned more successfully for Academy Awards, and handled its relations with critics more adeptly, than did Miramax. Late in 1998, however, there were rumors that Miramax might be shut out of the Oscar battle for the first time in years. These dire forecasts turned out to be false, as I discussed in the winter of 1998.

HOT RACE STOKES HARVEY'S HUNGER

Two roly-poly fellas, Santa and Harvey, can always be counted on to strut their stuff at this time of year, but, candidly, I've been skeptical about one of them. Not the one from the North Pole.

Harvey Weinstein, we were told, has been too fixated on launching his high-profile magazine with Tina Brown, too busy being a friend of Bill and Hillary, and too preoccupied with the New York social whirl to perform his customary end-of-year pyrotechnics. That's what people kept buzzing in my ear.

In the past, Harvey could always be counted on to upset the Oscar apple cart at year end—witness Miramax's 110 nominations and thirty wins, most from the last five years—but this year, they told me, he'd taken his eye off the ball.

Well, they were wrong: It's "Harvey Time" yet again. Two Miramax films, *Shakespeare in Love* and *Life Is Beautiful*, have emerged as serious Oscar dark horses and four or five others have a shot at least at a Golden Globe. And while Harvey does his thing, brother Bob has brought forth *The Faculty* to appease his loyal bloodlust demo.

It's no surprise therefore that Harvey's mood is downright festive as he suns himself in St. Barths this week. Despite Miramax's alleged "off-year," the company's profits, Harvey insists, reached $125 million, well ahead of last year's $71 million. Two holdovers from '97—*Good Will Hunting* and *Scream 2*—accounted for a hefty share of those revenues, to be sure.

Even Harvey would admit that many of his thirty or so releases each year do not exactly trigger a seismic shock in the marketplace. On the other hand, Miramax doesn't launch $50-million advertising fusillades to open its movies, as do the so-called "majors."

Thus Miramax made a profit on its overall program of live-action movies this year—a feat that perhaps only two of the majors could share in—and this despite occasional disappointments like *The Mighty* or Woody Allen's *Celebrity*.

Even Harvey now is playing his hand ever more cautiously. "We'll be releasing fewer movies in '99," he told me two weeks ago. "We're not starting any movie for the next three months and we've acquired only one movie since May."

These actions, he says, stemmed from prudence, not austerity. With several Miramax-like companies now crowding the market, prices have gotten surreal, Harvey believes.

Hence, while his company once depended on acquisitions, Miramax currently produces most of its own releases and, rumors to the contrary, is keeping the lid on costs. While the budget of *Shakespeare in Love* edged close to $40 million, that cost was split with Universal. "We're still making $5-million movies and we're keeping our average close to $14 million," he reports.

Harvey is keenly aware of the mixed signals sent forth by his association with Tina Brown, an editor who has never taken the Miramax pledge of parsimony. But, again, he insists this venture has been misperceived. He and Tina are seeking a fifty-fifty partner who will not only share start-up costs, but will also supply the back-office heft. He's convinced that ultimate revenues from TV magazine shows and movie spin-offs will make the new venture profitable.

If the networks indeed have an appetite for Tina, he may prove correct, given the felicitous economics of the *Dateline*s and *Primetime Live*s. Magazine insiders may remain skeptical about the prospects of yet another pricey version of *Vanity Fair* or the *New Yorker*, but they may also be missing the big picture.

Hence, while Tina and her partner, Ron Galotti, scout for new offices, Harvey is sunning himself and flashing his "what, me worry?" smile. In his mind, he is no longer merely a moviemaker, but rather a full-fledged media maven, and a unique one at that. Rupert Murdoch's toys may circle the globe, but he's never had the satisfaction of nurturing a brilliant work like *Shakespeare in Love* through the rough cinematic seas. Ted Turner may have his billions, but he doesn't have the instant gratification of reading a superb script and pressing a button to get it made.

And that's why, naysayers aside, no one enjoys Harvey Time quite as much as Harvey.

—*Variety*, January 4, 1999

.　　.　　.

Though Hollywood's power players tend to be tough-minded and resolute, the intense pressures and the temptations of the job have taken their toll on many. A classic case was that of David Begelman, a man who reached the summit of power only to come crashing to earth. I reflected on his saga in March 1998.

A SOCIOPATH'S SAD SAGA

It was precisely twenty years ago that this town's attention was riveted on a corporate melodrama far more intriguing than the plot of any movie. Even the judge hearing the case termed it "the most bizarre case" he'd ever encountered.

If David Begelman's life were reduced to a studio synopsis, it would read as follows:

The head of a major studio starts depositing checks intended for a star and star director into his personal bank account. He is discovered and suspended. His allies rally to his cause and get him reinstated. He's then forced to resign to face four counts of felony grand theft. A judge reduces his sentence to a misdemeanor and lets him off with the proviso that he produce an anti-drug documentary. A year later the very same studio chief is named chairman and CEO of yet another studio, whose owner insists that these "past transgressions" are irrelevant. Two years later he is fired for further unstated transgressions.

That, in a nutshell, is the remarkable saga of David Begelman, the erratic, charismatic agent-turned-studio chief. Why bring it up today? Because the Begelman case radically changed the lives of many people caught in its vortex and arguably had a permanent impact upon the manners and mores of the community.

Nonetheless, twenty years after the fact, the question is worth asking: Could something like l'affaire Begelman ever happen again? Talk to survivors of the incident and they generally agree that it could. At the same time, there were several elements to the imbroglio of twenty years ago that surely would never be replicated.

First and foremost, there was the enigmatic character of Begelman himself, a brilliant and bizarre man who, despite his impeccable manners and courtly presentation, pursued a singularly unkempt lifestyle. A man who loved to gamble, he was never especially discreet as to where he found the loose change to cover his debts. Why else would a man making millions a year in salary go to the trouble of forging checks worth a mere $60,000?

What made him especially frustrating to colleagues was that he had the makings of a superb studio chief. Under his regime, the once-pathetic Columbia was suddenly making pictures like *Close Encounters of the Third Kind*, *The Way We Were*, *Shampoo*, and many other movies that were commercial and innovative.

Hence it was no surprise that, when scandal first surfaced, his allies rushed to his side. Sure, David might be naughty, but he's David! The confusion as to how to deal with a check-kiting studio chief only exacerbated the turmoil between clashing power blocs on the board of directors.

After much hard-nosed negotiation, Begelman's downfall was followed shortly thereafter by that of Alan J. Hirschfield, the brilliant young president of Columbia Industries.

Begelman was finished. Or was he?

Surely no corporate officer who once faced grand theft felony charges would be hired to head yet another studio. Begelman's amazing "second chance" stemmed once again from the unique hold he had on the community—the image of the lovable rascal.

Kirk Kerkorian controlled MGM/UA at that time, as he does now, and he is a man who trusts his advisers, all of whom were attorneys. The advisers persuaded Kerkorian that Begelman had learned his lesson, that he was a changed man—thus proving yet again that good lawyers often make bad psychologists. To fortify their case, the lawyers even leaked news of Begelman's appointment and the stock promptly went up a few points.

To be sure, Begelman's "second shot" proved to be a disappointment. He spent a great deal of money on several dubious productions and within months there were whispers of behind-the-scenes intrigues. Soon Begelman was out of a job yet again.

Which brings us back to the issue, could the Begelman affair happen today? I put that question to several of the people who were enmeshed in it twenty years ago and their answer was yes.

"There's so much money out there," said one survivor, "that there's no reason why a sociopath like David couldn't have an even easier time siphoning off a few bucks into his own account."

True, the multinational companies that now own the studios have imposed stricter financial controls, they concede. Nonetheless, David Begelman never tried to make off with millions. He just wanted to soften the blow here and there when he had a bad night of poker.

And the reason he got away with it for so long—the lovable rascal syndrome—points up Hollywood's unique willingness to forgive sociopathic behavior. Whether you're an agent or manager or a studio chief, it's somehow OK to lie a little, to grab a little extra on a deal, to double-dip on commissions, et cetera. In a business where standards are fuzzy, why single out Begelman as a crook? He just pushed things a little further.

Hence, even though he was caught stealing money, there were powerful forces in town and in his own company that wanted to look the other way. They even rewarded him with another job.

On August 7, 1995, David Begelman took his own life. Paradoxically, many of those who were entangled in his troubles have gone on to lead satisfying lives. Hirschfield, who was canned as president of Columbia Pictures Industries in 1979, now lives in Jackson Hole, Wyoming, where he runs a fast-growing provider of real-time financial information, Data Broadcasting Corp., which has just formed a joint venture with CBS. He also owns a popular local restaurant in Jackson Hole.

John Cosgrove, the man who really made *Angel Death*, the documentary about the drug PCP that constituted Begelman's only "punishment," has made millions producing *Unsolved Mysteries*.

Cliff Robertson, the actor who turned in Begelman and who served several years in the wilderness, is now 72, and is trying to raise the money for a sequel to the film that won him an Oscar, *Charly*.

And Ray Stark, the onetime power broker at Columbia, at the age of 80 seems finally about to achieve a longtime dream—making *Houdini*, about a man who could escape any trap that anyone could devise, something David Begelman could never quite figure out how to do.

—*Variety*, March 2, 1998

.   .   .

One of David Begelman's protégés at Columbia, William Tennant, ironically came close to meeting a fate similar to that of his boss. The ultimate highflier in the late '60s and '70s, the charming and handsome Tennant ended up a homeless person and drug addict. In the years subsequent to publication of this column in February 1993, Tennant rehabilitated himself, launching yet another successful career as a video executive and manager in London. He still lives there with his wife and two young children.

EXEC COMES FULL CIRCLE
AFTER DESCENT INTO DESPAIR

Executives in Hollywood have always been adept at recycling themselves from job to job, but now and then someone gets put out to pasture. I recall coming upon one former studio exec— an important one at that—in a very distant pasture. He was sleeping in a doorway on Ventura Boulevard in the San Fernando Valley.

The name of the homeless person was Bill Tennant and I thought of him again this week after learning of the latest wrinkle in his bizarre career. Tennant, now living in London, had orchestrated the sale of Vision Video Ltd., a company he'd managed to resuscitate, to the Dutch giant Polygram. The man I'd seen sleeping in a doorway was back on his feet financially and emotionally— indeed, he had made yet another big score.

My career had intersected Tennant's several times over the past two decades—often enough for me to understand one crucial fact about him: While some people always manage to be in the right place at the right time, Tennant worked the other side of the street. Born in the slums of East L.A., Tennant had cut a swath as a superstar agent while still in his mid-twenties, but his rising star quickly went awry.

When the police needed someone to perform the horrific task of identifying Sharon Tate and the other victims of Charles Manson in 1970, for example, Tennant, as Roman Polanski's friend and agent, drew the grim assignment.

Tennant soon left agenting to become a vice president at Columbia, but once again, when the high-flying regime of David Begelman came crashing to earth amid the check-forging scandal, Tennant, who saw Begelman as a mentor, also bore the brunt.

Tennant went on to work beside some of the town's most enigmatic figures—men whose dealings seemed shrouded in legal imbroglios. There was Jonathan Krane at MCEG, Tom Coleman at Atlantic, and the late Neil Bogart at Casablanca.

Ultimately it all caught up with him. When it came time for Tennant's life to crash, it happened big. Cocaine addiction cost him his marriage, his savings, and, ultimately, even shelter. The man who once owned a beautiful home replete with tennis court now lived on the street, trading even the gold inlays in his teeth for a fix.

It was four years before Tennant managed to pull himself together. Predictably, the road back proved treacherous. Shorn of confidence or self-worth, Tennant was reluctant to call upon old colleagues. Yet, as a convert to AA, he was impelled to retrace his troubled past and to "make amends" to those who had worked with him.

I was one of those on his list, and I remember the sense of shock at being visited by this gaunt, battered figure. We stumbled through an awkward dialogue. He apologized for the error of his ways, and I cut him off, insisting that all that mattered now was his own regeneration.

Shortly thereafter, a friend called and asked, "Did you hear Bill Tennant is back in the business?"

"Terrific," I replied, "what's he doing?"

"He's selling sandwiches to movie crews off a catering truck." My friend thought this was funny. I cringed, flashing back to my first encounter with Tennant. A handsome kid with a natural swagger, Tennant had vaulted from the mail room of the old GAC to become a partner in Ziegler Ross. Tennant had come to talk to me about a new screenplay called *Butch Cassidy and the Sundance Kid*. He felt it was going to be hot. He was right, as usual.

Indeed, everything Tennant touched in those days seemed to acquire "heat." He made Peter Fonda's deal on *Easy Rider* and Roman Polanski's on *Rosemary's Baby*. When you met with Tennant you were talking about John Schlesinger and William Goldman. Everyone on his list seemed to be "happening," and Tennant seemed the fulcrum.

Later, when he became production VP at Columbia, the "action" followed him. Suddenly the once-moribund studio was turning out pictures like *Taxi Driver*, *All That Jazz,* and *Close Encounters of the Third Kind*. These projects were not all hatched by Tennant, of course, but he was a catalyst, an energy source.

He also kept flirting with danger. Friends had warned him to keep his distance from the trouble-prone Polanski, but Tennant paid no heed, becoming a regular in his circle. The shock of the Manson murders began unraveling him; in a sense, he had become the classic Hollywood victim.

How did he get from a catering truck to London? By chance, he had secured a job at Jonathan Krane's misbegotten venture, MCEG, and when the company foundered Tennant had been dispatched to the U.K. to salvage its video subsidiary, for which Krane had paid an absurd $83 million. Though uncomfortable in his new surroundings, Tennant managed to teach himself the video distribution business.

Within two years the newly renamed Vision Video Ltd. had been repackaged as a salable entity with gross revenues of about $40 million. Its library consisted of fourteen hundred titles, including six hundred features. Drawing on his Hollywood production experience, Tennant had begun to turn out successful videos for the U.K.

market built around local favorites like comedian Billy Connolly and radio talk-show host Danny Baker.

All this was good enough for Polygram, which grabbed up Tennant's venture to augment its own budding video empire. What this brought to Bill Tennant was something he hadn't had in many years—breathing room.

Newly married to a lovely young South African named Frances, who has a six-year-old daughter, Tennant feels at home in London now. His manner is calm, his style worldly and his eyes have lost that haunted look he had carried for so many years. For the first time he can look back across the lost years without flinching and without placing blame.

"I know I was my own worst enemy," he reflects. "Hollywood has always been a magnet attracting incomplete people who think that money and glamour can somehow make them complete. It can't, of course. You get consumed by it, not completed."

After all the troubled years, one senses Bill Tennant has found his own way to become complete.

—*Variety*, February 8, 1993

．　　．　　．

Even when a power player is rewarded with a golden parachute, the fall from corporate grace nonetheless is a stunning blow to the ego. Such was the case with Michael Fuchs, who held two of the top positions in show business, only to end up unemployed in 1995. I caught up with him in the fall of '98.

REVISITING FEISTY FUCHS

I've been having a curious on-again, off-again dialogue with Michael Fuchs over the past several months, which I initiated. "Michael," I will say, "it's been three years since your ceremonial beheading at Time Warner. What happens to a power person when he's stripped of his power?"

"Good question," Fuchs replies. "I think I have some good answers."

"Fine, give an interview. Or write a guest column. Speak out. It may be therapeutic."

"Yes," Fuchs will respond. Then a little later he will say, "No."

The "yesses" and "noes" have been going on for months now. I haven't experienced this much equivocation since breaking off with my high school girlfriend.

Three years ago when the brilliant, feisty Fuchs, the longtime chief of HBO, was suddenly fired as chairman and CEO both of HBO and the Warner Music Group after a six-month reign, the move sent shockwaves through many corporate hierarchies.

Backroom power struggles are a constant in corporate life, but this one had become public and at the world's biggest media and entertainment company. Having feuded with the Warner Bros. duo of Bob Daly and Terry Semel while running HBO, Fuchs now had ideas on how to re-create not only the music group but also Time Warner. And suddenly here was Gerald Levin, the stolid, stoic Time Warner chairman, nuking Fuchs and imposing order on his kingdom. Levin, it was said, had wearied of reading that Fuchs was his heir apparent.

It was all a vivid reminder of the evanescence of power. Corporate power in our society has lately become even more intoxicating than political power. The "suits" live in a rarefied cocoon of wealth and privilege while their political confreres must occupy a piranha-filled fishbowl. Politicians forever campaign and raise money, while CEOs, until recently, had only to worry about their boards of directors and their quarterly earnings.

The problem is that the giant multinational corporations are becoming as public and as political as our governmental institutions. The "suits" have to cultivate their constituencies just as carefully as a governor or senator, and the press is ever on the alert for missteps.

Which is why the Michael Fuchs episode was so intriguing. Young, single, and ever combative, his whole life was that of the corporate soldier, and suddenly it was gone. Did he overreach? Was he sandbagged? Was he too honest or too greedy?

Talk to friends of Michael Fuchs and they tell you that, on some levels, Fuchs is now happier and more fulfilled than during his years of soldiering. He travels constantly. He reads voraciously. He plays tennis and socializes. He serves on a couple of boards and hangs out with corporate players like Ron Perelman. A youthful 52, he is at once outgoing and utterly self-absorbed, convivial, yet intensely private. He talks not about TV ratings, but about watching the polar bears migrate in Canada or about his race-car lessons.

When relaxed, he may suddenly vent his anger. Semel and Daly, he will assert, are overrated power-players who, despite their mind-blowing compensation, are not delivering in either music or movies. Levin had given him a clear mandate to rebuild the music group, then pulled it away. The music business itself has gotten lost in a morass of double-dealing incompetence.

Michael Fuchs will say all this, and then will double back and fall silent. Having long since accepted the fact that he will not be offered another top corporate job—the opportunity at Sony was his last best shot—he still doesn't want to roil the waters too egregiously. Friends say, even if offered a top corporate post, he probably wouldn't accept it—after a few yesses and noes.

He is a man who, knowing on the one hand that, if given the chance, he could guide a corporate monolith with greater skill than most of the current power players, still relishes his autonomy and freedom on the sidelines.

He is, after all, quite rich. Thanks to Time Warner, he occupies one of Manhattan's most beautiful offices, with a panoramic view of Central Park. Sure, the phones don't ring that much, but he's his own man.

And as such, he chooses to remain silent.

—*Variety*, October 12, 1998

.   .   .

It is the rare executive in show business who "drops out," yet manages to return to the fray in an even more important post. Such was the case with

John Calley, who essentially disappeared for a decade only to return as studio chief yet again, first at United Artists and then at Sony. After this profile appeared in the August 1997 GQ, *Calley went on to experience a bumpy ride at Sony in 1998, with the studio dropping sharply in market share as even the much-heralded* Godzilla *proved to be a disappointment.*

THE OUTSIDER RETURNS

Five years ago, following a long exile in Los Angeles, my wife and I became enamored of New England's rolling hills and rustic barns and decided to do some house hunting around the community of Washington, Connecticut. As we quickly discovered, Washington had become a favored enclave of the wealthy arts elite, those strivers who had made financial scores in movies or TV or at such media sanctum sanctorums as Condé Nast and Time Warner. Indeed, the realtor who escorted us from house to house saw fit to drop frequent reminders of the artistic pedigree of our prospective neighbors, implying that proximity to a best-selling author or a film director would justify a loftier price. He seemed surprised, however, when one of the names he dropped resonated with me. We were surveying an ill-conceived clapboard structure that looked as if it had wandered away from its upscale tract, when, seeing our dismay, our guide noted that it was adjacent to the property where John Calley lived.

"You've heard of Calley?" the realtor inquired. When I nodded in recognition, he seemed almost apologetic. "He's a bit of a has-been, I know, but he once was a somebody in Hollywood, I've been told. That must have been some years ago." The asking price of the house, I sensed, had just been negotiated downward.

I changed the subject, but later Calley's name came up again. As the maître d' of the "hot" restaurant in town showed us to a table, he advised, "You'll like this table—it's John Calley's regular. I suppose you don't know who he is, of course."

Once we'd ordered, my wife asked, "This so-called has-been whose name keeps getting dropped—what really happened to him?"

I explained what I knew of Calley's legacy—how he had gone from producing trendy movies such as *Catch-22* in 1970 to a job as production chief at Warner Bros. only to wander off into self-imposed exile a decade and a half ago. Few in Hollywood ever mentioned his name anymore. As far as the power players were concerned, Calley had become a nonperson.

That was to change. As mysteriously as Calley had disappeared, he reemerged in 1993 as president of United Artists. And then, after a mere three years at that post, he levitated to an even higher profile as president and chief operating officer of Sony Pictures Entertainment. The reclusive has-been of Washington, Connecticut, was suddenly one of the most powerful figures in the entertainment industry; the country gentleman was now a global media star.

By Hollywood standards, Calley's career path may seem enigmatic, but then so is his personality. If Mark Canton, the previous Sony president, was the boastful, Armani-clad big spender, Calley is downright ascetic, a man who disdains Hollywood profligacy. If Jack Warner and Harry Cohn of olden days felt they shared the taste of the common man, Calley's personal tastes are unabashedly elitist. On some levels, he's as much of a snob as his best friend, Mike Nichols. While Hollywood mavens like Universal's Edgar Bronfman Jr. dwell in a cocoon of mansions and private jets, their movements sealed off by armies of security guards, Calley remains the free-spirited loner. Indeed, Calley's Sony coworkers, alarmed by a rash of robberies at this year's Cannes Film Festival, insisted that a colleague accompany their maverick boss to and from his hotel despite his protests that he wanted to go it alone.

Arguably, one reason for Calley's effectiveness in Hollywood is that no one can figure him out. Power players tend to typecast each other according to their styles and backgrounds—Warner Bros.' Robert Daly is Brooklyn Irish, Michael Ovitz is a Valley Jew (that's Los Angeles's San Fernando Valley), and so forth.

In contrast, John Calley is the ultimate Nowhere Man. The product of a broken home, he was born in Jersey City in 1930 and raised in poverty in California, working odd jobs as a janitor and a laborer in an ink factory. He knew little about his natural father other than that he was a car salesman whose "business friends" all had Italian names and spent a great deal of time getting manicures. At an age when other future Hollywood hotshots were earning their MBAs, Calley was serving in the army. Graduate school for him was the NBC mail room.

Despite this hardscrabble background, he presents himself as a well-read country gentleman. His manners are impeccable and his vocabulary erudite. In conversation he veers from topic to topic as though reminding you of his interests' disparate range. Though an ardent reader, he admits to having no artistic skills—yet writers and artists feel comfortable in his company (which sets him apart from virtually every other Hollywood suit). He is a notorious loner, yet his former girlfriends include Claudia Cardinale and Barbra Streisand. The three women with whom he has had longstanding relationships seem to have nothing in common. One was an Eastern European actress who spoke almost no English; the second was Sandy Lean, a shy Swiss-English woman who'd spent much of her childhood in the Himalayas and had been married to the great director David Lean. Calley's present wife is actress Meg Tilly, who is thirty years his junior.

Nor do the people he has worked with suggest a pattern in his movie tastes. During his decade at Warner Bros., he served as the key link to such artists as John Boorman, Mike Nichols, and the mind-bendingly eccentric Stanley Kubrick, but he also immersed himself in solid commercial fare such as *Dirty Harry*, *The Exorcist*, *Superman*, and that granddaddy of all disaster pictures, *The Towering Inferno*.

At United Artists, though Calley drew high marks for fostering *Goldeneye* (the first James Bond hit in some years) and Nichols' *The Birdcage* and for distributing *Leaving Las Vegas*, he also backed such ill-starred efforts as *Hackers*, a teenage computer adventure, and *Wild Bill*, a languid Walter Hill western. At Sony, Calley has reiterated his determination to turn out mainstream comedies and action fare to help create a rounded program of releases.

"Calley is a very realistic, bottom-line guy," says one member of his current production team. "The only thing you have to keep in mind is that you can never anticipate what his reaction will be to anything. As a human being, he's, well, off-the-wall."

In an industry increasingly dominated by lawyers and business-school graduates, Calley's management style has adapted to the times. In his first months at UA, following his long "retirement," Calley often expressed his discomfort in dealing with echelons of corporate management, reminding visitors, "I'm not a very good executive." When he tried to delegate tasks, he confessed, he usually ended up doing them himself. "One of the biggest problems in Hollywood," he told me at the time, "is that there are too many so-called executives. There are so many people whose job it is to say no that you can't ever find anyone to say yes."

At Sony, however, Calley's vocabulary began to grow more corporate from the outset, spilling over with unexpected references to "zero-basing," "value chain," and "re-engineering." At UA, Calley presided over an old-fashioned, single-product studio with a simple structure. But the Sony he encountered is a world-class corporate nightmare. And Calley's interaction with it has resulted in an ever-growing body count. Among the early casualties: Robert Cooper, the diminutive former head of HBO's movie unit, who only nine months earlier had been named president of production at TriStar Pictures, the Sony unit that produced such movies as *Jerry Maguire* and *Donnie Brasco*; David Saunders, the president of Triumph Films, a unit of Sony that focused on low-budget fare; and Barry Josephson, the youthful 40-year-old president of production at Columbia Pictures, another key filmmaking division of Sony.

Each departure was accompanied by the usual corporate euphemisms—all the men had made significant contributions to the corporation, et cetera. But the subtext was clear: John Calley may not be a typical corporate suit, but he has a vision for his company, and he intends to see that it is faithfully carried out by his chosen few.

Notoriously tactless, Cooper had done little to endear himself to his new boss, acquiring projects without consulting Calley's new management team. At HBO he and Calley had had an earlier run-in. Operating as independent producers, Calley and Nichols had brought in a long-form movie called *Fatherland* that Cooper had approved for production. At the eleventh hour, Cooper suddenly started overriding the producers' decisions on script and budget to the point where Calley and Nichols demanded their names be taken off the movie. Later Calley denied harboring any ill feelings toward Cooper over the incident; colleagues were skeptical.

But if heads were rolling at Sony, no one was really surprised. The previous occupants of Calley's corporate chair, Peter Guber and Jon Peters, had created a failure of almost operatic proportions. In 1994 Sony had taken a write-off of $3.2 billion on its Hollywood investment, an amount equal to almost half of what Sony had invested over eight years.

The patriarchal Japanese company was not accustomed to such debacles. Having started as a small-appliance manufacturer, it had grown into an electronics colossus. Calley's Tokyo boss, Nobuyuki Idei, was furious about the disasters of the Guber-Peters era. He was determined to build what he called "a total entertainment company" that would bring new luster to Sony's digital universe.

To signal this mood of change within the company, Sony released a twelve-minute video to its staff in which employees vented their complaints. At the end of the tape, John Calley himself took center stage to proclaim his openness to new attitudes. No longer, he said, can Sony betray "a Stone Age corporate culture facing the challenges of a space-age marketplace."

That Calley would be in a position to preside over Sony's "re-engineering" strikes his friends as the supreme irony. "Here's a guy who probably doesn't even own a suit, telling all these suits how to organize themselves," says a senior agent who has dealt with Calley many times over the years.

Irony aside, Calley, who turned 67 last month, seems fiercely dedicated to his new mission. He also has some talented manpower to help mobilize the effort, including Jeff Sagansky, the one-time CBS Entertainment chieftain whose main job is to oversee Sony's TV and overseas operations, and Howard Stringer, another ex-CBS executive, who was recently hired as president of the Sony Corporation of America to supervise Sony's sprawling New York–based activities.

To me, the long-term scenario looks like this: By restoring Sony's showbiz operations to respectability, the Japanese parent wants to pave the way for a public offering through which half or all of the company would become publicly owned. The hoped-for result: to turn the $3.2-billion write-off into a fiscal bonanza.

To get there, Sony will need more than re-engineering and cost-cutting. John Calley has to come up with hits—big hits. And that feat requires not only skill but also some damned good luck.

But fortune has often smiled on Calley. Witness the fact that upon taking over his new Sony job he inherited two box-office winners in *Jerry Maguire* and *Anaconda*—hits that followed a long string of Mark Canton losers. When I had lunch with Calley in early spring, he was still ebullient about this good fortune. "It's been a major morale builder for the marketing and distributing people," he observed. "It's so easy in this business to get a 'loser mentality.'"

Despite this enthusiasm, Calley seemed pale and edgy during lunch and admitted he felt under siege. With virtually everyone in town hurling projects his way, he was feeling pressure to close some big deals yet wary about moving too fast. Adding to the pressure was an unexpected setback—he had to undergo surgery for cataracts, which had rendered him temporarily incapable of reading scripts. "Here I am—I can't read a thing," Calley complained. "Producers and agents keep telling me, 'At last a studio chief who reads scripts,' and I can't read a goddamned thing till my eyes heal."

All this made Calley even more dependent on his two immediate production aides at Sony, Gareth Wigan, 65, and Lucy Fisher,

46, whose very presence reflects their boss's reliance on literacy and sophistication rather than on the sitcom mentality of the fast-talking young executives who populate rival studios. "Calley is reacting against the idea that the hotshots with their MBAs are the only ones who can tap into the mood of the market," observes one Sony colleague.

Indeed, it was this stance that motivated Frank Mancuso, president of MGM and United Artists, to bring Calley out of exile to begin with. No one knows precisely what prompted Mancuso to hire him. I had written a column in *Variety* earlier that year about successful managements of the past in which I singled out Calley's tenure at Warner Bros. Shortly after, I got a phone call from Mancuso saying, "I read your piece. Do you know where I can reach John Calley? I can't find a trace."

Coincidentally, Michael Ovitz, the head of the Creative Artists Agency who was working on reinventing MGM/UA, serving as a consultant to the Crédit Lyonnais Bank, had also called Calley out of the blue. "Ovitz and I had what seemed like a social meeting," Calley recalls. "He asked if I had a desire to get back into the fray. I replied that I was enjoying life in God's waiting room [Calley's code name for Washington] even though I was probably doing too much recreational sleeping."

Ultimately, Mancuso offered Calley the job of resuscitating UA. It was a four-year commitment, which Calley at first accepted and then turned down. Ovitz came back to him with another offer: Try it for one year, and if it isn't working, switch to a producing deal. Calley said yes.

Though I was acquainted with Calley, my own career directly intersected his only for one fleeting but memorable moment. When I was a young production vice president at Paramount in 1970, Calley and his then partner, Martin Ransohoff, were producing *Catch-22*, a project that left me befuddled. Like the rest of the world, I greatly admired the Joseph Heller bestseller, but the screenplay struck me as cold and convoluted. And the budget was even more disturbing. At $12.5 million—a lot of money in 1970—this seemed like a tough sell.

Both Calley and Nichols, the director, agreed. Prior to starting production, they asked for a meeting at Paramount to explain that they'd been unable to cut the budget and that, in their opinion, the movie was too costly. All the Paramount people concurred. As the meeting was breaking up, however, Charles Bluhdorn, the mercurial chairman of Gulf & Western, the conglomerate that owned Paramount, burst into the room and started fawning over Nichols. "I hear you are a very talented genius," Bluhdorn effused, and asked to know what the meeting was about. Nichols and his partner explained that they'd just canceled *Catch-22*, whereupon Bluhdorn exploded. It was ridiculous to cancel the film, he yelled—spend as much as $15 million if that is what it will take. "And most important," Bluhdorn added, pointing to his Paramount executives, "don't listen to these assholes."

The movie went forward and proved to be a major disappointment. The failure was a shock for Calley, who, with Ransohoff, had produced a string of successes, including *The Cincinnati Kid*, *The Americanization of Emily*, *Topkapi*, and *The Loved One*. At least *Catch-22* had been a noble failure—an example of artistic overreach.

John Calley is keenly aware that times have changed. The late '90s in Hollywood is the opposite of the late '60s. This is a time to make hits, not waves, a time to be a corporate player, not an innovator.

Can Calley fill that role? He's badly miscast in his current job, say the doubters. Both his age and his iconoclastic spirit militate against him.

Supporters challenge this thinking. Behind his eccentric facade, Calley is a skillful infighter, they say. His long years in exile have made him tougher, not gentler.

On this everyone agrees: There can be no more fascinating setting for the upcoming struggle than the battle-scarred playing fields of Sony. "We've seen everything over here," says one weary member of the Sony PR team. "It's been a war. We're ready for the next campaign."

—*GQ*, August 1997

.　.　.

Like John Calley, Joe Roth did not pursue the conventional executive career path, pausing along the way to try his hand at directing as well as producing. After this December 1997 article in GQ, *Roth's savvy as a filmmaker was much in evidence at Disney as he guided the studio to the top of the heap in 1998.*

CALLING THE SHOTS AT DISNEY

Even under the best of circumstances, my wife and I are not fond of black-tie banquets, but with this one we knew we were in trouble from the moment we were seated at our table. The faces around us were tense; the body language said, "How soon can we make our escape?"

The setting was the International Ballroom of the Beverly Hilton Hotel in Los Angeles, where in November 1996 more than one thousand of the entertainment industry's best and brightest had gathered to honor Joe Roth, chairman of the Walt Disney Studios. The funds raised from the sale of tables would go to the National Conference of Christians and Jews, an organization that inspires both admiration and humor. Indeed, each year at this event, whichever comic is working the dinner complains, "Which half of the room isn't laughing, the Christians or the Jews?"

Given the fact that their studio chairman was being honored, Disney executives were intent on demonstrating their fealty on this particular night, even though fissures were becoming apparent in the Disney corporate monolith. Adjacent to our table, for example, was one presided over by then president Michael Ovitz, who wore the haunted look of a prisoner of war. On the other side, looking equally ill at ease, sat Michael Eisner, the monarch of the Disney empire, who, we were soon to learn, had assumed a disdainful attitude toward his longtime friend Ovitz almost immediately upon hiring him.

Though our table was not directly enmeshed in the Eisner-Ovitz intrigue, it had its own dysfunctional cast of characters. There was Ted Harbert, who had lost his responsibilities as the programming chief of ABC (a Disney subsidiary) to be succeeded by a 32-year-old woman named Jamie Tarses, who, as luck would have it, was also at our table. A fidgety young woman with a shrill voice, Tarses made it quite clear she would have preferred any other table, with the possible exception of those hosted by Eisner and Ovitz.

A few tables removed from this vortex of discomfort was one presided over by Joe Roth himself. While colleagues around him fretted, Roth seemed to be having a jovial family dinner surrounded by his wife, children, and father-in-law, and assorted friends and relatives. When I went to his table to greet him, he rose and shook my hand. "Having a good time?" he asked, an enigmatic smile creasing his face. "I'm not sure," I confided. "I feel like a visitor to the Kremlin who happened to arrive in the midst of a palace coup."

Joe didn't break his smile. "Wait till you see the presentation," he advised cryptically. I didn't know exactly what he meant, but someone else was pressing in on us, and I decided not to ask.

About half an hour later, however, after the comedian of the evening complained, on cue, that either the Christians or the Jews were not laughing at his jokes, Eisner and Ovitz marched to the dais, with Joe Roth trailing behind. Though they were barely speaking at the time, Eisner and Ovitz had decided to jointly bestow the appropriate honors on their studio chairman. They got through it all right in a rather wooden manner. Roth seemed determined not to notice. He thanked his two bosses, congratulated the conference on its good work, and remarked how pleased he was that his family could be present for such a satisfying occasion. Then, still smiling, he shook hands with industry colleagues and honchos from the conference while most attendees fled to their cars as though a fire had broken out in the hall.

"Joe's amazing," my wife, Blackie, remarked as we filed out. "He creates his own environment around him. He didn't really attend our dinner tonight—he was having a nice little family get-together."

The ability of Joe Roth to seal himself in his own portable cocoon has been a key to his astonishing success in Hollywood. Though he neither thinks nor looks like a "suit," Roth at age 49 has managed to beat the suits at their own game. A calm, consistently courteous man who ambles around in jeans and sport shirts, Roth has worked for some of the toughest bosses in show business— Michael Eisner, Rupert Murdoch, and Barry Diller. Yet where others might have imploded, Roth continues to win at this perilous game.

This past summer was vintage Roth. While some of his arch-competitors, such as Warner Bros., stumbled badly with their summer movies, and while Sony, a chronic underachiever, produced the biggest crop of hits, Roth used guile and discipline to put together the most profitable slate of movies of any company.

His summer menu included the predictable action-adventure entrée *Con Air* (with a disciplined budget of $75 million), a soupçon of animation in *Hercules,* some tasty live-action children's fare in *George of the Jungle* (an unexpected $100-million hit), and two more surprises for dessert.

Shrewdly taking advantage of rival companies' alarm over soaring budgets, Roth picked up overseas rights to what turned out to be two of the biggest hits of the summer—*Face/Off* and *Air Force One.* Altogether he participated in five of the summer's ten $100-million hits and held his lead yet again in global market share.

This was no small feat, especially considering that live-action films had been the bête noire of Jeffrey Katzenberg, his predecessor. Though Disney had consistently made money on such animation hits as *The Lion King,* the studio had lost well over $150 million in the early '90s on live action.

Roth persuaded Eisner to approve another clever initiative: recycling parts of Disney's animated library as live-action films. Eisner had previously resisted this notion, but Roth had the idea of bringing John Hughes *(Home Alone)* into the equation as screen-writer and coproducer. The result: *101 Dalmatians.*

Indeed, Roth's summer success was so impressive that by early fall he was being rewarded with Hollywood's richest accolade—rumors that he was negotiating his departure. Though he vigorously denied the reports, they persisted. One story had it that a new independent company would be built around him, another that a rival studio was waving a big check. If Michael Eisner was to keep Roth at Disney, industry seers were saying, Eisner would have to do the one thing that he was most loath to do: utter something in Roth's ear about the possibility of succession. Eisner had demonstrated his irritability over this sort of talk three years earlier, when he tossed Katzenberg out of the company for campaigning too aggressively for the number-two corporate post.

The notion of Joe Roth ultimately sitting atop a corporate pyramid that generates $21.2 billion in annual revenues would strike those who have known him over the years as ironic. For among all the Hollywood power players, Roth remains the unlikeliest corporate soldier.

I first met him twenty years ago, when he was struggling to get his start as a film producer. Roth's first movie, a low-budget TV spoof called *Tunnelvision,* grew out of his association with a San Francisco improvisational comedy troupe, a sort of poor man's Second City that happened to include such future stars as Chevy Chase, Laraine Newman, and Howard Hesseman.

There was absolutely nothing in Joe Roth's demeanor at the time that hinted at his future. Slouching around in jeans and a T-shirt, the New York native seemed neither especially articulate nor even ambitious. I was serving as president of Lorimar Films, and I fostered one of Roth's low-budget comedies, an ill-starred effort called *Americathon.* The idea was an amusing one—a national telethon designed to save a financially bankrupt America from having its debts called due—but the film just didn't work. Some of my Lorimar colleagues got on his case, and it was then that I saw the real Joe emerge. The more he was battered, the more gracious he became—tough-minded about his objectives yet unstintingly reasonable in his responses. Hidden behind his hardened New York exterior, I realized, was a man who possessed both decency and resiliency.

But the life script that Roth had in mind did not entail a career in producing. He saw himself as a creative type, not as someone who hustled together packages. Even as he assembled his initial producing ventures *(Bachelor Party, The Stone Boy)*, he began stock-piling screenplays that he could direct.

Paradoxically, the man who would later prove astute in selecting hit screenplays for studios seemed unable to find a winner for himself. Between 1986 and 1990, Roth directed three films—*Streets of Gold, Coupe de Ville,* and the sequel to *Revenge of the Nerds*—all thoroughly professional but demonstrating no special style or point of view. Not given to self-delusion, Roth realized he wasn't setting the world on fire as a director. Besides, he wanted a stable family life, not the gypsy life of an itinerant filmmaker. In 1983 he and his wife, Donna, had lost their first child to sudden infant death syndrome, which left them both devastated. By the late '80s, with two more children inhabiting their household, Roth was determined not to be an absentee father.

His first move into the executive ranks was to form a partnership with a gruff, burly automobile wholesaler from Baltimore named James Robinson. They christened their company Morgan Creek. Robinson wanted to make a quick name for himself, and with Roth's help he did, fostering such movies as *Young Guns, Dead Ringers,* and *Enemies, a Love Story.* The duo was so successful that Roth was con-scripted, in 1989, by Rupert Murdoch to become chairman of the movie unit of Twentieth Century Fox. His immediate boss: Barry Diller, compared to whom James Robinson was a pussycat.

Brilliant but insistently confrontational, Diller had been president of Paramount before moving on to Fox to invent the fourth TV net-work. Roth and Diller seemed mismatched. Diller was a network-trained suit-and-tie man who loved to argue with subordinates, forcing them to rethink their positions. The soft-spoken Roth was not much for debate. As for the steel-willed Murdoch, his interest in movies was nil. He needed product for his global distribution platforms, and he didn't want to lose money obtaining it.

Roth's tenure at Fox was instantly brightened when he picked up *Home Alone*, the John Hughes megahit that Warner Bros. had passed on. From there he enjoyed what Hollywood likes to call a slam dunk—with projects like *Sleeping with the Enemy*, *The Last of the Mohicans*, and *Edward Scissorhands*.

After three and a half years, having produced a successful program of movies for Murdoch and Diller, Roth expected to be amply rewarded. But when he presented his fiscal demands, Murdoch saw fit to ignore them. With typical dispatch, Roth resigned to start a new independent film company with a longtime friend, Roger Birnbaum, that was to be based at Disney. Thrilled to return to filmmaking, the two set about fulfilling their new mandate. Jeffrey Katzenberg wanted to beef up his output of what he liked to refer to as "singles and doubles"—mid-budget movies that would make money without necessarily becoming blockbusters. Roth's new company, Caravan Pictures, churned out eleven such projects in the course of eighteen months, but the results were as dubious as the mandate. Roth found himself, as usual, making a great deal of money, but he knew that these mid-range movies were dying in the marketplace—witness *Angie* and *I Love Trouble*. Roth also felt that Disney wasn't supporting its movies with sufficient marketing clout, especially TV ads.

Then one day late in 1994 Roth received two invitations to the same party: Would he consider taking over the production reins of the Disney studio as a whole? The first contact came from Katzenberg, who expected to be moving into the number-two slot in the Disney hierarchy, formerly occupied by the late Frank Wells, and wanted Roth to succeed him. Katzenberg aggressively campaigned for Wells' old job before and after Michael Eisner's heart attack, which in Katzenberg's mind only underscored the need to clarify the issue of succession.

It was Eisner who next contacted Roth about the job, but Eisner knew something that Katzenberg did not: Katzenberg would be moving out rather than up.

As Katzenberg set about establishing DreamWorks SKG with his two partners, Steven Spielberg and David Geffen, and filing a $250-million lawsuit against his old employer, Roth began reinventing the way Disney did business. Whereas Katzenberg seemed to savor bureaucracy, Roth sliced the staff by more than twenty-five percent. Whereas Katzenberg intended to release as many as fifty films a year, Roth stated sharply, "I want to make pictures, not meet quotas." More important, Roth said he was simply not interested in the old "singles and doubles" strategy—a studio like Disney needed blockbusters.

Talk to Hollywood's principal dealmakers and they uniformly give Roth high marks for achieving his objectives. "He does his homework, and he gives you answers," reports the chief of one talent agency. Says an important showbusiness attorney, "Joe is one tough dog, even if he doesn't bark much. He knows exactly what he wants."

What he wants most urgently is to do his job and still have a life. Rising at six every morning to speed-read at least one script, Roth heads for the studio early but returns home virtually every night for dinner, ducking nearly all social functions. Friday afternoons are reserved for his son's soccer team, which he coaches. As one Disney colleague puts it, "I hate the expression, but Joe Roth is a true-blue family man, circa the 1950s."

Not that his job doesn't get to him on occasion. Roth was furious not long ago when a young filmmaker he had nurtured closed a rich deal at another studio even as he was editing a movie at Disney. Says an agent involved, "Joe is the king, and the king wanted me to come to his office and grovel. I groveled. I apologized. I kissed his ring." Roth is not a shouter; his deep voice becomes deeper and colder in anger and his accents more clipped. "He doesn't have to yell at you to let you know you're dead," says a lawyer who's had his Roth run-ins.

Though nearly everyone credits Roth with keen intelligence, this quality is also a point of criticism. "Joe is in a position of complete power, and instead of intelligent movies, what does he give us? *Con Air* and *GI Jane*," fumes one producer. "Somewhere along the way, he's lost his passion to make good movies."

Ask Roth about this criticism and he doesn't flinch. "I am probably more risk averse than I need to be," he says. "But Disney is a big company with a multitude of stockholders. Sure, I often go with what is safe, because the company deserves to have a return on its investment." Roth notes that amid the would-be blockbusters on his schedule, such as *Armageddon,* a $100-million disaster film destined for release next summer, there are movies that aim higher. Two of these projects, shepherded by Robert Redford, are *The Horse Whisperer,* based on the bestseller, and *A Civil Action,* based on a nonfiction book chronicling a lawsuit against a company accused of toxic-waste dumping. He also notes that over the years he has given a "go" to such estimable movies as *Barton Fink, Grand Canyon,* and *Grosse Pointe Blank* (which his wife coproduced).

Colleagues believe that as Joe Roth becomes more secure in his job, he will start taking more and more chances. On the other hand, few think his commitment to Disney will be a long-term one.

There are several theories about Roth's future. Some friends believe he will leave after his five-year contract expires and find a productive but noncorporate playing field. Michael Eisner has the right to renew Roth's deal for another two years, but some Disneyites feel that as Roth's power and respect continue to grow, Eisner may find him as much a threat as a resource. "Michael doesn't want a number two—the Katzenberg and Ovitz incidents reminded us of that," says one agent.

Insiders, however, believe that Eisner has mellowed following his searing experiences with Ovitz and Katzenberg and that he will fight to retain Roth. The board of directors, moreover, respects Roth much more than it did Katzenberg. "Look at Joe's credentials and you find an amazing similarity to those of Eisner when he got the Disney job," says one Disney veteran. "Both come from the creative side, and Disney's future is tied to its ability to innovate. Disney cannot be run by some numbers guy. An empty suit will drive us into oblivion."

Well, Joe Roth is the opposite of an empty suit. In the end, destiny will determine whether he will be the next ruler of the Disney empire. That is, once Joe Roth decides if he wants to be.

—*GQ*, December 1997

. . .

Hollywood executives habitually are loath to put their thoughts into writing, lest they come back to haunt them. The voluble, hyperambitious Jeffrey Katzenberg, however, was the exception. He wrote a thoughtful, well-circulated manifesto about the movie business in 1991 and, sure enough, five years later I decided to take a retrospective look at his assessments.

KATZENBERG MANIFESTO REVISITED

MEMO TO: Jeffrey Katzenberg

It was just five years ago that *Variety* published your twenty-eight-page document, the Katzenberg Manifesto, which marked perhaps the only time that a major executive attempted to write a comprehensive state-of-the-industry analysis.

At the time, many of us admired the pronunciamento as being both insightful and tough-minded. Reading it five years later, however, one overriding conclusion stands out:

While your memo set forth all the right information, it advanced the wrong prognoses.

Now, I realize it's easy to second-guess someone from the perspective of five years. I also accept your protestation that you wrote your manifesto for internal consumption, not for public perusal.

Having said all this, consider the following:

You wrote that "bloated event films" had left behind a trail of red ink and represented a blueprint for disaster. Wrong. A quick look at this summer's box-office results confirms the fact that "event pictures" have proven to be the salvation of Hollywood. Megapics yield megabucks, Jeffrey.

You predicted that Disney would succeed with a contrarian strategy of mid-range, "high-concept" pictures that were not star-driven. You even predicted that *The Rocketeer* would prove a proto-type of the hits of the future because it had "no giant stars, no big gross participants, and we own the rights and control the licensing." Wrong, Jeffrey. The Disney program of mid-range, live-action pic-tures ended up losing money (I don't want to get into an argument as to how much) and *The Rocketeer*'s domestic box-office returns dropped dead at $46.7 million.

You predicted that Disney's "maniacal, hands-on approach" would yield big returns for the studio, provided "the decision-making pyramid remained short and squat with a minimal distance between the place where the ideas come in and the verdicts get delivered." With this in mind you built a complex of "squat pyra-mids" like Hollywood Pictures, Touchstone Pictures, Walt Disney Pictures, et cetera. Interesting idea, but did it pan out? Why is Joe Roth now at work stomping on your pyramids and transforming the once-sprawling Disney executive corps into a tight hit team making half as many movies as under your regime?

Your memo even advanced the basic formula for a hit movie: "There should be a sympathetic protagonist who goes through some transforming experience with which the audience can relate." Arguably this formula did not apply to the two biggest hits of summer 1996, *Independence Day* and *Twister*. These pictures levitated themselves into megapics because they offered theme-park rides, not sympathetic protagonists who underwent transforming experiences.

Now, having said all this, Jeffrey, I don't want to suggest that your manifesto was utterly lacking in merit. Quite the contrary. You were very perceptive in your warnings about soaring production costs and superstar salaries. You were right on in cautioning the industry that "like lemmings, we are all racing faster and faster into the sea, each of us trying to outspend the other."

Similarly, who would not sympathize with your gutsy assess-ment of *Dick Tracy*. While praising its artistry, you wrote, "*Dick*

Tracy was about successful filmmaking, but it was also about losing control of our own destiny. And that's too high a price to pay for any movie."

Where your manifesto ran into trouble was in its unbridled optimism. Having succeeded with early films at Disney, like *Down and Out in Beverly Hills*, you seemed to conclude that a studio, if it were tightly managed, could grind out moneymaking, high-concept films with great consistency.

In all fairness, Jeffrey, your memo concluded that "filmmaking is not a science." While setting forth your rules "go for singles and doubles, hold down costs, keep hands on," you quickly added, "there are always exceptions to the rules."

Indeed, with this in mind, Jeffrey, I would like to invite you to write a guest column, a sort of updated Katzenbergian Manifesto. In it, you could reflect on the Disney experience and the emergence of "effects pictures," and, more important, set forth some rules that might govern the future of your new company, DreamWorks.

To be sure, you now have a couple of partners named Steven and David. In recent weeks, I've had occasion to talk to both of them about the state of the industry. I've come away with the feeling that they really don't believe in rules, but rather in making the best movies possible on a case-by-case basis.

Maybe that would be the most prudent manifesto for the next century, Jeffrey. No rules.

Remember when Hemingway wrote, "There is no one thing that's true, it is all true." Now there's a manifesto for you.

—*Variety*, September 3, 1996

. . .

As one executive after another got fired at Universal in 1998, I finally wrote the following open memo to Ron Meyer, the president, about his vulnerable role as the "last survivor." The story ran December 14, 1998.

NO MORE MR. NICE GUY

TO: Ron Meyer

I never thought I'd be saying this to you, Ron, but I think you need an agent.

I realize, of course, that you have performed this function for others over the years, and with great success. But now suddenly you've ended up with what can only be described as "the job from hell" and, candidly, you need a smart strategist at your side.

On paper, of course, you're king of the hill. Only three years away from agenting, you're now president of Universal Studios, in charge of all its activities, including movies. That's the rub. All the corporate buffers between you and that dreaded green light have been erased. With Casey Silver and the others gone, the buck stops with you.

How did you let this happen?

If you want a reality check, Ron, take a quick poll of your fellow corporate suits around town. The one job no one wants is that of studio chief, and it's not hard to see why. The movie business isn't a business anymore except for the stars and their agents. None of the corporate owners want to make movies. They just want to find a sucker who'll put up the money. If it wasn't for the Justice Deptartment, they'd all implement the equivalent of the NBA player-lockout.

And your company, Universal, is hardly an exception. Edgar Bronfman Jr. was not exactly thrilled last week in disclosing that Universal's film division would lose $65 million in the current quarter and perhaps even more in the next two quarters. That's a helluva time to take over a studio, Ron.

I'm only saying this to you because I consider you a friend. Come to think of it, almost everyone I've met in town considers you a friend. You're so tactful you could melt butter on an ice cube. You're the only person I know who can fire someone and make them feel good about it.

Well, you'll need that gift in the coming months, Ron. As studio chief you'll spend nearly all of your time saying no. Instead of telling stars how much money you've just made for them, you'll be informing them you won't pay them what they're asking.

A glance at Universal's problems in '98 clarifies your mandate. You'll have the dubious pleasure of instructing someone such as Martin Brest that he'll have to take a full hour out of *Meet Joe Black* in order for audiences to accept the movie. Marty's a lot of fun in meetings like that.

You'll have to tell a director such as George Miller that he'll have to deliver his movie at least a month prior to its release date so that the studio can test the film and make its changes. No more monkeying around with special effects until the eleventh hour. The George Millers of the world react very nicely to deadlines.

That's why you need someone else to take the heat, Ron. There has to be some poor slob with a fancy title for directors to scream at and superstars to abuse. There has to be an intermediary who can tell a producer, "Take $30 million out of the budget or take a hike." Then you can step in as the benevolent uberfuhrer who strives for an accommodation and makes everyone feel better.

Of course, all these problems become even more dire when a studio is on a cold streak, Ron. The level of tension rises exponentially. The stakes grow higher, tempers shorter.

I realize trends can be reversed. Studios that are "losers" can be reinvigorated. Two or three hits can turn things around.

But turnarounds like that don't happen unless someone plays the role of the bad guy, and guess who fills that role at Universal? It's you, Ron, the man who is everyone's friend.

Make that, was everyone's friend.

—*Variety*, December 14, 1998

. . .

The ultimate face-off between Michael Eisner and Jeffrey Katzenberg in a faux courtroom turned up more about business practices in the industry than anyone wanted to know. In the August 1999 GQ, I looked at some of the issues leading up to that trial.

FEAR AND LOATHING IN
THE MAGIC KINGDOM

The story was related to me by a TV executive—not your ordinary network bureaucrat, but a major player. Nearly a decade ago, Michael Eisner and Jeffrey Katzenberg, he told me, had decided to come in together to pitch an idea to his network. It was a truly bold and innovative idea that, if successful, would have represented a huge programming coup for Disney. Hence the joint effort, with Eisner and Katzenberg presenting their case with unusual fervor. There was even a hint of a threat in their presentation, as though to suggest that if they were rebuffed there might be repercussions from a higher corporate level. After all, this wasn't a normal meeting; this was the Michael and Jeffrey Show. This was big league.

Their proposal proved to be overaggressive, however, and despite their effort at intimidation, it was rejected by the network. An appeal was forcefully delivered to a higher level, but to no avail. The network executive survived the onslaught, ultimately moving on to a more exalted position. As for Eisner and Katzenberg, they shortly resolved their frustration by making an even more cosmic move: They bought a network of their own, ABC.

The anecdote is indicative of the folklore that came to surround the Disney team—tales of a megalomaniacal zeal that redefined corporate leadership in their generation. A tall, shambling man who delivered his orders in a rough, gravelly voice, Eisner was the innovator, the idea-a-minute management machine. Katzenberg, short and aggressive, was the implementer, the nonstop get-it-done apparatchik who came to be known as the "golden retriever." Orchestrating the duo was a rather princely individual named Frank Wells, who was Disney's senior business brain, a diplomat who could assuage the ruffled feelings of Eisner and Katzenberg when they clashed and also of those they trod upon in pursuing their objectives.

It was a neat arrangement. Until 1994, that is, when the Disney team imploded, causing Katzenberg to leave and later seek reparation through the courts.

I was in Europe this past spring when the most publicized phase of the Eisner-Katzenberg trial got under way. Time and again, key figures in the European entertainment industry would ask me incredulously, How could this happen? How could the guardian of a fabled brand like Disney permit an acrimonious dispute to end up in court? How could scores of sensitive internal documents find their way into the press, documents suggesting that Disney had shortchanged its creative partners in movies and TV?

Given Europeans' propensity for corporate secrecy, the episode seemed to them more akin to an executive suicide pact, and even in Hollywood, which is accustomed to displays of narcissistic greed, the Eisner-Katzenberg trial seemed surreal. In Hollywood, at least, the level of understanding was aided by two essential insights:

1. Though money was formally the issue (Katzenberg claimed Disney owed him bonuses totaling more than $250 million for his ten years of service), this was really more like a classic divorce trial, with feelings of rejection and animosity constantly bubbling to the surface. Hence a principal reason Eisner declined to offer the sort of secret settlement he had achieved with Michael Ovitz was that he truly disdained "the little midget" (as he once admitted calling Katzenberg) and was nauseated by the prospect of signing away $250 million without a helluva fight.

2. To Hollywood insiders, the sheer nastiness of the battle came to reflect the near paranoia gripping Hollywood's power players, a syndrome brought on by shrinking profit margins and the relentless demands of Wall Street for better numbers. If this particular battle seemed crazy, it only affirmed the craziness that had overtaken Hollywood's corporate culture.

The ultimate irony was that Disney would end up the battleground— a company that for years had represented a glowing success story in the business world. When Michael Eisner and his late partner, Frank

Wells, took over a sleepy animation factory in 1984, its sales were $1.7 billion. Fifteen years later, the company has become a nation-state unto itself, with worldwide sales in the $23-billion range.

Scan the photos on the walls of Disney headquarters and you see old Walt and his sidekicks looking like prairie folk who accidentally wandered onto the alien turf of Hollywood. Walt didn't much like show business and was vocal in his distrust of "those Jews" who, in his view, ran the town.

In annexing Disney, it was the plan of the Bass brothers of Texas and their partners to install Wells as president, with Eisner as his creative lieutenant. When Eisner balked at being number two, Wells gracefully stepped aside, agreeing to accept the role of consigliere. Eisner promptly imported the hyperactive Katzenberg, who had served him faithfully for years at Paramount, where both worked under Barry Diller.

The new Disney regime seemed to click instantly. Suddenly, the studio parking lot, long empty, was filled by 8:00 A.M. The previously torpid work ethic was supplanted by one that seemed almost pathologically frenzied. Katzenberg's personal idiosyncrasies became instantly mythic: his propensity for scheduling three breakfast appointments back-to-back; his 8:00 A.M. Saturday-morning meetings; his insistent phone calls to agents that uniformly began with "Whatcha got?"

The Disney style reflected a sort of institutional scrappiness. Consider the great Six Flags war of several years ago. The setup: An obscure theme park named Six Flags decided to run commercials on Los Angeles TV stations, aggressively pitching its virtues as a downscale alternative to Disneyland. Within days this routine act of self-promotion was to trigger a series of confrontations akin to a corporate Cuban Missile Crisis.

Pitted against each other were Time Warner, then the proprietor of the seven Six Flags amusement parks, and Disney, a company that basically believes it owns the theme-park business. Before order could be restored, this sequence of events unfolded: Disney refused to let the ads run on its local station, KCAL, causing Time Warner to call Disney a corporate bully. Disney canceled all its advertising in Time Warner's magazines. Time Warner canceled a major corporate meeting it was about to hold at a Disney resort near Orlando. Disney questioned the competence of Gerald Levin, Time Warner's chairman, pointing out that Time Warner kept tagging along on Disney ideas—opening retail stores, for example, and emulating Disney's afternoon-TV cartoon block with its own Tiny Toons. Time Warner started running commercials for Six Flags on other TV channels, asking why a family would want to go to an overcrowded place like Disneyland to see "a mouse and some dwarfs."

But wait. Time Warner and Disney, though bitter rivals, were also into each other's pockets: Each was a customer or a supplier for the other in records, cable TV, books, and, until recently, the overseas distribution of motion pictures. Suddenly, the big boys blew the whistle. Epithets stopped flying; nasty commercials were instantly canceled. Even in the bellicose, in-your-face '90s, executives were reminded, certain rules of corporate politesse were to be observed.

Futile as well as fratricidal, the Six Flags spat nonetheless provided a vivid glimpse into the corporate cultures of two of the most important players in the global entertainment industry. If Katzenberg was a demanding taskmaster, his boss, Eisner, was even more so. While Disney was regarded as the hot new place in town,with annual revenues that shot up sevenfold in a decade, there was also a steady exodus of senior executives who had either wearied of the tension or made so much money on their stock options that they were ready to move on to calmer shores.

But Katzenberg remained an ardent loyalist. As the years progressed, the face he presented to the industry became less that of the fervid "golden retriever" and more that of a budding corporate statesman, perhaps even the heir apparent. He gave speeches at industry functions. His manner became less abrupt. Most of all, he shrewdly positioned himself when it came to taking credit for major company successes. So much so, in fact, that some other key players took offense.

The glossiest success story was that of *The Lion King*, an animated feature released in June 1994 that went on to become the *Gone with the Wind* of its genre. Before *The Lion King*, feature animation was considered a solid business, with a bountiful video aftermarket. After *The Lion King*, animation became the miracle cure for the industry's ills. Not only was there a dependable audience awaiting each new release, but there were also no big stars waiting in line to grab their hefty percentages. *The Lion King* spewed out a billion-dollar profit for Disney and changed the face of the industry. And, not surprisingly, the movie also triggered a fierce competition at Disney to bask in its afterglow. Katzenberg, for one, clearly relished his association with the film. Whenever *The Lion King* was mentioned in the press, Katzenberg's name magically popped up. Given the dwindling returns on Disney's live-action movies, this was hardly an inept maneuver.

But there were other hierarchs in the Disney power pyramid who resented the perception that Katzenberg was the godfather of its animation. One of these was Roy Disney, Walt's nephew, who had focused on animation throughout his studio career. Roy Disney complained to Eisner that Katzenberg was trying to hog credit and was rudely dismissive of Katzenberg's contributions. Another dissident was Peter Schneider, a slight, rather diffident man who had come out of the Chicago theater to head Disney's animation effort. Schneider applauded Katzenberg for lavishing company resources on the animation program and for leading the marketing charge. At the same time, Schneider felt he'd led the way creatively; Katzenberg, in his view, was veering away from Disney's basic mission. Schneider saw animation in terms of whimsy and myth. Katzenberg, he felt, tended to view animation within the context of live-action characters and story lines—hence features like *The Hunchback of Notre Dame*.

At the time, none of Katzenberg's colleagues knew he was accumulating not only plaudits from the press but also formidable sums of money, thanks to a generous but secret bonus program. When

Eisner and Wells were granted a rich stock-options plan several years earlier, Katzenberg was excluded. Apparently out of guilt, Wells had designed a special bonus that would give Katzenberg two percent of all revenues from the motion pictures and TV programs made while he was studio chief there.

While Eisner and Wells soon were accumulating fortunes in the hundreds of millions through their options, Katzenberg, too, was getting rich, but no one, including Katzenberg, knew how rich. In designing his plan, Wells had left a lot of fuzzy areas. Would ancillary revenue streams, such as merchandising, be included in the two percent? What would happen if Katzenberg left the company before the expiration of his contract? No one knew the answers to these questions, not even Sanford Litvack, now Disney's chief of corporate operations, who claimed at the trial that he'd never heard of the bonus plan until preparations for litigation got under way. And because Wells died in a helicopter crash in April 1994, the precise definitions of what would become Hollywood's most discussed perk became even more of a mystery.

It almost seemed as if Wells, in his hubris, assumed the Disney team would go on forever. But in fact his death contributed to its breakup: Without Wells as the mediator, tensions at Disney became ever more intense, and Eisner seemed oddly uninterested in resolving them. Associates observed that as Eisner's money and power increased, his ability to admit mistakes or praise colleagues all but disappeared. As Katzenberg saw it, Eisner had also developed a tendency to forget past promises, such as his oral promise that Katzenberg would become his number-two man if anything ever happened to Wells.

The flash point occurred when Eisner suffered a heart attack in July 1994. Recovering in the hospital, he was prodded by his wife, Jane, and by others to appoint a number-two man—someone with operating experience. Eisner knew they were right, but he also knew that the individual he selected would inevitably come to be regarded as his heir apparent, and that bothered him. Also irritating

Eisner, by his own account, were frequent phone calls from Katzenberg, presenting himself as the only viable number-two man. As far as Eisner was concerned, this pressure was unconscionable. (Katzenberg denies campaigning for the job.) It also was a reminder to Eisner that Katzenberg, with all his talents, lacked the tact for the top post. A cooler head was needed.

That person was Eisner's close personal friend Michael Ovitz. The naming of Ovitz astonished key players at Disney. Though respected for his agenting skills, Ovitz was a complete outsider. He had no understanding of the Magic Kingdom's intricate geopolitics. The Disney empire had evolved into a collection of feudal fiefdoms, each with its own self-protective hierarchy. More important, Ovitz was hardly the sort of operational whiz Eisner required. He'd never run anything other than his relatively small talent agency. He was a dealmaker—indeed, a deal junkie—not a manager. The Ovitz experiment was, of course, a debacle. In his eighteen months on the job, Ovitz seemed like an organ transplant that the Disney corporate body had massively rejected.

But if the Ovitz choice proved a major headache, Katzenberg would soon become an even bigger one. Marching off to form DreamWorks with Steven Spielberg and David Geffen, Katzenberg before long was bidding up the prices of animation talent and otherwise positioning himself as a Disney competitor.

It was shortly after his self-exile from Disney that I encountered Katzenberg in Santa Monica. Attired in a T-shirt, shorts, and kneepads, Katzenberg had been rollerblading furiously along the beachfront, as though working off his rage. His indignation at Eisner's betrayal was so intense that he was incapable of rational discussion. As we sat down for a quick lunch, I could see the anger pulsing through his body. He seemed at once the battered wife and the rejected son.

And he clearly was not one to accept his fate passively. Though his new company, DreamWorks, had begun to enjoy considerable success, Katzenberg still burned. He had played a pivotal role in one of his industry's great success stories, and, by God, he was going to be rewarded for it. But no one knew what form his reward would take—not until the beginning of the big trial this past spring.

The trial, held before a judge who was acting as a sort of referee, was supposed to take place behind closed doors, the way the Disney crew had planned it. When I learned of this arrangement, however, I filed on behalf of *Variety* to open up the proceedings. With our case argued brilliantly by attorney Pierce O'Donnell, the court readily agreed, and the circus began.

It was clear from the beginning that the proceedings would be nasty. The Disney attorneys sought to depict Katzenberg as a scheming loser, even though doing so put the company in a bad light. His live-action movies were $231 million in the red at the time he departed in 1994, it was argued. They also claimed that by leaving before the expiration of his contract, Katzenberg had forfeited his bonus. Despite Katzenberg's claims of having tried to ameliorate the dispute, one of Disney's lawyers quoted a memo in which Katzenberg told his lawyer, "I want to be an absolute killer on this point."

Responding to this onslaught, Katzenberg's attorneys argued that Disney's reneging on the deal stemmed from Eisner's personal animus—evident in Eisner's comment to writer Tony Schwartz (who'd assisted him on his memoir) that Katzenberg was a "little midget." According to Katzenberg, he once tried to present a document spelling out his two-percent deal to Eisner, but when he handed it to him, Eisner "physically backed away," as though it were a bomb, and ordered his deputy to leave his office. The bonus was "an annuity for my children," Katzenberg said. Rebutting the charges that his live-action program was a failure, Katzenberg insisted that, over their full ten-year life spans, the films would turn out to be profitable, while his animated movies were a huge success.

Even as Katzenberg's attorneys were presenting their case, documents came pouring out into public view suggesting Disney was systematically underreporting revenue and overreporting expenses to its creative partners. Since Katzenberg was now in effect one of

those profit participants, these documents were germane, if inflam-
matory, as they surely would generate further litigation. To those
observing the case day by day, Katzenberg's side seemed to be winning—a notion confirmed shortly by the judge, who ruled that
Disney did indeed owe its former executive the two-percent bonus
despite his early exit to DreamWorks.

The implications of this decision were startling. It meant the
true cost to Disney of brushing aside Katzenberg would total somewhere north of $1 billion—surely one of the most expensive man-
agement decrees in corporate history. The actual dollars committed
to the Ovitz and Katzenberg settlements will total nearly half a billion. The incremental cost of doing business in a vastly more competitive environment spawned by the creation of DreamWorks
conservatively adds another half billion to that figure. Also to be
factored in is the impact on Disney stock: During a year when the
value of Time Warner shares was doubling, Disney stock tumbled
by some thirty-five percent, with part of that loss inevitably stem-
ming from a decline in public confidence in Disney management.
The aura of invincibility had been shattered.

Could it all have been avoided? While Eisner loyalists insist the
relationship between the two men was beyond repair, there are
those within the Mouse House who vehemently disagree. They
argue that, having worked together for almost two decades, both
sides could have made accommodations. Katzenberg had been anx-
ious to bring in Joe Roth as his chief of production. After he left,
Roth, the former production head at Twentieth Century Fox, was
given that job at Disney. Had Katzenberg remained, Roth's presence would have placed a buffer between Eisner and Katzenberg,
and Roth's expertise at live-action movies would have comple-
mented Katzenberg's strength in animation.

The alienation of Katzenberg, in their view, reflected two key
flaws in Eisner's character: his unwillingness to let anyone encroach
upon his power base and what some associates call his "Park
Avenue snobbishness." "Michael was born rich and grew up rich,

and, plain and simple, he feels he's better than those around him," says one former employee.

So while other executives might have tolerated Katzenberg's growing megalomania and found ways to deflect it, it was in Eisner's character to want to simply wash the slate clean. To this day, there is still no number two at Disney—indeed, no one who even approaches that status.

Yet, to Eisner, his former golden retriever's behavior during the trial only confirmed his worst suspicions. Speaking in harsh, blunt terms, Eisner testified that Katzenberg was greedy and that he "was negotiating with me through the press," manipulating the media through leaks and the release of sensitive documents. Katzenberg's conspiracy theories "would have made Oliver Stone proud," the Disney side charged. "I didn't hate Mr. Katzenberg," Eisner growled at one point. "I still don't hate Mr. Katzenberg."

Perhaps not, but he sure had me fooled.

—*GQ*, August 1999

.   .   .

Few in the history of the entertainment industry have been counted out more often, only to emerge on top of every struggle, than Gerald Levin of Time Warner. Not long after publication of this column in Variety *in April of 1999, Levin was to make another of his Machiavellian moves, sweeping aside the powerful team of Robert Daly and Terry Semel from the corporate hierarchy.*

SAGA OF SURVIVAL

It's hard to think of another corporate executive who's been fired more often than Gerald Levin. In the press, that is.

Over a span of ten years, Levin's ignominious fate has been sealed in the pages of *Forbes*, the *New Yorker*, and many other magazines. Even *Fortune*, a magazine owned by Levin's company, Time Warner, suggested that the CEO had a dangerous predilection for "risking his own neck."

Now approaching his sixtieth birthday, having survived ten turbulent years since helping to engineer the prodigious merger of
Time Inc. and Warner, Jerry Levin certainly deserves some sort of
special trophy as the Ultimate '90s Survivor.

Especially since he has more than just survived. His empire
today is Wall Street's darling, its stock showing a five-fold increase
from the level at which it was stagnating a scant five years ago.
While much of that rise can be traced to revisionist evaluations of
the future of cable, the company's individual units at this moment in
time are exuding good health. Its magazines are looking sharp under
the guidance of Norman Pearlstine, and even the long-somnolent,
entertainment assets suddenly are percolating—witness the performance of *The Matrix* and *Analyze This*.

Were it not for the fact that Jerry Levin is a rather somber, rab-
binical sort, one could say that he has the last laugh. Perhaps, in the
privacy of his home, staring at stock options worth more than $300
million, he's at least enjoying a chortle.

After all, *Business Week* reported a mere four years ago that
Levin was "attempting nothing short of a corporate revolution that
could easily blow up in his face." One news story after another
emphasized that Levin's lack of "charisma" had rubbed off on his
company—witness its limp stock price. That veteran stock tracker,
Harold Vogel, said Wall Street "had a betting pool" as to whether
the Time Warner CEO would last more than six months.

Why was Levin so uniformly discounted? Part of the answer
related to the corporate culture. Levin's measured, studious manner
posed a startling contrast to the style of his predecessor, Steven J.
Ross, a rambunctious, extroverted type who enjoyed glitzy parties
and the company of stars, and was also uninhibited about
spreading around the big bucks. Indeed, under Ross, big bucks
defined the corporate culture, creating, as John Malone once put it,
"a feudal state in which the barons had all the power."

Nor did Jerry Levin fit the tweedy, post-preppie stereotype that
long characterized Time Inc. Levin came from Philadelphia, not

Greenwich, Connecticut, the preferred Time Inc. enclave; also, he went to Haverford, a small Quaker college, not Harvard or Yale.

Apart from culture shock came corporate shock: First the shotgun wedding of Warner and Time Inc., the marriage that couldn't work, but did, followed by yet another cataclysm, Time Warner merging with Turner. Clearly the freewheeling Ted Turner could never coexist with Levin, yet they seem to be doing so.

Amid this "Sturm und Drang" there were continuing complaints about Levin's steadfast commitment to the world's most unglamorous industry: cable. By 1994 and 1995 the cable industry's cash-flow growth stalled, government regulation was stepped up, and, thanks in part to propaganda from the phone companies, Wall Street had concluded that other technologies had made cable an anachronism. Having emerged from the HBO cocoon, critics said, Levin was blind to the new horizons.

There were other land mines as well. The firing of Michael Fuchs, only six months after anointing him the savior who'd "clean up" the mess at Warner's music division, gave everyone in the empire a bad case of nerves. The deal with US West, aimed at reducing debt, struck critics as an example of balance-sheet shuffling so convoluted that the company could never extricate itself from its complexities. Then came the Teletext news-on-demand debacle, not to mention subscription TV. Amid all this, Levin's son was found murdered in his Manhattan apartment.

So how did Levin survive all these traumas? Ask those who worked for him, or negotiated against him, and you get a cacophony of explanations.

Despite his scholarly exterior, "he has enormous inner strength," observes the Capital Group's Gordon Crawford, a major investor.

"He's mind-bendingly lucky as well as being very tough ," says one high-ranking Time Warner executive. "It sure helped when Bill Gates decided to pump $1 billion into Comcast a couple of years ago, signaling Wall Street that cable would be the key in connecting households to the Internet. Cable was in style again."

Whatever the reasons, the furious infighting has stopped. The stock is soaring, the divisions are doing well, and the doomsayers have long since been put to rest.

And history will have to judge whether Levin, in inventing the concept of a media monolith encompassing all branches of information and entertainment, has created a brilliant corporate organism that will infuse the media with fresh capital and innovation, or will suffocate it in a financial and intellectual tyranny.

When the *New Yorker* profiled Levin on the brink of the Turner merger, it stated: "Twenty years ago, Gerald Levin had a very big idea. Now he desperately needs another one."

Guess what: He got it.

—*Variety*, April 19, 1999

PART II

DEALMAKERS

Of all the managers and lawyers who have woven their way into the center of Hollywood dealmaking and intrigue, none operated with more "cool," or effectiveness, than Sidney Korshak. Indeed, after I left the New York Times *to go to work at Paramount, I had always assumed that, at the very least, I would be able to write an interesting book about my studio adventures, drawing from my Paramount experience. As I described in the* GQ *of June 1997, it was Sidney Korshak who helped persuade me that this would be, shall we say, a problematic exercise.*

THE MAN WHO KNEW TOO MUCH

A span of twenty-five years wreaks great change on individuals. When I first met Al Pacino, a quarter century ago, he was clean-faced and hungry. Today he conveys the gravitas of a grizzled veteran. James Caan, the tough street kid, has mellowed into silver-haired beneficence. And Francis Ford Coppola, once tentative and unkempt, with his scruffy black beard, has become the proto-typical padrone, his demeanor suggesting a man who has seen it all and has surely shot it all, from the vineyards of the Napa Valley to the rice paddies of Vietnam.

These impressions swept over me not long ago as I attended a commemorative twenty-fifth-anniversary screening of *The Godfather.* Invited to the old Castro Theater in San Francisco were most of the movie's principals, including cast members Pacino, Caan, and Robert Duvall. Marlon Brando had also been invited, but always the glutton, he had demanded a $100,000 "appearance fee," which no one intended to pay. Also on hand were the producer, Al Ruddy, and the two Paramount executives who had patched the movie together, Robert Evans and me, as well as representatives of present-day Paramount, led by the steadfastly ebullient Sherry Lansing.

If Brando's grandeur was missing, Coppola's was very much in evidence as he embraced his guests, exchanging reminiscences about the shooting of a film that has achieved cinematic immortality. The astonishing legacy of *The Godfather* has been a mixed blessing in his life, Coppola acknowledged. It brought him wealth and power but also wrenched him from the career he had scrupulously laid out for himself—one devoted to making small, experimental films like *The Conversation* rather than big Hollywood star vehicles.

Coppola, the world-weary patriarch, stood in sharp contrast to the naïve and very straight young man I'd first encountered twenty-five years earlier. Working with Evans at Paramount, I had acquired an option on Mario Puzo's novel, and while others were trying to corral big-name directors, I became fixated on Coppola. Though Coppola had never made a hit picture, he excelled as a screenwriter, and his early directing efforts showed great promise. Most important, Coppola saw the movie as a great family saga, not as just another shoot-'em-up Mafia flick.

Initially, there were two problems: (1) his reluctance to direct a big Hollywood movie and (2) his lack of worldliness and total ignorance of Mobdom. His family was middle-class Italian. His father was a musician and a composer, not a Mafia capo. In fact, the only person who knew less about the Mafia than Coppola was Mario Puzo, the rotund, kind-spirited novelist. "Everything I know about 'the boys' I learned from books," he told me at our first meeting. Having written two novels that were embraced by critics but not by book buyers, Puzo had decided to write a commercial novel on a subject he knew nothing about.

Paradoxically, the innocence of Puzo and Coppola worked to their benefit. What distinguished their work was their focus on family and character. Others had held forth on the intricacies of Mafia tactics, but until then no one had so effectively scrutinized the bonds and traditions of a family like the Corleones.

What neither Coppola nor Puzo knew at the time was that, even as they were inventing their vivid Mafia power players, the company that was financing their movie, Paramount Pictures, was rife with real-life prototypes of characters in their movie. One of the most influential members of this group would later die in an Italian jail in a rigged suicide. Another would rise to infamy as a Mafia front man. The Paramount lot itself would ultimately become a beachhead for the Mob, a substantial piece of it owned by a company with shadowy connections to "the boys."

While Coppola and Puzo were prepping *The Godfather*, did they sense that, with the melodramas being played out in Paramount's corridors, they could have done their research simply by keeping their ears open? I'm convinced they didn't.

But the evidence suggests that, years later, Coppola decided to do some retrospective fact-finding. There are remarkable similarities between the plot of *The Godfather III* and some of the incidents that took place at Paramount and Gulf & Western (as its parent company was then called). Even the name of the bad guys' company in that movie, Immobiliare, struck a chord: Charles Bluhdorn, who ran Gulf & Western and Paramount, sat on the board of a real-life company called Immobiliare alongside Michele Sindona, a Sicilian financier who was also a key financial adviser to the Gambino family and other Mafia clans. Bluhdorn was fascinated with his Sicilian ally, who seemed to have total access to Europe's rich and famous, as well as a remarkable knowledge of the Vatican Bank's convoluted finances.

My own insight into all this advanced in stages. When Paramount recruited me for a senior production job in 1966, I'd been working as a reporter for the *New York Times* and so could hardly plead terminal naïveté. I knew Bluhdorn was a highflier—a dynamic, utterly reckless Austrian-born wheeler-dealer who had come very far, very fast. The corporate environment was so volatile I was convinced that within a year Bluhdorn would crash and burn or I would be fired along with Evans, who was as inexperienced at studio management as I was. Hence, in accepting the job, I promised myself I would keep careful notes so that, in a worst-case scenario, I would be able to write an incisive insider's account of studio life in the fast lane.

At the end of the first year, I realized that Evans and I were becoming adept at our jobs and had begun preparation on some formidable movies (our term in office ultimately lasted eight years). I also realized that the single most prudent thing I could do with my notes was not simply to discard them but to incinerate them. They were quite accurate; they were also quite dangerous.

In looking through these notes, I'd finally started to put together an assessment of Bluhdorn and his company. It was at first amusing to scan the vignettes: Bluhdorn secretly meeting with Fidel Castro, trying to persuade him to join in launching the ultimate capitalistic caper, a global sugar cartel; Bluhdorn boasting how he could make huge losses from the Julie Andrews movie *Darling Lili* disappear into thin air by shuffling the numbers into a phantom subsidiary (the SEC later tried to throw him in jail for these maneuvers); Bluhdorn declaring that new European friends, like Sindona, now gave him virtually limitless funding for expansion, even to the point of allowing him to launch hostile takeovers of A & P and Pan American Airlines.

In retrospect, it's easy to see that Bluhdorn was over the edge—a maverick bent on self-destruction. At the time, however, the perspective wasn't so clear. Raucous and ill-mannered, Bluhdorn presented himself as a spirited outlaw who was raiding the sanctum sanctorum of the entrenched corporate power players. While the CEOs were playing golf at their country clubs, Bluhdorn was stealing their companies out from under them. Besides, Bluhdorn was operating in New York and Europe. Evans and I were out in Los Angeles, working with a skeletal staff and supervising a program of twenty-five pictures a year. In the frenzy of Hollywood dealmaking, it was easy to overlook Bluhdorn's corporate machinations.

And there was more than enough to consume my attention at the studio. *Rosemary's Baby* was in production, with Roman Polanski directing Mia Farrow—an inexperienced young actress who had just become the bride of Frank Sinatra. Polanski was stretching Farrow to the limit, putting her through as many as thirty takes in an effort to elicit an appropriately tortured performance. Early in the shoot, I received a visit from a Sinatra consigliere, who urged me to intervene with the director. The number of takes must be limited to two or three, he instructed. He even offered me a strong incentive to take action—namely, that neither of my legs would be broken.

My retort was that I had no intention of passing that message on to Polanski and that, even if I did, he would ignore it. The incident brought home to me, however, the Wild West atmosphere that permeated the studio.

The reasons for this atmosphere went beyond Paramount and Bluhdorn. The entire industry was in a sad state then. Television had robbed the movies of much of their audience, the blockbuster hadn't been invented yet, and video was still in the laboratory.

Paramount in particular had been a pathetic invalid. Now, suddenly, Bluhdorn was pumping in big money. Since he was an outlaw, all sorts of fellow outlaws descended on the studio. It was both exciting and hairy. And there I was, taking scrupulous notes, keeping track of the players and their demands.

It was a vivid character named Sidney Korshak who indirectly made me decide to burn my notes. Always immaculately attired in a dark gray suit, the tall, somber Korshak had become a fixture at Paramount, constantly on the phone with Bluhdorn and visiting Evans almost every day. I always found Korshak to be impeccably polite but also utterly humorless. I don't think I ever saw him smile, but I was keenly aware of the folklore surrounding him. He and his brother, Marshall, had come of age in the Chicago of Al Capone, and he clearly felt at home in a number of power circles—not only big labor and big business but also "the boys." Korshak could settle a nettlesome labor dispute with a single phone call. Indeed, he could shut down Las Vegas. He never raised his voice, but seated each day at his favorite restaurant, the Bistro, two phones at his table, Korshak had extraordinary reach.

One day he dropped by my office to tell me that his son would be producing a movie at Paramount. I had never heard of the project, but Korshak assured me that it would be starting immediately. "Peter, my son has not produced anything before," Korshak confided. "I would be greatly in your debt if you kept an eye on him. He doesn't have your savvy."

When Sidney Korshak asked a favor, it wasn't smart to decline, especially when it was such a reasonable one. Korshak seemed relaxed that day. He started chatting about the state of Hollywood. His comments were, as always, clipped and discreet. At one point, he glanced at his watch, then excused himself and dialed a phone number. "Hello, Lew," he began. It soon became clear that he was conversing with Lew Wasserman, then chairman of MCA and the most powerful man in the entertainment industry. It was also clear that Korshak had accessed a private line, bypassing the customary secretarial intermediary.

After hanging up, Korshak praised Wasserman, noting how effectively and prudently the MCA boss ran his affairs. "Peter, do you know what's the best insurance policy in the world that absolutely guarantees continued breathing?" he asked. I shook my head. "It's silence," he said. He peered across at me as if he had just imparted great wisdom. In a way, he had. After all, how often did one receive advice from the man who was arguably the world's best fixer?

It was an especially persuasive reason to go back and burn my notes.

Inevitably, there have been times when I've regretted not having a journal to remind me of my years at Paramount. Myriad books and articles have been written about the making of *The Godfather*. Indeed, the movies of the late '60s and early '70s have achieved near legendary status, and Paramount made some of the best—*Chinatown, Paper Moon, The Conversation,* Franco Zeffirelli's *Romeo and Juliet, Rosemary's Baby, True Grit,* and *Goodbye, Columbus.* These movies were created amid promises and threats, blandishments and epithets, which by now have all blended together. The in-house detonations and the Bluhdorn tantrums have merged with those of the stars and the star directors with whom Evans and I interacted each day.

It would be fascinating to re-create precisely who did what to whom. On *The Godfather*, why was Francis Coppola almost fired after the second week of shooting? It would be great to have a record. On the other hand, I have felt a sense of security over the years, knowing that I took out Sidney Korshak's recommended insurance policy.

Korshak himself is permanently silenced now, having died quietly of heart failure. In his final days, he still put on his dark suit every morning, walked into his den, and watched television. He told family and friends he couldn't remember things anymore. Maybe he was simply acting out his code of silence.

Bluhdorn, noisy and rambunctious to the end, died of cancer in the Dominican Republic, though his associates put out the official word that he'd had a heart attack while flying back to New York.

Francis Coppola has outlasted them all, still directing movies and buying up wineries in his beloved Napa. Whenever he makes a star vehicle, the critics say it's not as good as *The Godfather*. And whenever he goes back to his original plan and directs a small movie, the critics admonish him for not aiming high enough.

For him *The Godfather* is at once his greatest accomplishment and his greatest curse. At the start of Mario Puzo's novel, Balzac is quoted: "Behind every great fortune there is a great crime." Part of Francis Coppola regards *The Godfather* as his greatest crime.

—*GQ*, June 1997

.   .   .

Even as Sidney Korshak was plying the corridors at Paramount, some deal-makers with even shadier pasts also were in evidence—men who ultimately helped inspire the plot of Godfather III. *In the* Variety *of January 7, 1991, I disclosed how very close the Mafia came to owning an important piece of Hollywood.*

HOW PAR WISED UP TO WISEGUYS

With *The Godfather Part III* rolling up strong box-office numbers, some insiders are wondering whether there's a hidden, almost subliminal, subtext to the film.

This story, like the plot of the film itself, cuts across generations and involves convoluted twists of fate.

At about the time Francis Coppola was preparing his first *Godfather* at Paramount some twenty years ago, a fascinating power struggle was gripping the studio. Interests closely linked to the mob had managed to establish a secret beachhead at Paramount. Using a satellite company, they'd even bought a major holding in the Paramount lot. Their incursion was the closest the mob ever came to exercising influence over a major movie studio.

It had been Charles Bluhdorn, the brilliant if mercurial founder of Gulf & Western (the conglomerate that owned Paramount), who had discovered this mess, was shocked, and took rapid steps to disentangle himself. Even as he did so, Bluhdorn watched in dismay as his erstwhile associates were sentenced to prison, fell victim to mysterious "suicides," or were "hit," Mafia-style.

Bluhdorn knew he had ventured dangerously close to the "black hole" and had saved himself. Paradoxically, throughout this period, two frequent visitors to his office were none other than Francis Coppola and Mario Puzo, the earnest young chroniclers of Mafia intrigues, both of whom had remained oblivious to Bluhdorn's behind-the-scenes machinations.

Their obliviousness carried great irony. At the time, both Coppola and Puzo, while confident of their story, were insecure about its factual underpinnings. The reason was that neither had actually met a real Mafioso. Puzo's best-selling novel, despite its air of authenticity, had stemmed purely from library research and his own imaginings.

It was only years later that Coppola and Puzo were to learn that some of the Mafia's key financial brains also were plying Paramount's corridors at the time. These men loved Puzo's novel so ardently that they actually toted it around with them, giving away copies as gifts. In his frequent visits with Bluhdorn to discuss *The Godfather*, Coppola would overhear heated phone conversations about schemes that were mind-bending in their complexity, and he sensed their ominous tone. But Bluhdorn, wary of the possible consequences, did not make his contacts available to the filmmakers.

Now, a generation later, Coppola and Puzo have had the last word. Having searched for years for a viable plot for the second sequel, their minds meandered back to the mysterious emissaries who had circled around Paramount some twenty years earlier.

And this time they were far more secure about their facts, thanks to subsequent revelations exposing the extent of the intrigue. In their script of *Godfather III*, Coppola and Puzo used the real names of some key entities involved in the struggle; Coppola even dedicated *Godfather III* to Bluhdom's memory.

Godfather III relates the efforts of Michael Corleone (Al Pacino) to achieve respectability for his family enterprise by acquiring control of a giant but shadowy European conglomerate called Immobiliare. In his quest, Michael opens up a hornet's nest of intrigue. The acquisition requires the consent of the Vatican. And there are some all-powerful European financiers who do not want Michael to achieve his objective.

In the film's operatic climax, Michael narrowly escapes assassination, and an assortment of schemers and Mafiosi fall before the onslaught. Even the newly anointed pope, who had been examining Vatican finances, falls victim to a veiled assassination.

Ring a bell? Think back to the mysterious death of Pope John Paul I in September 1978. In his thirty-three-day reign, the so-called "Smiling Pope" had launched an investigation into the Vatican's convoluted financial affairs. Those events, too, touched off a wave of hits and suicides.

And how about Immobiliare? There really was such a company—Societa Generale Immobiliare—and Charles Bluhdorn had served on its board along with a man who would come back to haunt him, a Sicilian financier named Michele Sindona.

Bluhdorn had helped Sindona raise the money to buy a twenty-percent share of Immobiliare that the Vatican wanted to dispose of. Immobiliare in turn purchased a major interest in the Paramount lot in Hollywood, thus giving the studio a much-needed infusion of cash.

In Bluhdorn's estimation, Sindona was a fascinating highflier with access to Europe's rich and powerful who now wanted to expand to the U.S. With this in mind, Sindona had become the biggest shareholder in the ill-fated Franklin National Bank, one of America's twenty largest banks, and even financed construction of the Watergate complex in Washington, D.C.

Then Sindona's bubble burst. He was sentenced to twenty-five years in prison for fraud and sixty-five other counts. The Justice Department revealed that Sindona also had functioned as financial adviser to the Gambino family, among other Mafia clans. Later extradited to Italy, Sindona was convicted of murder and died four years ago in a rigged suicide.

By the time Coppola had completed *The Godfather II*, Bluhdom had purged his company of the Sindona taint and had set it back on a solid course. In the final years of his life (he died in 1983 at the age of 56), Bluhdorn, who venerated Coppola, tried repeatedly to persuade the director to do a second sequel. He even jotted down story outlines that he hoped might interest Coppola.

The one thing he never did was sit down with Coppola and explain in detail what he knew about Michele Sindona, about the Smiling Pope, and about the other shadowy figures who had dominated his life briefly. Had he done so, he might have prompted an earlier start of *Godfather III*, avoiding the sixteen-year gap between sequels.

It's as though Coppola were reminding Hollywood's power players that he understood the secrets of the past. He knew how Bluhdorn, like Michael Corleone, had stepped too close to the edge and had barely saved himself. The message is there—how the lure of money and power can destroy the boldest of thinkers, whether they be denizens of the legitimate business world or of the subterranean world of the Mafia.

—Variety, January 7, 1991

. . .

Agents and managers play a unique role in Hollywood. They pitch the projects, make the deals, spread the gossip, and, in a sense, set the tone. In August 1996, I described in GQ *what happens when a talent agency experiences a sort of nervous breakdown.*

THE TROUBLED TEN-PERCENTERS

In show business, there's always been a tacit understanding of the relationship between "talent" and their agents. The talent (actors, directors, and the like) are the children who look to their agents as surrogate parents, dispensers of wisdom on career decisions, marital spats, or whatever. Hence, when Mae West was traveling in Europe with her pet chimp and became worried about its stomach problems, it was Johnny Hyde of the William Morris office who found a veterinarian and put him in touch. The venerable Lew Wasserman, back in his agenting days, was occasionally called upon to mediate divorce settlements for superstar clients like Clark Gable and Myrna Loy—he even divided up the personal property between Loy and her first husband, producer Arthur Hornblow Jr. And when Sylvester Stallone some months ago became nervous that his career was ebbing, he turned for solace to his Creative Artists Agency (CAA) representative, Ron Meyer, who has since been anointed president of MCA. Meyer rewarded Stallone with a three-picture deal that would pay him $20 million per picture—an arrangement that magically elevated the Italian Stallion's mood.

Lately, however, several events have disrupted this longstanding agent-client relationship and have raised serious questions as to who are the parents and who are the children.

A case in point: the implosion of the United Talent Agency. Formed five years ago, UTA quickly established itself as a highflier agency, having built the careers of such players as Jim Carrey, Sandra Bullock, and *Jurassic Park* screenwriter David Koepp.

Suddenly, the Big Three—CAA, International Creative Management (ICM), and William Morris—realized there was about to be a Big Four.

Then last April UTA began to self-destruct, the events unfolding in rapid succession. One Sunday night, the youthful principals of the agency convened an emergency meeting to fire one of their partners, a self-styled "warrior" named Gavin Polone, who represents such up-and-comers as Koepp, Conan O'Brien, and *Seinfeld* creator Larry David. A succinct statement was issued to the press, explaining that the 31-year-old Polone had demonstrated "inappropriate behavior" toward a fellow agent named Nancy Jones. "Inappropriate behavior," of course, has become the standard euphemism for sexual harassment.

The ferocious Polone promptly warned that he would not go quietly and was prepared to level charges of his own. Three days later, his former UTA partners, under duress, granted Polone a hefty settlement and issued a public apology for terming his behavior "inappropriate," declaring, oddly, that it was only the media coverage that was inappropriate. How this turnaround came about has been the subject of much speculation. The young warrior then disclosed that he was planning to become a manager and would take his substantial client list with him.

Now the virus started to spread. Martin Bauer, a founding partner and former president of UTA, contemplated suing his colleagues on the grounds that he'd been opposed to firing Polone all along but that his partners had excluded him from the Sunday emergency meeting. Jay Sures, a sharp young TV agent, abruptly quit, citing "intolerable working conditions," and hired the same lawyers used by Polone. UTA insiders first mumbled about Sures trying to "blackmail" the agency, then hired him back, promoting him to co-head of the TV department. Meanwhile, Nancy Jones, the supposed victim of Polone's "inappropriate behavior," signed on with CAA.

Viewing the confusion, Polone declared publicly, "I feel vindicated. I'm extremely happy."

There were a lot of agents around Hollywood, however, who did not share Polone's good cheer. The UTA implosion represented just one in a series of incidents that have blemished the image of the agency business and helped shake client confidence. The latest round of disruptions commenced a year ago, when Michael Ovitz and Ron Meyer resigned from CAA to assume important corporate posts, Meyer at MCA and Ovitz at Disney. Some felt their departure would energize the business of agenting, but instead it has destabilized it. The level of competitive angst among the agencies has become so intense that agents now spend the bulk of their time not servicing existing clients but maneuvering for new ones. "My job security rests on signing new clients," says one of the town's senior agents with some exasperation. "That's just the way it is, and I don't like it."

Agents have always courted new clients, but until recent years, the "rules of the club" were strictly observed. This meant that it was verboten to approach a client of another agent unless that client had indicated dissatisfaction and hence declared himself to be "in play." Now, however, there are no more rules and no more club. It's open season on every client, all the time.

The upshot is that many things simply don't get done. Scripts aren't read. Deals aren't closed. Phone calls aren't returned. "It's getting a lot harder to do business," one studio chief says. "The machine is sputtering."

One important manager reported that it took him an entire week to make telephone contact with a key CAA agent with whom he shares a client. The purpose of the call was simply to inform the agent that he had closed a lucrative new deal for their client. "I was just trying to report good news to someone who's supposed to be on my team," the manager says. "Imagine if I'd been trying to pitch him something."

Adding to the static are agents who have come to regard themselves as bigger stars than any of their clients. They go to extraordinary pains to get their names in the trade papers and to secure the best tables at restaurants. Like TV anchors, they obsess about branding themselves with a special look and style—hair, clothes, and phone manner.

Again, Gavin Polone is a vivid example. His black beard, like his black clothes, is designed to intimidate. Indeed, he wrote a magazine article earlier this year to explain the secrets of his rough trade. The only way to think of Hollywood is as "the Wild West for Jews," he wrote. "I see myself as the guy protecting the townsfolk (my clients) from the greedy landowners (the studio executives)." As such, Polone explained, the key to success is to "think of yourself as a warrior. . . . My goal is to erode my opponent's self-confidence, to make him doubt whatever leverage he thinks he has. . . . Experience has taught me that unless my gun jams or I am ambushed, these tactics will usually leave my rival lying in the dusty street."

Words like these may inspire Hollywood's whiz-kid agents, but they sow distrust among clients. As one director friend of mine puts it, "I want to build a career, not start a war. I need an agent, not a Green Beret."

Clients admire tough negotiators, to be sure, but more and more, the key to dealmaking is conciliation, not combat. In an era of spiraling costs, it requires give-and-take among stars and star directors to accommodate their salaries and contingent compensation. As it is, macho dealmakers have all but eliminated the two-star picture that characterized Hollywood's halcyon days. In that period, the goal was to "team," say, a John Wayne and a James Stewart or a Tracy and a Hepburn. The idea was not only to achieve "chemistry," but also to take the onus off a star to "carry" a picture. Today it's rare to find more than one superstar on a marquee, because their deals won't fit.

"There's a pervasive nastiness in the business today," says Martin Bauer, who survived the UTA wars and was restored as president. "Agenting used to be fun. The fun is gone."

As a kid starting out at Paramount, I was a witness to the earlier generation of freewheeling, pre-warrior agents. I remember the great agent Ted Ashley bouncing into a meeting to pitch a package involving two major stars. He was full of enthusiasm, ribald anecdotes—and candor. "If you want this deal, then I'm gonna stick you with a kid director that you don't want," Ashley tossed off. "You may feel that he'll screw up your movie, but I've got to get him a job and this is the only way I can do it."

It was hard not to respond to this cheerful gonifry. When my colleagues and I agreed to take a chance with his untried director, Ashley promptly summoned an aide, who entered carrying four bottles of champagne and some hors d'oeuvres. After all, a deal had been agreed upon, and it was time to celebrate.

Ashley's ebullience would seem out of place in today's abrasive, gray-faced, deal-making environment. When a Gavin Polone marches into your office, you need a Valium, not a champagne party.

"Talent agencies used to attract people who loved show business," notes Harry Ufland, a onetime agent for Robert De Niro and Martin Scorsese who left the field to produce. "When I was an agent, I worked for my clients. Today's kids work only for themselves."

"I take offense at agents pushing to get their names in the paper," says Dan Melnick, once the studio chief at Columbia. Jeffrey Berg, the CEO at ICM, agrees: "I wince when I see a story in the trade papers naming the agents who made a particular deal. It's wrong to insert ourselves into the process. We shouldn't seek to be singled out for doing something we're paid to do."

Why did things turn sour in the agenting business? Some showbiz denizens say it's simply the Zeitgeist—a reflection of the fiercely competitive, downsizing, mean-spirited '90s. Others put much of the blame for the changed atmosphere at the feet of Mike Ovitz. "It was Ovitz who made agenting a paramilitary exercise," says a CAA rival. In order to fortify loyalty within CAA, it's pointed out, Ovitz paid salaries of more than $1 million a year to either ten or twenty of his senior agents, depending on whom you ask. The result was to sharply increase compensation throughout the agency business.

"When you reached the era of the million-dollar agent, you began to get your 'warriors,' your egomaniacs, your agents wanting to be bigger stars than their clients," says one of the town's top producers. "You can't blame it all on Ovitz, but he started the ball rolling."

Ovitz himself is well aware of this criticism, but in his new role as president of Disney, he carefully avoids any discussion of the agency business. It's clear he got bored with agenting or, as one detractor puts it, he created the monster, then fled when he saw what he had wrought.

Ovitz's defenders insist he made a formidable contribution by inventing a more disciplined, sophisticated agenting machine. In its heyday, CAA captured the top stars because it was a better-run business. During my own tenure at film studios, when I submitted a project to CAA for a star or a director, the response was prompt and lucid, though often accompanied by a proposal involving an absurd amount of money. Submissions to rival agencies elicited a much more complex cacophony of replies. Different agents working for the same agency would pitch their own stars or directors in competition with other clients. The CAA of Mike Ovitz spoke with one voice; ICM and William Morris, in contrast, often spoke with many voices—and sometimes they propounded more interesting ideas.

Typically, the mail room and other training programs at CAA recruited young lawyers, MBAs and even Ph.D.s, all of them attracted by the prospect of big money. The fabled William Morris mail room of old, which produced the likes of Barry Diller and David Geffen, rarely boasted anyone with a college degree. "Our aim was to attract kids who possessed a genuine love of show business," reflects Leonard Hirshan, a forty-five-year veteran of the Morris office who still represents the likes of Clint Eastwood and Walter Matthau.

During his first week with the agency, Hirshan recalls, William Morris Jr. watched him open his first paycheck, for $38.50. "Ah, another young capitalist is born," Morris said, with a tinge of irony.

Like other veterans of his trade, Hirshan is appalled by the magnitude of the changes. In 1960, he recalls, the *New York Times* published an article by Dore Schary, a onetime studio chief at MGM and the playwright responsible for *Sunrise at Campobello*. Schary credited Hirshan with coming up with the idea of casting Greer Garson as Eleanor Roosevelt in the film version of *Sunrise* and went on to write, "Many people in show business enjoy making scathing remarks about agents, but I think agents perform highly useful and creative functions." It would be hard to imagine anyone volunteering that sort of praise for the agenting profession as it exists today, Hirshan observes.

In his well-crafted book *The Agency*, published last year, Frank Rose cites the long list of companies and individuals who tried to kill off talent agencies in the early years—vaudeville circuits, producers, movie exhibitors, and even a few stars intent on saving themselves some money. In the end, the pioneer agents outwitted their antagonists.

Today's agents, far brighter and better capitalized, confront a new set of rivals. Managers are playing a vastly more important role in the lives of stars, directors, and even writers. Entertainment attorneys are also gaining heightened visibility, and some players, like Kevin Costner and Joel Schumacher, who directed *Batman Forever* and this summer's *A Time to Kill*, have chosen to be represented by their lawyers and not use agents at all.

It was Raymond Chandler, in a novel appropriately titled *Ten Percent of Your Life*, who wrote, "Wherever the money is, there will the jackals gather, and where the jackals gather, something usually dies." Many showbiz veterans, noticing the ingathering of jackals, are determined not to be part of the body count.

—*GQ*, August 1996

.   .   .

Increasingly of late, agents and managers have been getting in each other's way in Hollywood. In the January 1999 GQ, I explained how this came about and the role the ubiquitous Michael Ovitz played in the imbroglio.

ENTER: THE MANAGERS

Now more than ever, if you want to start an argument in Hollywood, all you have to do is utter two words: Mike Ovitz.

Ovitz, of course, was the talent agent who, in reinventing his craft, made the mistake of upsetting the balance of power in the entertainment industry. At the core of his strategy was a very basic concept: In a celebrity culture, the clout of the superstar extends far beyond big salaries and gross participations. In wielding this clout, however, Ovitz, still technically the seller, became more powerful than the buyers and hence made himself the target of a great deal of fear and loathing.

And now, after an unfortunate intermission as president of Disney, Ovitz is at it again. No one knows quite what he's up to, but it's clear he's reinventing things, and thus disrupting the status quo. This time the target of his reinvention is the management business, which has always existed side by side with agenting. As between the Israelis and the Arabs, an uneasy truce has long existed between the two sides, interrupted by brief episodes of combat. The fear is that, once Ovitz completes his realignment, this truce will be irrevocably severed, resulting in an unholy war between the two factions.

Even prior to Ovitz's intervention, tensions had been rising. The titans of the agency business have become increasingly upset as bright young members of their fraternity have quit only to be reborn as managers, enjoying the broader entrepreneurial opportunities that profession offers. As a result, turf wars have broken out between agents and managers; not surprisingly, agents have derived a perverse pleasure from the lawsuit filed by Garry Shandling against his manager, charging a wide array of conflicts of interest.

These clashes may seem frivolous, but huge amounts of money are at stake, not to mention egos. The business of representing talent is an ancient trade—the William Morris office celebrated its hundredth anniversary last September—but only recently has it become an enormously remunerative one. There are at present at least a hundred agents and managers in Hollywood earning well over $1 million a year, and they have no intention of seeing their money and power eroded.

The distinction between a manager and an agent is at once meaningful and arcane. Reduced to simplest terms, the job of an agent is to find gigs and negotiate deals. The manager is forbidden by state law and by rules of the talent guilds from doing these tasks (though exceptions can be made on a case-by-case basis). He is supposed to be the deep thinker who masterminds clients' careers and holds their hands. "The way things used to be, you saw the managers in the clubs scouting new talent, but you never saw the agents there," observes Bernie Brillstein, the loquacious, leonine veteran manager who before his putative retirement was a partner in the powerhouse management firm of Brillstein-Grey Entertainment. "Managers found and nurtured the talent and hired and fired the agents. Managers shaped careers while agents made the deals and, now and then, came up with a piece of material."

What may have seemed like a logical division of labor has broken down in recent years. Many managers blatantly flout the rules, searching out work for clients and cutting deals. Agents, in turn, have anointed themselves as the deep thinkers who strategize and package—and still perform all the duties agents traditionally do.

And, not surprisingly, a growing number of stars, filmmakers, and even writers, out of sheer confusion, now retain both an agent and a manager. This can prove an expensive arrangement: Generally, agents and managers each take a ten-percent slice of the action, with another five percent usually going to an attorney, and still further fees finding their way into the pockets of business managers and publicists. "I like the security of having both an agent and a manager," one famous but aging actor confided to me recently. "Now I have two guys who don't return my phone calls."

Indeed, the problem with all this is that, in the end, it's still unclear exactly who is working for whom. The big management firms have become even more affluent by selling ownership stakes to huge corporations which themselves employ talent. Brillstein-Grey is partially owned by Universal Pictures, and Industry Entertainment (formerly Addis Wechsler) by Interpublic, a holding company for ad agencies and other businesses. A couple of the talent agencies have also been in similar negotiations, and on occasion they have taken on studios as clients—witness Creative Artists Agency (CAA) representing MGM at the behest of Crédit Lyonnais during MGM's period of reorganization. As a result, an actor may find his avowed representative negotiating on his behalf with a buyer that owns a major piece of his manager's company.

To be sure, the big law firms have gotten away with conflicts of interest like this for years and have been the targets of lawsuits as a consequence. The attorneys wave off these charges on the grounds that they are credentialed professionals and by demanding that clients sign forms acknowledging these conflicts, but managers have found themselves more vulnerable.

Hence the Garry Shandling suit, an especially nasty internecine squabble. The comedian, who created and starred in *The Larry Sanders Show* on HBO, not only was a client of Brad Grey's for eighteen years, but also considered himself a close friend. Shandling is known as a gifted, if highly neurotic and obsessive, individual who can be at once loyal and vengeful. The 41-year-old Grey, a savvy, meticulously polite man, is a study in understatement; he speaks softly, dresses modestly, and avoids displays of ego. Grey has effectively erased certain nuances of manner that once struck clients as neo-Ovitzian—reassuring hand gestures, effusive expressions of praise, et cetera.

Aspects of the Shandling suit cut to the heart of manager-client relationships as redefined in '90s corporate Hollywood. The comedian claims Grey used Shandling's celebrity to help build his huge business but didn't cut Shandling in on the action. According to the suit, Grey also double-dipped by taking his cut of Shandling's salary at the same time he was earning a fee as the executive producer of Shandling's show. Grey contends he amply rewarded his client for contributing to the growth of Grey's overall business and that it's standard for managers to take producer fees when they truly perform services in that capacity.

Most insiders believe the Shandling suit, set for trial in June, will either be settled or thrown out, but it has nonetheless provided an unnerving subtext to many maneuverings involving managers and agents. Agents are fiercely jealous of the fact that managers are allowed to serve as producers and executive producers of clients' movies and TV shows while they are barred from doing so. It isn't a matter only of money but also of ego and competitive advantage.

One manager, Chuck Binder, a cheerful, rotund man who represents Sharon Stone, Daryl Hannah, and a string of other prominent actresses, openly boasts that the studios cover his management fees by paying him as a producer, thus letting him serve his clients for nothing. This drives the agents crazy—they still deduct the standard ten-percent fee and don't have the ego satisfaction of calling themselves producers.

This may sound like a trivial complaint for an agent making $1 million or so a year, but it's precisely because of their big salaries that agents have become increasingly insecure. One partner in a major agency, who understandably doesn't want his name used, defined the problem as follows: "I represent a top star who has a lawyer making his deals and buzzing into one ear and a manager lining up roles and buzzing into his other ear, and what's left for my agency? We funnel him material. We give him access to our top writers." The unstated question is whether this particular star will continue to deem it good value to pay ten percent of his salary to his agent in return for these modest services.

And that, indeed, is why talent agents have become as nervous as they are wealthy. Some big agencies have responded by reducing their traditional ten-percent fee to five percent or less. Though some stars, such as Clint Eastwood, have remained stalwart in paying ten percent and never firing their agents (Eastwood has been represented by Leonard Hirshan of the William Morris Agency for more than thirty years), other stars who are self-styled dealmakers, Warren Beatty in the vanguard, have negotiated their fees to less than five percent. Indeed, a few decline to pay any fee, arguing that their residual value to the agency is sufficient—the ultimate product of the Ovitzian celebrity culture.

The emergence of agents as plutocrats, albeit insecure pluto-crats, has become an amusing sideshow in '90s Hollywood. Since many of the senior agents are relatively uneducated and unworldly, having started out in the mail room and having never imagined themselves as millionaire businessmen, they seem genuinely embar-rassed by their riches. Some agents, awash in unexpected capital, have retained their original houses but habitually buy neighboring houses as they become available, ending up the owners of vast, unwieldy compounds with weirdly structured add-on homes that look as though they were put together with Erector sets. Others obsessively buy homes in Santa Barbara and apartments in New York, which they admittedly never visit.

Working in a personal-service business and schooled in a rigid work ethic, most agents limit their vacations to a skimpy two weeks a year, but they spend lavishly on their brief escapes. One top agent leases a Greek tycoon's yacht each year; another rents castles in Tuscany, replete with huge staffs. Friends are invited along to par-take of the short-lived regal opulence. Then the agents return to their cell-like offices, put on their headsets, and immerse them-selves in their clients' problems again. "I concede it's crazy-making, but that's the way it is," acknowledges one agent now heading into his fifties. "I live like a king, but in the office I spend much of my time like an overpaid concierge, demanding my client get a better Winnebago on his next picture or persuading a studio to pay for his bigger jet and more expensive chef."

This oddly bifurcated lifestyle was one reason Mike Ovitz ulti-mately deserted the agency wars. Having effectively realigned the balance of power in Hollywood, he had become a bigger celebrity

and a more important player than any of his clients. He was orchestrating corporate acquisitions and management upheavals at the
same time he was counseling clients on marital problems and
helping them decide whether or not they should grow a mustache
for an upcoming role.

A shrewd manipulator of power, Ovitz upset some rival power
players who felt threatened by not only his weaponry but also his
cunning. David Geffen, among others, made no secret of his determination to derail Ovitz, but, paradoxically, it was Ovitz's erstwhile
friend Michael Eisner who did the most effective job. According to
Eisner, Ovitz failed to master his operational responsibilities during
his brief tenure at Disney. Reverting to his agent instincts, he conducted himself like a deal junkie, striking new alliances for the giant
company. Ovitz's allies paint a different picture: Eisner, a true control freak, refused to give Ovitz line responsibility and, indeed, saw
to it that no one reported to him. The heads of the major operating
divisions at Disney, who function like feudal lords, effectively froze
the newcomer out of their fiefdoms.

In any case, Ovitz has been at work lining up a new career, and
not surprisingly, his moves are deemed threatening to some of the
town's power players. The press-shy Ovitz has steadfastly refused to
outline his new venture. He declines even to admit he has one. It
would seem, however, that Ovitz wants to establish a diversified
enterprise with stakes in entertainment, sports, and management.
He already has a major interest in Livent Inc., which owns theaters
and produces musical extravaganzas such as *Ragtime* and *Fosse*. He's
trying to bring a football franchise to L.A. (see the August 1998 *GQ*
article "Crazylegs Ovitz"). He's an investor in a variety of high-tech
ventures and is convinced the distribution side of show business,
more than any other, will undergo a radical change. He's been
talking to important stars, directors, and managers about coming
together in an innovative, combined management-and-production
entity that would span these activities. Among the young managers
he's been importuning are Rick Yorn and his sister-in-law, Julie

Silverman-Yorn, who between them represent Leonardo DiCaprio, Cameron Diaz, Claire Danes, Matt Dillon, and Minnie Driver. The Yorns were intrigued by Ovitz's proposals but have to extract themselves from their contracts with Industry Entertainment. One reason the Yorns are willing to leave the firm is that, in selling fifty-one percent of their company to Interpublic in 1997, founders Keith Addis and Nick Wechsler didn't offer them ownership positions, which typifies the problems management companies encounter when they try to transform themselves into moguls.

If Ovitz can land the Yorn team and other bright young managers and mobilize top-line talent, the industry fears he will have the same impact on the management business that he had on agenting. In short, nothing will ever be the same.

More important, the balance of power between agents and managers, already unsteady, will permanently shift toward managers. It happened in the music business some years ago. Agents found their position weakened as lawyers and managers made the deals and wielded the power. More and more Hollywood stars and star directors may decide that, like DiCaprio, James Cameron, and Harrison Ford, among others, they just don't need the big agencies anymore.

If all this comes about, Hollywood's topography will be permanently rearranged and everyone will know precisely whose fault it is. It's that man again—the name that will, more than ever, start arguments all over town.

—GQ, January 1999

· · ·

With more and more agents pondering a shift in their role to that of manager, in October 1998 I wrote a hypothetical column in Variety *reporting (facetiously) that one major agency, United Talent, had furtively become a management firm, surrendering its agency status. Though many in the community realized the column was a joke, agents at UTA cried "foul," complaining that many outraged clients were demanding to know what was going on.*

THE CASE OF THE ANTSY AGENTS

This is one of those "now it can be told" stories that are always grist for newspapers. Two weeks ago, under a veil of secrecy, UTA, the United Talent Agency, officially switched its status from agency to management firm. No other major agency has ever made such an overnight switch.

I learned about the shift through one of the UTA clients who'd been asked to sign a new set of agency contracts. Since his original papers still had several months to run, he asked his then agent, now manager, for an explanation.

"Don't worry about it," came the reply, "I'm a manager now, but you're still my client. And you still have to pay me ten percent, except now I'll also be able to produce your next movie so the studio will cover my fee instead of you. It's a win-win deal."

The client, a friend of mine, was stunned. "But I thought there were these constraints—managers can't solicit work for clients and can't negotiate deals. Stuff like that."

"Don't worry about it," the agent-turned-manager replied. "No one pays attention to that stuff anyway."

As news of the UTA shift filtered out, the reaction at rival agencies was rather testy. "This redefines the whole structure of the industry," one senior CAA agent intoned. "And I thought Mike Ovitz was our only threat."

There were other tremors as well. The official staff psychiatrist at UTA submitted his resignation, stating that his services were no longer required. "Agents need day-to-day care," he said. "Managers are a less neurotic lot because they call themselves producers to help their self-esteem."

Jim Carrey, who is UTA's biggest client, was understood to have called his young agent, Nick Stevens, about the shift. "Don't worry about it," Stevens told him.

"Will the credits on my next project read, 'A Nick Stevens Film?'" Carrey asked, half-seriously.

"I'll never be a credit grabber, even as your new producer," the agent-cum-manager replied.

UTA's decision to become a management firm came at a time of rising tensions between agents and managers. A growing number of agents have been defecting to enter the management business. A prime lure, of course, is the chance to become more entrepreneurial by producing clients' projects and ultimately selling a stake in their firms to networks or other multinational corporations.

Managers have been watching developments in the Garry Shandling case with some concern since it raises conflict-of-interest issues that cut to the heart of the manager-client relationship.

As management firms have become ever larger, and their ownership more complex, some clients have been trying to figure out whether they actually work for their managers, or their managers work for them.

An ever greater number of actors and filmmakers presently find themselves in the position of paying ten percent to their agent, another ten percent to their manager, five percent to their attorney, and other fees to publicists and business managers. The pie has gotten bigger, but the number of people taking slices has also proliferated.

Given this climate, the UTA decision was considered inevitable by some.

The reaction of SAG and the DGA was benign. "We're studying the situation," said a SAG spokesman, adding that his guild liked to study situations. Networks and studios also were taking a wait-and-see attitude. "All it means to us is that we end up paying still more managers to be producers," said one production chief. "If they deliver their stars to us, what do we care? We don't know what a producer does anyway."

Indeed, the sharpest reaction to the UTA decision emanated from those managers whose clients are represented by the agency. The Gold-Miller Co., for example, represents Jim Carrey, who suddenly now has an abundance of managers and no agent. "We refuse to be alarmist about the situation," said a spokesman for the management firm.

As things turned out, he was right. Three days ago, an emergency meeting was called at UTA. Speaking with high emotion, several of the younger agents confessed they were having second thoughts. One said that, in his first week as a manager-producer, he found that studios were not returning his phone calls. Another complained he'd lost his prize tables at both The Grill and The Palm. Since agents tip far better than producers, they get the best tables, he was warned by Gigi, the resident guru.

"When I was an agent, people begged me for things," acknowledged one young agent. "As a producer, I'm doing the begging. It sucks."

A secret vote was taken and it wasn't close: UTA reverted to its status as an agency, effective late last week. The industry was not breathing easier as yet, however. A meeting has been set at CAA for this week to discuss emulating UTA's lead. "We're the true Masters of the Universe," one CAA agent remarked. "They couldn't make it work, but we could!"

Note: The events described in this column are fictitious—at least for the moment.

—*Variety*, October 28, 1998

.   .   .

The agency business is fiercely competitive and, from time to time, things get out of control. During one intense period of client shifts and agent raids in spring 1995, I took the occasion to propose some guidelines to agency presidents. Not surprisingly, they were ignored.

MEMO TO TALENT AGENCY CHIEFS

SUBJECT: Reality Check

In accordance with this column's custom of giving advice where none is solicited, I would urge you to pause for a moment from your frenetic activity to consider the following question: Is there a subliminal message in the fact that ICM's answer to Watergate occurred just as the calamitous baseball strike nears its climax?

If baseball is out of control, so indeed is the agency business. The rules of the game have long since been trashed. Competition has given way to chaos.

When I became editor of this newspaper, one of my first moves was to step up coverage of the agency business. Agenting, I felt, represented an important microcosm of show biz, all energy, flash, and big bucks.

As things turned out, this was one of those decisions I lived to regret. The level of competition and paranoia in the agency business is such that every story is greeted by cries of anguish. The whole exercise has proved to be more trouble than it's worth.

Agenting, it is clear, should be relegated instead to the sports pages because that is basically what the business has become. And, as such, it is clearly time for the people who preside over the agency business to get together and adopt the sorts of rules that helped baseball reach its primacy before the crazies took control.

Step One

A commissioner should be appointed (Fay Vincent is one candidate) to administer new Rules of the Game. He would have the final say in settling conflicts between agencies.

Step Two

An anti-raiding code should be adopted and enforced by the commissioner. This would simply codify the practices that prevailed before the 1980s: Namely, no agent may pursue a client unless that client had effectively let it be known that he is looking to change his representation. The late Stan Kamen of the William Morris Agency, one of the most successful agents in the annals of tenpercenteries, built up a solid client list without ever raiding anyone. A Stan Kamen Award should therefore be given to the practitioner who most clearly lives up to that tradition.

Step Three
A system of orchestrated trades should be administered by the commissioner's office, governing both agents and clients. Given the fact that young agents are feral by nature, they require frequent change of habitat; hence it should be possible for a third party to negotiate a trade whereby ICM and UTA could simply exchange two or three malcontents.

Similarly, if an edgy client like John Hughes wishes to leave CAA for ICM, only to return to CAA a week later, the commissioner's office should create a "Ricochet Rule" for clients who need to attract attention to themselves. In that particular week, for example, an ICM client would also be permitted to bounce back and forth to equalize things.

Step Four
Given the growing demands of hot young agents and the shrinking margins of the agencies, a salary-cap mechanism should be created along with what the baseball mavens call their "luxury tax" to facilitate revenue-sharing. This would help to create parity on the agency playing field.

Step Five
To complete the sports analogy, clients should have access to some sort of information about the effectiveness of their agents—the equivalent of a batting average, if you will. If an agent is batting .300 on his pitches, the client has a right to that information. The same goes for an agent who bats .150. At present it's the client who's paying the bills—and who is also in the dark as to performance.

Now, I realize that industry seers will pooh these proposals on the grounds that the top agents could never work together. I should point out, however, that, as the agent raids have mounted, the august chieftains of every major agency have called this newspaper to lobby for a reduction in the noise level. Specifically, each proposed that news of client shifts be taken off page one and relegated instead to a space inside the paper—a column we have labeled "The Ten-Percenters."

This rare show of unanimity bodes well for the future. At least everyone is on the same page.

And certainly the events at ICM this week should reinforce this phenomenon. The specter of four young agents in a late-night attempt to transport their files from ICM with the aim of forming their own agency poses a nightmare image for senior agents. Inevitably, threats of lawsuits and other punishment have quickly ensued.

In a way, the ICM melodrama seemed oddly anachronistic. Why were these guys piling papers into cartons? What ever happened to disks or even Xerox machines?

The incident reminded some of the confrontation a decade ago when one bright young agent resigned from William Morris with the intention of joining CAA. One of the senior graybeards from William Morris's inner sanctum confronted him in the hall outside his office. "You're fired," he shouted angrily at the startled agent, promptly locking him out of his office.

"You can't fire me—I've already quit," protested the agent.

"Then I'll take away your car," screamed his elderly boss.

The agent found himself trudging along El Camino in the rain, looking for a taxi.

The old-timers at the Morris agency in that era expected a certain level of decorum that has long since vanished.

Thus the time has come to consider the proposals advanced above. With their adoption, a new era of sanity and stability could return to the agency business. The dealmakers could stop banging into one another and return to the business of making deals.

They could also put their lives back in perspective. In Irving Lazar's memoir, published this week, the revered "Swifty" succinctly sets forth his philosophy of life. "The way I see it," he said, "you get to do what you want to do and you have a great life, and then you have to die—and that's the deal."

That, Swifty felt, was the best deal he could make. Perhaps it's time for the town's dealmakers to ponder their best deal, as well.

—*Variety*, April 3, 1995

.   .   .

When they're not raiding rivals, some agents play a constructive role in shaping the careers of their clients. Under Arnold Rifkin, for example, the venerable William Morris Agency devoted more and more of its resources not just to the big stars and big pictures, but also to the independent sector, and from time to time their forays were highly remunerative, as I explained in the October 1995 GQ. In 1999, the agency nonetheless removed Rifkin, replacing him with Jim Wiatt of ICM.

THE AGENT AS ENTREPRENEUR

The late Irving Lazar was the brashest (and shortest) agent I've ever met. He once pitched a project to me with a million-dollar price tag. I passed. Three days later, he was back on the phone, pitching the identical project but with a still higher price. When I reminded him of our earlier conversation, he was anything but fazed. "I thought you'd have the good sense to realize that it had improved with age," he shot back.

Swifty, as he was called, set forth his philosophy of dealmaking in his recently published autobiography. "Always shoot for the moon," he wrote. "That's the only way to make a deal. It's also the only way to have any fun."

Given this philosophy, I'm afraid Swifty might not have had much fun in the sector of dealmaking that now preoccupies a small but growing band of agents in Hollywood—the world of independent filmmaking. The trick to putting together movies like *Pulp Fiction* is usually to ask for less, not more. Instead of shooting for the moon, dealmakers find themselves caught up in negotiating esoterica like bridge financing, completion-bonding, and tricky back-end deals that substitute for cold cash. The universe of the niche picture is one of making do, of finding ways to stretch a

dollar and of arguing grips and gaffers out of things like meal penalties and medical benefits.

Though Swifty would not have been comfortable in this universe, Arnold Rifkin, the chief of the William Morris Agency's
motion-picture division, positively thrives in it. Not long ago, he
set up a special division at his ninety-seven-year-old agency whose
assignment is not to sign superstars or even to represent talent but
rather to stitch together the sorts of movie projects that top
Hollywood agencies traditionally disdain. The objective: to connect the right projects to money and also to a distributor.

Ever since movies like *Pulp Fiction, Four Weddings and a Funeral,*
and *The Crying Game* proved that there is a large audience for independent films, each of the major talent agencies has taken an
increased interest in putting together what *Variety* calls "niche pix."
CAA has its own experts in offshore financing, led by John Ptak, and
ICM has Peter Rawley, but the prime focus of these mega-agencies
has continued to be on major studios like Warner Bros. and
Paramount. "Rifkin's Raiders," meanwhile, have been beating the
bushes not only at independents like Miramax and Goldwyn, but
also at more arcane funding sources in the United States and abroad.

That Rifkin would lead the charge is a bit ironic, because he is
the sort of agent with whom Swifty would have felt at home—at
least on the surface. And there are those who would argue that
Rifkin, like many agents, is all surface. The slick 47-year-old agent-
warrior always looks as though he's just emerged from the shower—
he's well scrubbed, fresh-faced, and impeccably groomed. His
custom-made white shirts with their rounded collars (he shares his
shirtmaker with friend and fellow clothes-hound Pat Riley) look as
if they've never been worn before. "If Armani made pajamas, Arnold
would sleep in them," says one colleague.

Rifkin is unembarrassed about his obsession with appearances.
"The Armani fit seems complementary to my body," he says casually,
and he even lectures his class at the University of Southern California,
not to mention his agents, on the art of "self-presentation." "My

body fat is down to twelve and a half percent," he tells you matter-of-factly, as though reporting the time of day.

Not surprisingly, Rifkin is also a proponent of motivational slogans, spouting New Age aphorisms with an exuberance that would daunt even gurus like Tony Robbins. "I tell my people, 'Negativism is unacceptable,'" says Rifkin. "'Start hearing your own voice and your own success.'"

This positive thinking is particularly important, Rifkin believes, in helping clients deal with the ever-present specter of failure. "If a client of mine goes in the tank with a project," he says, "I surround him; I fill every room in his life. I compel him to see the positive side. No matter how great the failure, I always ask for more money for his next picture."

It was vintage Rifkin when, after Bruce Willis, his biggest superstar client, took a bath with *Hudson Hawk,* the agent marched into the market with sharply higher salary demands. On the other hand, he also encouraged Willis to do something most stars won't do—take small but flashy roles in niche pictures. Willis did this to great effect in *Pulp Fiction,* among others, and has increasingly been perceived as an actor's actor, not just another action star—a designation that should enrich and prolong his career.

Rifkin's renunciation of all things negative was put to the ultimate test three years ago, when he merged his Triad Agency with William Morris and took over as head of the combined motion-picture department. "I knew William Morris was a troubled place, but I was not prepared for what I found," Rifkin acknowledges. Not only had the agency lost most of its star clients—including Kevin Costner, Mel Gibson, and Julia Roberts—but a mood of defeatism had also permeated its hallowed halls. For too many years, the place had been run by somber old businessmen who were not agents but self-anointed "keepers of the legacy"—indeed, they had no feel for '90s-style rough-and-tumble agenting.

The agency had experienced many ups and downs in the decades since the original William Morris, a Jewish immigrant from Germany, hung out his shingle as a vaudeville agent. The major theater chains coveted his commissions and almost succeeded in putting him out of business, but Morris fought back. Mob domination of Las Vegas threatened to choke off revenues, but the agency hired its own in-house mobster to deal with "the boys." Lew Wasserman's MCA powerhouse pulled major clients away from William Morris four decades ago, but the Kennedy-era Justice Department decreed that MCA would have to choose between production and the agency business—it opted for production.

The Morris office had always been remarkably resilient, and Rifkin was determined that it retain this quality following the merger. He gathered his troops, delivering messianic lectures about the art of success. He refused to hold meetings in the dusty old conference room, spending an estimated $1 million on a sharp new one.

He also recruited new agents, breaking with the orthodox wisdom that newcomers should arrive with agenting experience. For example, the two new heads of the independent-film division, Rick Hess and Cassian Elwes, had never been agents—the 33-year-old Hess had been a development executive, while the 35-year-old Elwes had been a producer.

Rifkin demanded enthusiasm and total commitment from his staff. "Sometimes I would see Arnold prowling the corridors, looking for some poor soul hiding behind his desk rather than working the town," says a young agent. One of Rifkin's dictates was that every Monday night, four-man teams of William Morris agents would march into an important restaurant where industry figures gather, take a table, order some food, and then aggressively circulate. "I want my agents to show the town that they're out there," Rifkin says. "I want them to demonstrate their camaraderie."

The message: By mobilizing its own assault teams, William Morris could match the paramilitary Zeitgeist that prevailed at CAA.

In marshaling his forces, Rifkin knew there were solid assets on which he could build. Despite its setbacks, William Morris had remained a very wealthy company; there was no debt load such as that carried by ICM. The William Morris television department had retained its strength, as had Triad's music department. And despite the exodus of movie clients, such important stars as Clint Eastwood, Bruce Willis, Quentin Tarantino, John Travolta, and Daniel Day-Lewis remained.

Motivational speeches notwithstanding, Rifkin realized that there was little chance in the short term of stealing superstars like Tom Cruise from CAA and Arnold Schwarzenegger from ICM. But if he couldn't sign a big star, at least he could build a new one—hence the frontal assault on niche films. William Morris might not have had Mel Gibson, but it did have Tarantino. Perhaps it could synthesize a few more.

When *Pulp Fiction* exploded, Rifkin's lieutenants feverishly pored over Tarantino's early writings, and before long they'd pasted together an all–William Morris cast for Tarantino's very first script, *From Dusk Till Dawn*—one that includes Tarantino himself, George Clooney, Juliette Lewis, and the ubiquitous Harvey Keitel. The director, Robert Rodriguez, is an ICM client, but as Rick Hess explains, "In our division, we make pictures; we don't poach clients." The film started shooting last May.

Rifkin's team also lined up financing for *Shockwave,* to be written and directed by another client, *Waterworld* screenwriter David Twohy, whose only previous film was produced for Showtime; a newly signed client, Charlie Sheen, was given the lead role. It did the same for another successful young writer, Desmond Nakano, whose first directing effort, *White Man's Burden,* pairs the newly reborn John Travolta and Harry Belafonte. And Kevin Spacey, a talented young actor, was given the chance to direct his first film, *Albino Alligator* with Matt Dillon and Gary Sinise.

Rifkin and his lieutenants figure they've put together close to thirty of these niche pictures, and they feel they're just getting started. Says Hess, "We think of ourselves more as executive producers than as agents. Our job is to sell start-dates, not scripts."

To be sure, there can be a sale only if there's a buyer, and to this end the Morris mafia has proved quite imaginative. Instead of pitching only to the major studios, Rifkin, Hess, and Elwes focus on the satellite enterprises, such as Peter Guber's new company at Sony Pictures and Lakeshore Entertainment at Paramount—entities that can green-light their own projects, which a major will then distribute.

Also in Rifkin's sights, of course, are such independent-minded companies as the Ted Turner-owned New Line Cinema, the Disney-owned Miramax, and Goldwyn, not to mention new players like Rysher Entertainment (funded by Cox Enterprises) and overseas distributors like France's UCC. Rifkin's warriors have already hit on Live Entertainment, which is moving out of video movies into the mainstream, and Spelling Entertainment, owned by schlock-TV giant Aaron Spelling (and ultimately by Blockbuster), which is expanding into niche pix. Plus, there's a broad spectrum of foreign banks, like Newmarket in the United Kingdom, and foreign-sales companies, like J & M, that finance or partially finance independent films.

"Despite what anyone may tell you, there's a voracious appetite for niche product out there," says Hess. The key is to aggressively seek out the new players and tailor deals that are a good fit for them. In return, the agency takes a fee for bringing together the elements, or a piece of the picture if the budget can't encompass a fee. The agency also earns commissions from as many clients as it can fit into the package.

The agents at CAA might pooh-pooh these fervid efforts. That agency's take from *Forrest Gump* alone vastly exceeded total revenues that William Morris has elicited from its niche-pix division. Tom Hanks and director Robert Zemeckis ultimately could make over $70 million from that project, which would translate into a neat $7 million for the house that Ovitz built.

But this much must be said for William Morris's young guns: They are helping to build new careers, not just booking superstars. They are also spawning a new genre of edgy films in the $10-million to $20-million bracket that could serve as an alternative to the glitzy $60-million popcorn product of the major studios. *Albino Alligator* may not win an Oscar—it may not even make much money—but it will almost certainly display more freshness and energy than *Judge Dredd*.

"We're building something," says Rifkin. "We haven't signed Dustin Hoffman, but Dustin Hoffman is starring in a new film, *American Buffalo*, directed by our young client Michael Corrente, who we think will be the next Scorsese. But we can't sign Scorsese either, at least not now." However, the recent departure of CAA head Mike Ovitz for Disney and of his former number two, Ron Meyer, for MCA should level the playing field. William Morris has an incentive to shoot for the stars again, in addition to the indie players.

Rifkin stiffens in his chair, straightening his Armani jacket. "But you know Hollywood," he says with a smile. "'Now' can be a very short time."

—GQ, October 1995

.   .   .

Late in 1995, the International Creative Management Agency momentarily found itself in a position of virtual control over the key players in the action-movie genre. Its dominance inspired the following analysis, in a November column in Variety *that year, about the decline and fall of the Hollywood action movie and what ICM might do about it.*

ACTION IN TRACTION

MEMO TO: Jeff Berg and Jim Wiatt, ICM

With the wars between the talent agencies picking up in intensity, you've convincingly demonstrated that you're combat-ready. Indeed, as the agency business more and more takes on the tone of an action movie, perhaps it's no coincidence that ICM has effectively cornered the market on action stars. With the defection this week of Sylvester Stallone from CAA to ICM, your agency now represents Sly, Schwarzenegger, Steven Seagal, and Jean-Claude Van Damme, among others. I'm beginning to see why you identify with these warriors, and they with you.

The only problem, however, is that ICM's agent-warriors seem to carry almost more clout than the stars they represent, judging from recent box-office results. Both Stallone and Seagal, in particular, have taken their lumps lately; in fact, the action genre as a whole, once considered the mainstay of the international market, seems to be in trouble. Twenty years ago, half of the fifty top-grossing movies were of the action genre, while today's action movies dominate the lists of the biggest losers—expensive losers, at that. Look no further than two of Stallone's latest—*Judge Dredd* and *Assassins*.

If you plan to turn your action oligopoly to good advantage, and prevent the studios from self-destructing in the process, perhaps it's time to consider some drastic remedies.

Now, I wouldn't represent myself as the oracle of action, but, in talking to some veteran practitioners of this dying trade, I've come up with a few recommendations you might put before your hyperkinetic roster of action stars:

1. The classic action films used to be about character, not explosions. Hits like *The Magnificent Seven* or *The Great Escape* were essentially character pieces that meticulously built to a suspenseful climax. Look at *Fair Game* and you see what the genre has been reduced to—a series of detonations in search of a plot.

2. When the studios put together their great action films, they would entrust them to their best filmmakers, not their neophytes. John Sturges directed some classic action films, and does anyone out there remember a fellow named Cecil B. DeMille? By contrast, projects like *Fair Game* and *Judge Dredd* were directed by newcomers, as though the producers felt the genre was no longer deserving of seasoned hands.

3. The obsession with the international market has done more to subvert the action genre than any other influence. It's true that *Die Hard: With a Vengeance* managed to grind out $250 million overseas, but look at the subject matter of films that are scoring

big around the world today and you find more and more surprises—movies like *The Bridges of Madison County* and *A Perfect World* and comedies like *Casper* and *Dumb and Dumber,* which, according to conventional wisdom, aren't supposed to "travel." The assumption that the international audience doesn't give a damn about plot or empathetic characters may prove the biggest threat to Hollywood since the invention of television.

4. Action can't exist in a vacuum. Classic action set pieces usually took place within a broader framework—witness the action scenes in *Star Wars* or *From Here to Eternity* or *Ben-Hur* or, more recently, *The Fugitive.* On the other hand, *Fair Game,* a textbook on how not to make action films, sends Billy Baldwin and Cindy Crawford (she plays a lawyer, no less) racing from explosion to explosion without conveying to the audience who's doing what to whom. It's not action, it's nihilism.

5. The size of the gross does not increase in direct proportion to the size of the body count. There are signs around the world that audiences are pulling away from mindless violence—there's enough of that in everyday life. Only four people died in *High Noon* and you had to wait to the end to see it happen, but audiences could never forget that movie.

6. Instead of mass destruction, how about trying a little style—or is that now a dirty word in the action business? Take a look at the new James Bond movie, *Goldeneye:* Director Martin Campbell and co-writer Bruce Feirstein actually introduce the unthinkable—elegant settings, self-referential wit, sophisticated mind games. And it works.

7. Since I keep coming back to *Fair Game,* how about one last measure: Why not strip away the license from those who have vulgarized the craft? Joel Silver, for example—the man who gave us *Assassins, Fair Game, Demolition Man, Predator,* and *The Last*

Boy Scout. Silver's been dining out on *Lethal Weapon* for a long time now, but the bottom line is that his movies have become bogus and gross. Silver should still be allowed to blow away a few of his assistants each year, but keep him off a movie set.

So you see, Jeff and Jim, you have your work cut out for you. You have a great franchise over at ICM, and no doubt you will further embellish it. Along the way, however, you have also taken on a bigger obligation: The movie business is in a bit of a mess these days, and the decline of the action picture is one big reason. Just asking for bigger paychecks is not the answer. Indeed, as the CEO of one company points out, the burgeoning above-the-line fees already are "cheating the audience out of production values." The time is at hand when the major agencies need to add some constructive ideas to the mix.

Congratulations, guys. Now it's time to get down to work.

—Variety, November 13, 1995

.   .   .

Most talent agencies are hotbeds of intrigue, marked by intense rivalries between senior agents and junior hotshots. That generational clash inspired the following remarks in March 1993.

DRAWING THE BATTLE LINES

Here's another one of those issues that everyone's aware of but no one wants to discuss: generational angst.

Generational what?

I'll make it simpler: The kids coming of age in the entertainment business resent the hell out of their elders, and the "old-timers"—those in their forties and fifties—feel the kids are a bunch of avaricious upstarts.

That's what's known as war, folks, and you can see the manifestations when you walk the corridors of the talent agencies, the networks, the studios, or wherever Hollywood does business. It would be nice to ignore it, but it would also be self-defeating, for all this fear and loathing, unless confronted, could result in defections at the agencies, ferment at the studios, and an upsurge in business for the shrinks.

You come upon the symptoms at unexpected times. The other day I was visiting the head of a talent agency—an important one—when I bumped into a young agent whose mood was as blue as his Armani jacket. The kid had once worked as a gofer for me and I knew him to be bright and fiercely ambitious.

"I need some advice," the kid said, grabbing my arm and guiding me into his small office. He explained his dilemma: The president of his agency had just ripped into him for failing to return phone calls.

"The old farts who run this agency think that's the most important thing on the agenda," the kid complained. "If I called back every has-been who calls me, I'd never have time to put together my own deals."

He held up his phone list and it was imposing. One name on it was David Picker.

"Did you call back David?" I asked.

"Who is that guy?"

"Well, at one time or another he's been head of production at just about every studio in town, and he has a new deal at Paramount. He's going to make a lot more pictures."

"What's he done lately?"

I looked at the young agent and shook my head. "I think this issue is bigger than both of us," I said. "Just do me a favor and when you call back David Picker, give him my best."

Phone etiquette is a small issue, but it's emblematic of the factors fueling generational angst. Talk to top players in the agency business, like Ron Meyer of CAA or Jerry Katzman of the William Morris Agency, and they'll tell you they never go home at the end of a day without returning every phone call. It's not just a question of good manners, it's also fulfilling a sort of social contract.

"I talk myself blue in the face, but I can't convince my young agents to return phone calls," says the chief of a huge agency. "Just to rub it in, one of my best young agents today didn't even return my call."

To the seasoned agents or studio executives, show business runs on relationships. If you help solve one person's problems today, he'll be there to help you tomorrow.

The kids don't see it that way, and one reason is that they don't come into the business through the agency mail rooms. Today's new recruits arrive in town armed with MBAs from Harvard or law degrees from Stanford. They have come because Hollywood is perceived as the land of opportunity. The law firms are shrinking. The investment bankers are bailing. Show biz is "in," and the newcomers intend to invent their own rules.

"I don't believe the old-boy network works except for the benefit of the old boys," is the way one youthful, Ivy League–bred, development executive put it to me a few days ago. He'd cornered me at a reception because he wanted to ask some questions about *Daily Variety.* "Your paper is like a diary of how the old boys help each other," he said. "How about my generation? Where do we fit in?"

Their only shot, he said, is to put their own unique backgrounds to work for them. That means networking, and coming up with new schemes that their elders wouldn't think of.

The task of the elders, of course, is to mobilize their talent without getting ground under by the new wave. "If only the kids had any sense of history, any curiosity about what went before," one senior agent told me. "Mention any filmmaker who worked before 1980, and they roll their eyes."

This attitude is felt at many levels. At the Writers Guild Awards this week, Del Reisman, guild president, said "ageism" is turning into "an American tragedy. Talent does not know age. I find it to be a cruel and unusual punishment."

Reisman may be worried about the refusal to employ writers over the age of fifty, but others fret simply about getting their phone calls returned.

"There was such a sense of family in this business when I was a kid," one studio chief reflected. "A dysfunctional family, but a family nonetheless."

He paused for a second and grimaced. "Listen to me, I sound like an old man."

He's forty years old. But to the well-dressed kid delivering his mail, he was already extinct.

—*Variety*, March 29, 1993

PART III

STARS

Sly Stallone had just fired his fourth agent in four years and his career seemed on the wane when I decided to offer him some unsolicited advice in February of 1998. Less than a year later he'd shifted yet again.

SLY DIAGNOSIS: ASIAN FLU

MEMO TO: Sylvester Stallone

It was just twenty-two years ago, Sly, that you decided you weren't going to sit around passively and wait for that "perfect role" to materialize, you would get to work and create it. *Rocky* demonstrated more than testosterone; it showed real promise.

Well here we are in 1998, Sly, and candidly, some of us are wondering what happened to that promise—even to that testosterone. Your career has gone flaccid and your principal displays of macho seem focused on firing your agents. All your agents. In four years you've gone from CAA to ICM to William Morris to CAA and back to ICM.

Now, there's nothing wrong with whacking ten-percenters, Sly, but serial agent-firing, like serial marrying, suggests deeper problems.

One of those problems is rather obvious: Talk to action directors around town and they're offering their best parts to the likes of Chow Yun-Fat, Jet Li, or Michelle Yeoh. Hence the man who once was Rambo has fallen victim to the Asian invasion. The whirling, twirling Yeoh is credited with adding as much as $20 million to the gross of the last James Bond epic, *Tomorrow Never Dies*. Those are hot numbers, Sly.

All of which underscores the dilemma of being an action star: What happens when you start approaching the senior-citizen circuit? In Charles Bronson's latest movies, he looked more worried about his arthritis than his adversaries.

The action industry has changed. Heroes don't tote around automatic weapons anymore, like Rambo used to do. They rarely even land a solid punch. It's more about gravity-defying pirouettes and chopsocky pyrotechnics.

In your day, Sly, an action hero could get away with talking about his dream of winning a championship. Today, action stars don't talk at all.

Which brings us back to career choices: Since you don't trust your agents, I've taken it upon myself to set forth some of your options.

You can take a hiatus from moviemaking and focus on business. Certainly the Planet Hollywood burger chain, which you started with fellow action star Arnold Schwarzenegger, among others, could use some attention. At a time when the stock market is booming, Planet Hollywood's shares are as lifeless as one of Michelle Yeoh's chopsocky victims.

You can try your hand at directing. Another onetime action star, Clint Eastwood, has certainly created an illustrious afterlife as an auteur. Indeed, he's removed himself so far from his former genre that some who saw *Midnight in the Garden of Good and Evil* felt that it needed a little more action. A lot more action, in fact.

You can cut your price and try some "serious" acting. One of your myriad former agents, Arnold Rifkin, has regenerated several careers by putting big stars into small pictures at reduced salaries—witness Bruce Willis's star turn in *Pulp Fiction*. Unless I'm mistaken, he recommended that you appear in *Cop Land*, Sly, and that seemed like a step up from *Judge Dredd* or *Daylight*. But, of course, Rifkin got added to the body count not long ago.

You could reverse the Asian invasion by moving to Hong Kong and starting a new Hollywood-style action industry over there. Everything is topsy-turvy in Asia, Sly; moviegoers in that part of the world might be eager to see some Retro Rambo. It's been years since audiences witnessed the heartwarming image of an enemy being blown apart by an M-16.

These are just a few of the possible choices, Sly. I'm sure you are considering others as well.

But one word of caution: Whatever you do, try not to fire anybody for a while. It's gotten too confusing. There are rumors that you've been calling ICM, asking for Arnold Rifkin. Word has it that you've even called Ron Meyer at CAA to find out when your two-year-old, $60-million, three-picture deal would kick in. Meyer, of course, is now at Universal trying to figure that out too.

The most ridiculous rumor of all, Sly, is that you terminated one recent agent because he didn't return your phone calls promptly. Give it a rest, Sly—who do you think you are, Chow Yun-Fat? These are different times that call for different rhythms.

A suggestion: If you are angry with your agent, don't fire him; just turn up at the office, do a few kicks and whirls, deck twenty or so senior ten-percenters, then calmly fold your trampoline and return to the parking lot. It's amazing how quickly your next calls will get returned.

—*Variety*, February 9, 1998

. . .

Fresh from his unexpected triumph in Titanic, *Leonardo DiCaprio was careening around the party circuit and capriciously committing to unlikely roles in movies that would never get made when I decided to send him a friendly memo in the summer of 1998.*

LUBRICIOUS LEONARDO

MEMO TO: Leonardo DiCaprio

I've been watching you ricochet between movie offers lately, Leo, and frankly it's not been a pretty sight. Depending on whom one believes, you've been flirting with the idea of playing a cowboy, a Hemingway hero, a yuppie murderer, a schizophrenic law student, and, in this week's latest "leak," a wanderer who's in possession of a map to paradise. Each step of the way your salary has theoretically escalated to $20 million, then to $21 million, and upward.

All this has created a degree of confusion about your true intentions. And your publicist hasn't helped, leaping into the fray at one point to announce that you "may do the project or may do another project." OK, that clears everything up.

Now, I realize it's not easy being an instant superstar, Leo, but frankly your act already is getting a little old. Watching you lurch from offer to offer, reminds me of Marlon Brando in his later years when he'd wake up, yawn, scratch himself, and decide to say yes to whatever his next offer was. I once asked Marlon why he chose one particularly grotesque role and he responded, "They offered me twelve and a quarter percent of the gross. I always wanted someone to offer me a quarter percent of something." I told him that I understood completely.

Anyway, Leo, I honestly feel you should find a better role model for both your career and your diet. Most of your rivals in your age group seem quite adept at choosing roles. Matt Damon, for one, is either the smartest, or luckiest, kid around—go to see *Saving Private Ryan,* and there he is again, in another great role.

Now I don't want to be presumptuous, but I thought it might be helpful to suggest a few "do's" and "don'ts" that you might consider in plotting your career path. I hope these may be helpful.

First the "Do's"
Take off a couple of years and go to college, Leo. Think how great it would be to read something else besides scripts. Consider how refreshing it would be to be rejected by some college woman who thinks you're too callow.

Let go of that dream for the $20-million salary. At those prices you'll have to carry the picture. Think back to those olden days when studios could afford two stars or even three in a movie. That made for better movies, and also longer careers.

With this in mind, hire an agent, Leo. Sure, I know you trust your manager, and rightly so, but a good agent might connect you with the right material, not to mention directors and costars. It's helpful to get advice from different quarters.

Much as you may hate awards shows, you can't snub all of them. Your absence at the Oscars was graceless—you lost a chance to look magnanimous. By snubbing the MTV movie awards and accepting an award via videotape, you invited ridicule (and you got it: Witness the parody called "The Making of the Leonardo DiCaprio Acceptance Speech").

And Now a Few "Don'ts"
Don't take up Scientology, Leo. It's worked for Travolta and Cruise—they've certainly learned the secrets to self-assertiveness—but your fans respond to your self-effacing, nonassertive manner. Besides, you'll never be asked to plead with the IRS or other branches of government if you keep your autonomy.

Don't count on your female teen constituency for loyalty. They're a notoriously fickle lot, favoring bland, blond androgyny one moment, then suddenly demanding steroidal masculinity the next.

Don't pacify a producer by telling him you're "interested" in a project. Not only do you encourage premature press releases, but you also risk Kim Basinger–like lawsuits. And Kim lost that case, Leo.

Now, you may want to dismiss my list of "do's" and "don'ts," Leo, but I would urge you to think about the past career choices of "hot" young leading men of generations past. After *Star Wars,* Mark Hamill did *Corvette Summer.* Oops. Michael J. Fox followed *Back to the Future* with *Bright Lights, Big City.* Bigger oops. Macaulay Culkin followed *Home Alone* with *Getting Even with Dad.* That was a Freudian "oops." Tom Cruise followed *Risky Business* with *The Outsiders.* OK, he got away with that, but he was born lucky. And how about the other kids in that movie—Rob Lowe and C. Thomas Howell, for example.

It's tough being the hottest young leading man around, Leo. All you've got to look forward to is fame, fortune, and women. Come to think of it, I think I'll lavish my sound advice on someone who really needs it.

—*Variety*, July 13, 1998

.   .   .

The perennially extroverted Arnold Schwarzenegger seemed to be everywhere in early summer of '93, pitching his ill-starred movie, The Last Action Hero, *with an almost fervid desperation. The press, however, started hammering him instead of applauding him—something he was not accustomed to. In the* Variety *of June 21, 1993, I directed this memo to him.*

PRESCRIPTION FOR ANXIOUS
ARNOLD'S "IMAGE WHIPLASH"

I don't customarily dispense unsolicited advice, but in view of the vicissitudes facing Arnold Schwarzenegger this week, I'm tempted to make an exception. Now one might well ask, does anyone who makes $15 million a picture really need advice? Probably not, but even Arnold can stumble now and then. Hence the following:

MEMO TO: Arnold Schwarzenegger

SUBJECT: Image Whiplash

I've been thinking of you this week, Arnold, wondering whether you were falling victim to that ailment known as "Image Whiplash." This is the condition that occurs when, for no apparent reason, everything that appears in the press about you changes overnight from white to black, when reporters who on Monday were fawning are suddenly frowning on Tuesday. Arnold the Magnificent instantly becomes Arnold the Mendacious.

Knowing how seriously you take your career, I can imagine you sitting there, marshaling your advisers, feverishly analyzing the cause of the flip-flop. Hence I thought I might chime in.

First, some strategic observations. The anti-Arnold missiles have been fired from all directions. The *New York Daily News* depicts you as uncharitable. The *Los Angeles Times* suggests you cater only to reporters who ask cream-puff questions and who, like David Sheehan, are willingly "Schwarzeneggered." *USA Today* headlines "Schwarzenegger's star dimming . . ." and asks whether Arnold "can beat the bad vibes."

Why the sudden onslaught? One reason is simply that the press enjoys being fickle—it's an expression of power. "There's a gravitational law that goes beyond Newton," theorizes one Hollywood philosopher, Sylvester Stallone. "No one stays on top. There has to be a fall." Stallone should know. He's been down; his new film, *Cliffhanger,* may pull him up.

But let's be honest, Arnold: Part of the problem is of your own making. In your exuberance at achieving stardom, you've managed to develop some serious syndromes:

The Madonna Syndrome, otherwise known as hyper-hype: It's one thing to sell your wares, Arnold, but at the preview of *Last Action Hero* did you really have to say, "I've turned out another great movie and everyone seems to love it and the critics have already said that it's a great summer hit"? Chill out, Arnold—just because they gave you executive producer credit doesn't mean you have to sound like you're selling used cars.

The Bill Clinton Syndrome, otherwise known as overexposure: You don't need to be everywhere, overexplaining everything, Arnold. In the old days of the studio system, the superstars were remote figures—almost amorphous. By contrast, you're positively ubiquitous. It's understandable that you want to pitch *Last Action Hero,* but how many Planet Hollywoods can you open in one year? Most stars do an occasional magazine cover, but the newsstands these days present a sea of Schwarzenegger. You've done three *GQ* covers alone in the past six years!

The Mickey Rourke Syndrome, otherwise known as taking the press for granted: It's fine to make yourself available for interviews,

Arnold, but it's also gauche to boast about your PR productivity. At a huge dinner at Cannes last month, you announced with great pleasure that you had given more than sixty press interviews that day and had honed your answers so efficiently that the average interview took under three minutes. Now, Arnold, we're all gratified that you talk so fast, but a reporter doesn't want to be thought of as a Volkswagen on an assembly line. You're supposed to tell an interviewer how clever he is, not how quickly he can be processed.

Now, in saying all this, I don't want to fall into yet another syndrome—namely, becoming mindlessly overcritical.

You deserve high marks in a number of areas, Arnold, and I want to be up-front about these. In a business where rudeness is venerated, you are meticulously courteous. You stand behind your work. You take a keen interest in the world around you, although your politics make Charlton Heston seem like a '60s pinko.

You understand more about the specifics of distribution and dealmaking than any other top star I know, with the possible exception of Warren Beatty. Again, the difference is that Beatty shrewdly masks his knowledge while you flaunt it. Ask Beatty about the definition of adjusted gross in his newest deal, and he'll start talking about Jack Nicholson's art collection. By contrast, you sometimes sound like you're preparing your doctoral dissertation in film finance at Harvard Business School.

Again, there's a lesson to be learned from the past, Arnold.

When stars of a previous generation, like Steve McQueen or Robert Mitchum, suffered image whiplash after the press turned on them, their mentors gave them some sound advice. Both cautiously withdrew from the fray. Both also mastered a type of StarSpeak—a marvelously arcane rhetoric that was essentially incomprehensible to a normal human being. Hence, on the rare occasion that they granted interviews, a reporter would listen carefully, then go home and stare at his notes with total helplessness. What they had transcribed was, in fact, a form of gibberish: The words themselves made sense, but, assembled into sentences, they made positively no sense at all. The Hedda Hoppers of that era would thus take pity and invent their own felicitous responses.

Arnold, perhaps you should take a lesson in StarSpeak. Forget the bravado, the hard-sell aphorisms, the self-hype. Forget about Planet Hollywood and all your other adventures in commerce. Cool down. Relax.

All of a sudden everyone will forget you're the bad guy of the moment and start loving you again.

—*Variety*, June 21, 1993

.   .   .

At a time when most superstars were stubbornly holding out for the glitziest roles and the fattest deals, Bruce Willis was succeeding with a different strategy of supplementing his action films with artistically ambitious independent efforts. Hence the following words of opprobrium in March 1996.

AN ARTFUL GESTURE

MEMO TO: Bruce Willis

Forgive me if this column seems a bit awkward, Bruce, but, you see, I'm not in the habit of tipping my hat to a movie star—especially at this moment in history when every star in town seems to be demanding $20 million as his price for accepting a role. At the risk of sounding rude, that seems like an absurd amount of money—it's downright vulgar. I remember when you first started tossing around incendiary devices in *Die Hard*, Bruce, and, candidly, I never figured you for $20 million. I was wrong—you have several such offers on the table, I am told.

So you win my plaudits, Bruce—not for joining the $20-million club, but for starting an entirely different type of in-group. Time and again, while other stars keep whining about being typecast and pigeonholed, you've put yourself on the line by accepting offbeat roles at sharply reduced prices. Your delightful tour de force in *Pulp Fiction* was the most celebrated of these acting escapades, but you also played supporting roles in *Four Rooms, Death Becomes Her,* and *Nobody's Fool,* among others.

Hence, besides being the ubiquitous fish-out-of-water action hero, you've also been a nebbish plastic surgeon, a shell-shocked Vietnam vet, and a crooked boxer on the lam.

And not only do you seem to be enjoying yourself, but it's also enhanced your career. Studios haven't stereotyped you; they actually think of you as an actor!

Meanwhile, your agent, Arnold Rifkin of William Morris, has not only not been blocking your strategy, fearful of blowing off some fat commissions, but has also been actually encouraging these capers.

"I think a movie star has a responsibility to make good things happen," Rifkin says matter-of-factly. "When you reach that level of success, it becomes a question of commitment to one's craft. I think it's an absolutely terrific idea."

To say the least, Rifkin's opinions are not exactly universally accepted. Most top agents and managers in this town are dead set against Willis-style price-cutting on several grounds: If their star bombs in a small role, they're afraid it will cause major career damage. The "cut-rate" fee may then actually stick. Most of all, agents fear being second-guessed by other agents, especially now that client-swiping has become a Hollywood obsession.

Hence, prodded by their brain trusts, most stars continue to hold out for exorbitant fees as they march sullenly from one bad role to the next. It's no mere accident that some of the biggest turkeys of late boast considerable star power—Julia Roberts' *Mary Reilly* will be a huge money-loser, not to mention other vehicles starring the likes of Sylvester Stallone, Harrison Ford, Demi Moore, and Denzel Washington. It's getting scary out there, Bruce, and you know it better than most; after all, you, too, have lived through the likes of *Hudson Hawk, The Bonfire of the Vanities,* and *North.*

Given the failure of so many superstar vehicles, will the spending spree abate? If anything, the wind seems to be blowing strongly in the other direction. Nicolas Cage's reward for getting totally swackered in

Leaving Las Vegas is that his price has doubled from $3 million to $6 million. Robert De Niro, who seems to be in a new picture every couple of months, suddenly is demanding $14–$16 million for his next role. The ubiquitous John Travolta has seen his price soar from $150,000 *(Pulp Fiction)* to $18 million. Kurt Russell and Wesley Snipes have become $10-million actors. Demi Moore and Julia Roberts have hit the $12-million mark, and Sandra Bullock, who was paid $250,000 for *The Net,* now asks $10.5 million. And George Clooney will get a $10-million payday when he becomes the next Batman.

Meanwhile, what are you up to, Bruce? The way I hear it, your total up-front pay for *Pulp Fiction, Four Rooms,* and *12 Monkeys* combined for under $1 million. That's not exactly philanthropy, but, by the standards of your profession, it comes close.

Here and there, a few actors are following suit, of course. Jack Nicholson did *The Crossing Guard* for scale out of friendship to Sean Penn, who directed it. It goes without saying that Nicholson will receive far less money from his fifteen-percent stake of the gross receipts than he did from his famous supporting part in *Terms of Endearment.*

A couple of other stars also have worked for sharply reduced prices, but mainly to jump-start their directing careers—for example, Kevin Costner in *Dances with Wolves* or Mel Gibson in *The Man Without a Face.* But that's far different from what you've been up to, Bruce. You've actually put yourself on the line for your craft— acting. And as a result, you've helped some pretty good movies get made that, were it not for you, would have fallen by the wayside.

As I said at the outset, tipping my hat to a movie star doesn't come easily to me. But, there's always a first.

—*Variety,* March 4, 1996

.   .   .

Like Bruce Willis, Jack Nicholson as well had rung up remarkable successes in a series of idiosyncratic roles. I summed up his approach in this column in November 1992. Of course, he was later to top himself with the quirky hit, As Good As It Gets, *in 1998.*

JUDICIOUS JACK

Since the big stories lately have been about angst and turmoil, it might be therapeutic to focus for a moment on someone who embodies a vastly different quality—durability. Studio mavens may come and go, but Jack Nicholson, quirky and idiosyncratic as ever, has quietly embarked upon his fourth decade as a megastar. Indeed, with riveting performances in *A Few Good Men* and *Hoffa,* Nicholson's presence dominates the holiday slate of ambitious and expensive pictures.

Robin Williams put it aptly at a recent Oscar show: "There's Jack Nicholson—and then there's everyone else." But what makes Nicholson's durability all the more remarkable is that he has invented a whole new category of stardom. Sifting through an immense pile of offers, he can find that unique role which, while it may only encompass three or four scenes, can totally transmogrify a film—and also make him countless millions of dollars. Witness *A Few Good Men* or *Terms of Endearment.*

Nicholson took on *Terms of Endearment* for no money up-front and gave an edge to what could be seen as a "soapy" film. For a mere $500,000 a day, he transformed a potentially static and stagey show like *A Few Good Men* into compelling drama. Doubtless millions more will gush forth. Jack Nicholson is surely the highest-paid character actor in the history of movies.

And he deserves to be. I feel strongly about this because I remember the Jack Nicholson I first met in the '60s—a genial, rough-around-the-edges, Irish kid from Jersey who had begun to run out of dreams.

In those days Nicholson was already a battle-scarred veteran of the B-picture circuit. He'd worked as a writer, actor, associate producer, and occasional grip on the kinds of movies even Roger Corman would just as soon forget. He'd fought dysentery doing two-bit action pictures in the Philippines. He'd even trekked to Cannes to peddle foreign rights to biker pictures. His friends and partners were gonzo '60s filmmakers like Dennis Hopper and Bob Rafelson—men with big egos and also high ideals.

Nicholson felt he had learned filmmaking from the bottom up, but no one seemed particularly interested. When I first intercepted him, he had just finished shooting a biker film but had no idea how it would cut together. He'd originally been an associate producer on the film, but when Rip Torn dropped out, Nicholson had been eased into one of the key roles. The film was *Easy Rider.*

Things were so lean for Nicholson that when Paramount offered him a supporting role in a big-budget musical, *On a Clear Day You Can See Forever,* he accepted the part even though he hated the project. Robert Evans had initiated the idea of using Nicholson; he had seen him in a B picture and felt there was something in his lopsided, sardonic smile that lit up the screen. When they finally met at Evans's Sherry Netherland suite, Evans offered Nicholson $10,000 to play the role. Nicholson blanched, then sent his agent from the room. He walked over to Evans, a total stranger at that time, and pleaded his case: "Look, pal," he said, "you're talking to a broke actor facing child support and alimony. Make it $15,000." Evans, an ex-actor himself, was touched by the direct appeal. They settled at $12,500, but Nicholson's key scene—the only time he actually sang in a movie—ended up on the cutting-room floor.

It didn't matter, because *Easy Rider* burst upon the scene and suddenly Jack Nicholson had a career. His filmography since then is well known and amazingly eclectic.

It spans *Five Easy Pieces* to *Witches of Eastwick, Carnal Knowledge* to *Broadcast News, Chinatown* to *Heartburn.* There have been turkeys along the way: Witness the recent *Man Trouble* or the stillborn *Ironweed.* But somehow a debacle like *The Fortune* would always be followed by *One Flew over the Cuckoo's Nest.*

His occasional forays into directing have been equally unpredictable. *Goin' South* had freshness and energy, but *The Two Jakes* seemed ill-fated from inception. Now Nicholson talks of a desire to return to directing, as though yearning to master a craft that had eluded his grasp. "I feel I'm ready for another try," he says pensively. "Maybe another road picture. Something. I want another go at it."

Spend some time chatting with Nicholson about his films and you quickly realize his success is no fluke. I know of no other Hollywood actor with a sharper mind, and his street smarts are reflected in business dealings as well. Nicholson understands how to shape a deal to gamble on his instincts—when to go for the big up-front deal, when to ask for no money but a heavy back-end participation. He abjures the high-profile agents and managers; his coterie of advisers has been unchanged for decades and none has ever got his name in the paper.

The results have been extraordinary. His take on *Batman* alone was $50 million. Some believe Nicholson to be one of Hollywood's three or four wealthiest actors, but no one would know it from his attire or lifestyle. Says one longtime friend: "Jack is so frugal he lives in a house that's probably worth $500,000, but it contains his art collection which is probably worth $150 million."

Nicholson is diffident about discussing his art collection—"my pictures," as he calls it. The "pictures" comprise an eclectic assortment that Nicholson himself accumulated at auctions. They literally spill out of his house—a Chagall in the bathroom, a Picasso in the hallway. "I bought what I liked," Nicholson explains casually, as though talking about a collection of ties.

Just as he bought what he liked, so he lives as he likes. Though he has a girlfriend and two children, they live in a separate house some distance away. Nicholson understandably is loath to discuss his idiosyncratic family life, but if he wants to do it "my way," it's understandable considering his own personal history. He was well into his thirties before he learned his family secrets: The person he'd thought was his sister was actually his mother while the person he thought to be his mother was in fact his grandmother. When he'd sorted it all out, sisters ended up as aunts, nephews as cousins, and so on.

Perhaps he's found a way to use the eccentricities of his past to fuel his acting career. Who else could summon up such resources of humor, malevolence, and pathos to suit character after character?

Who else could levitate those eyebrows and invent such a superbly lopsided, sardonic smile?

—Variety, November 16, 1992

. . .

Even as Willis and Nicholson were plying their unique career paths, most of the big stars still seemed bent on pursuing the big bucks and their work increasingly showed it, as I pointed out in GQ *in October 1996.*

GRAND DELUSIONS

I do not pretend to be a confidant of movie stars and have never run with anyone's coterie or rat pack. On the other hand, I have, over the years, found myself in lengthy deliberations with many stars and those who thought of themselves as stars. I'm not referring here to that pathetic form of interaction known as the celebrity interview, but rather to the grimmer, more businesslike dialogues involving scripts, directors, locations, costars, and, to be sure, money.

Indeed, thinking back on these discussions, I am bemused by how differently stars present themselves when they are talking business from when they're acting out their roles for a magazine interview. These are actors, after all, and as such they come off as rational, lucid, self-possessed individuals. That's not the way they talk when the tape recorder clicks off.

I remember talking to the late Steve McQueen for half an hour before realizing there was no point in going on without a lexicon—when McQueen was stuck for a word (which was often), he simply invented one, assuming his listener would catch his drift; I didn't. I once chatted with George C. Scott at some length and was puzzled by his apparent hostility, until I realized he was so drunk he was about to fall off his chair.

Back in the days when he was a big star, I thought I was having a conversation with Robert Mitchum, until I realized he was actually talking to himself. I doubt if he even knew I was present. Mel Gibson and I were engaged in a rather urgent colloquy about the choice of director on one occasion until, right in the middle of a sentence, he simply walked away, which was all the more puzzling since it was his sentence, not mine. Paul Newman in his younger days suggested we talk about a script while taking a drive. It soon became apparent, however, that he was more interested in demonstrating the prowess of his souped-up Volkswagen Bug than in dealing with script problems—the little car had been equipped with a Porsche engine, which enabled it to blast past startled motorists.

My purpose here is not to argue that all movie stars are cads and ingrates. Some are both gentle and genteel. Clint Eastwood is such a good-spirited sort he cannot bring himself to ask fellow actors to read or test for roles in films that he directs. He feels that process is demeaning, so he casts his projects on the basis of viewing their previous work.

The point is simply, that intrinsic to the nature of stardom are pressures that induce extraordinary degrees of paranoia and narcissism. This was also true back in the era of Chaplin and Pickford, but these pressures have exponentially increased in recent times.

It's not hard to figure out the reason. It's all about money.

Movie stars have always been amply compensated for their unique "look" and other gifts, to be sure. During the days of the studio system, major stars like Spencer Tracy and Clark Gable made between $300,000 and $600,000 a year, which would translate into big bucks today. They were, nonetheless, employees of the studio, subject to suspension and dismissal. More important, they were not permitted to share in the ultimate earnings of their films—no cut of the gross. They were in the business of being actors; they would be shocked that the business of being a celebrity has turned out to be vastly more lucrative.

But today's big stars are celebrities first and actors second. As such, they have taken on the status of multinational corporations, with phalanxes of advisers and vast holdings in businesses and real estate around the globe.

A big star today doesn't just perform in a film; he effectively owns it, or at least a major portion of it. Mel Gibson, Arnold Schwarzenegger, Tom Cruise, and other members of this elite fraternity earn between $15 million and $20 million in up-front compensation against gross participations ranging from ten to fifteen percent. What this means is that Tom Hanks can make $50 million from *Forrest Gump* and Tom Cruise can equal that take for *Mission: Impossible.* And all for perhaps two or three months' work.

Thanks to the new math of filmmaking, top stars and star directors are becoming vastly more wealthy than the studio executives for whom they presumably work, amassing fortunes in the hundreds of millions of dollars. Steven Spielberg, who produces pictures *(Twister),* directs *(Jurassic Park),* and is a partner in a production company (DreamWorks), could become one of the five wealthiest Americans by the end of this century, a billionaire many times over. His gross participations in his movies slide up to as high as fifty percent as revenues from each project accumulate.

What impact is all this having on the delicate psyches of the top stars? We're still too early into the new epoch of the celebrity super-rich to draw any firm conclusions, but going by early anecdotal evidence, I would suggest the following: The impact is crazy-making.

We're not just talking temper tantrums or flights of egocentricity here. We're talking about paranoia and self-destructive behavior. And the results, more and more, are up there for the public to observe, both in the work and the nonwork.

Witness the case of Jim Carrey, the once amiable young Canadian who was principally responsible for one of this year's serious turkeys, *The Cable Guy.* A while ago, Carrey was living in his car, sending home a few bucks to help his family whenever he happened upon a gig. Then along came surprise hits like *Ace Ventura: Pet Detective* and *The Mask,* and the young comic was instantly wealthy. He moved into a new multimillion-dollar home in Brentwood only to realize that he had few possessions. He dispatched his valet to buy basics like soap, towels, and silverware, not to mention dog food.

It was Mark Canton, the mercurial chairman of Columbia TriStar, who officially anointed Carrey a superstar by offering him $20 million to assume the lead in *The Cable Guy*, a decision that was greeted by hoots of derision from other studio chiefs. Carrey had not built a suitable track record, especially overseas, to join the elite $20-million club, they argued.

Canton not only doubled the young actor's salary, but also turned control of the project over to him. The original script was a simpleminded buddy-comedy by an aspiring writer named Lou Holtz Jr. who'd been working in the office of the Los Angeles County district attorney at the time. The script was judged to be good enough to elicit the tidy sum of $1 million. Nonetheless, Carrey and a young director named Ben Stiller decided to turn it into something they considered to be much more interesting—a satire of psycho thrillers like *Fatal Attraction*. This appealed to Carrey because it would supposedly afford him the chance to stretch as an actor.

As things turned out, the entire movie proved to be a stretch. The first third seemed a replay of *Dumb and Dumber*, only to turn abruptly into *Cape Fear*, Part II. Carrey was terrible—"a volatile comic talent in free fall," as Janet Maslin wrote in the *New York Times*. And though Mark Canton still insisted that the film ultimately would make money for his studio, it would certainly be the least successful Carrey vehicle on record.

The entire experience left Carrey cranky and confused. He steadfastly refused to talk about *The Cable Guy*, burying himself instead in his next project, *The Truman Show*, for which he was to be paid a mere $12 million.

John Travolta's behavior on *The Double* provided yet another scenario of the movie star as unguided missile. This past June, Travolta, fresh from the success of *Broken Arrow* and *Get Shorty*, was to start a movie for Roman Polanski in Paris, based on an obscure novella by Dostoyevsky. His salary: $17 million, plus the usual back-end emoluments.

Before committing to the project, Travolta had met with Polanski, discussed the role, and agreed to the script, along with certain changes that were to be implemented by the writer, Jeremy Leven. He then had his $200,000 made-to-order trailer shipped to Paris. Travolta has a reputation as the most demanding star around in terms of his expensive list of perks, including his own chef and a caterer for the crew—so they'll all be happy. Mandalay, the production company founded by Peter Guber, late of Sony, embarked upon preproduction; expenditures totaled $13 million, encompassing an elaborate set and the services of some special-effects wizards.

Everything seemed on course until the star arrived with his entourage of eight. Then Travolta met with Polanski once again, and together they read through the script. As Polanski recalls it, Travolta seemed to read his part in a bored monotone. It was as though he had either lost enthusiasm for the film or was fearful of the challenge of acting out both the character and the character's alter ego—his "double."

Suddenly, things got weird. According to Mandalay, Travolta's handlers requested a week's delay, which added some $200,000 to the budget. Travolta indicated that he was not in sync with Polanski's very specific stage directions and that he wanted creative control. In the future, Polanski would have to submit his "creative vision" in writing to Travolta and abstain from making suggestions about his performance. As the entire crew stood by, the rumors flew: Would Travolta walk? Would Polanski be replaced?

As usually happens in situations like this, the worst-case scenario soon played out. Travolta headed for the airport, the production was stalled, and the lawsuits started flying. The star's high-powered attorneys claimed that Travolta, upon arriving in Paris, had found that changes had been made to thirty-seven of the hundred and ten pages of the screenplay. They also alleged that Polanski had wanted Travolta to portray his part in "an overboard, comedic style" rather than the "subtle, complex portrayal that had been contemplated."

Given the impasse, the lawyers said, Mandalay had proposed two alternative directors to replace Polanski, with the star agreeing to pay Polanski's fee out of his $17-million salary. Mandalay denies offering such a choice.

Travolta's capricious behavior surprised most Hollywood seers. After all, Travolta had become an instant star in his early twenties with *Saturday Night Fever,* only to crash and burn. This was his second time around, and it was thought that he would jump at the chance of working with an actor's director, the man responsible for *Chinatown* and *Rosemary's Baby.* Travolta proved them wrong.

Still, in a matter of days, Travolta's handlers had nailed down two new gigs at superstar salaries. The reason: Despite all the trauma, studios stand ready to pay whatever it takes to sign a star. In Hollywood the mantra of the moment is to make a star-driven product. Talk to Joe Roth at Disney or Peter Chernin, the chairman and CEO of Twentieth Century Fox Filmed Entertainment (where Roth formerly worked), and they'll set forth the same philosophy: The biggest trap is to make mid-range movies that lack the big star or the potential for a glitzy marketing campaign of the sort that drove *Independence Day* into the box-office stratosphere. The most prudent course is to pay the big bucks and take your shot rather than get lost in the pack.

Given this pervasive point of view, star salaries (and gross percentages) will continue to soar because the demand for superstars greatly surpasses supply. The only question: Where's the lid?

My theory is that, since superstars already own the store metaphorically, they will probably end up owning it in fact. By "the store," I am referring to the product, not the studio which produces and distributes it.

Under this model, the Schwarzeneggers and Gibsons, having effectively priced themselves out of the market, will find that the only way to build a body of work will be to fund some of their own projects and own the negatives. This strategy could also be applied to the publishing world by superstar writers like John Grisham and Tom Clancy. Since these authors have created an extraordinary "brand name," no publisher can afford to pay them what they demand. Hence some publishing veterans believe the authors will end up self-publishing and owning the copyrights.

All this might sound like a big leap, but the entrepreneurial spirit is already running rampant among major stars. As evidence one need look no further than Planet Hollywood, that mother of all burger chains, whose principals include Schwarzenegger, Sylvester Stallone, and Bruce Willis and Demi Moore. Simply by hurtling their superstar bodies to the restaurant openings around the world, these celebrities have helped create a chain of thirty-three eateries. Earlier this year, the company completed an initial public offering that was so successful the company's market value at one point reached $2.8 billion.

Though it's chic to look down on it, Planet Hollywood is the ultimate symbol of the surpassing power of celebrityhood, a reminder that, for today's superstar, acting is simply the start of the revenue stream. Just as a major film generates its big bucks in ancillary markets, such as video, TV, music, and theme parks, so the top celebrity also stands ready and eager to exploit his ancillaries. And each superstar is surrounded, indeed all but suffocated, by an army of lawyers and licensing wizards eager to cash in on the celebrity bonanza.

Along the way, to be sure, a few minor things might get lost in the shuffle. Once an artist is transmogrified into a multinational corporation, it's not unreasonable to suspect that his craft will suffer. With astonishing megabucks being spread around, no star is going to take any artistic chances. More and more movies will resemble Schwarzenegger's shrewd but cynical summer hit, *Eraser*, a $120-million movie that looked like it had come off an assembly line, with all the action scenes and jokes turning up on computerized cue.

The superstar who lives his life surrounded by number-crunchers increasingly comes to resemble a corporate apparatchik rather than an artist. An example: Until the mid-1980s, it was no big deal for a recognized director, producer, or studio executive to obtain a meeting with a top star to discuss a new project or script. Such sessions are growing increasingly rare. An agent or manager will say, "Make me an offer—my star doesn't have time for frivolous meetings." The subtext: Don't distract my star from his principal calling—making money.

As I said at the outset, I've never hung out with a major star, never aspired to be part of the inner circle. It's a rush to walk into a restaurant in the company of a Schwarzenegger—to have everyone's attention focused on you, to share a tiny glint of the limelight. But with today's superstars, even that isn't much fun. The self-important security men are always scurrying in your way. There always seems to be a lawyer or an accountant elbowing you aside. Indeed, taking a superstar to lunch these days is akin to dining with the president of AT&T. You find yourself talking about money.

Being a celebrity is a growth business nowadays—that much I understand. It happens to be a business that I fail to find very interesting, however. It's also one that already is seriously getting in the way of a process that I respect—making good movies.

—*GQ*, October 1996

.   .   .

While the studios continued to up the ante in the superstar derby, there was growing concern in Hollywood that their policies were increasingly counterproductive, as I argued in April 1998.

CAN HOLLYWOOD AFFORD SUPERSTARS?

I ran into a director the other day who complained that he found himself in what he described as "the classic good news/bad news situation." It seems a top star had just committed to his next movie. That was the good news. The bad news was that the director now had to wait ten months for the star to become available. "The studio won't make the movie without him," he explained. "At the same time, they say he's not worth his money. So I have to wait ten months for someone neither of us really wants."

The director's dilemma vividly illustrates Hollywood's "dirty little secret"—one that finally is being discussed openly along the corridors of power: At a time when the studios are firmly committed to the star system, it has become increasingly clear that the economics of the star system simply don't make sense anymore.

A quick look at some of the evidence:

The number of nonsuperstar hits over the last year significantly outnumbered hits with superstars. This was the year of *Titanic, Men in Black, The Lost World, Good Will Hunting,* and *George of the Jungle,* not to mention sleepers like *Bean.*

Defying the axiom that superstars always "open" a picture, this was the year of *The Postman, Mad City,* and *Father's Day*—superstar movies that opened to very dim, nonsuperstar numbers.

There was ample evidence this year that the fast-growing "youth audience" seems determined to discover its own stars rather than support those anointed by their elders. Witness *Good Will Hunting, Scream,* and *I Know What You Did Last Summer.*"

Of all the indicters, the latter one is the most daunting. The teenage population will soar to more than fifty million by 2005, more than twice the growth rate of any other age group. Both the studios and the networks already are tilting their schedules heavily toward the vaunted "youth demo."

The message to studio chiefs is clear: Why fork out $20 million for a superstar who may be spurned by young moviegoers?

"I simply don't believe the market today supports $20-million movie stars," the president of one studio tells me. "The only argument to pay that kind of money is the overseas market."

But while the star system still resonates in Europe and Asia, there's also growing evidence that the world filmgoing audience is fast becoming more homogeneous. Not only is there vastly less support internationally for the Sly Stallone–type action movie, but films like *My Best Friend's Wedding* ($160 million overseas) and *The Full Monty* ($191 million overseas) are also doing surprising business around the world.

Moreover, the huge wave of multiplex construction worldwide is bringing a younger audience with accordingly eclectic tastes into movie theaters.

Where does this leave the superstars? In big trouble, it would seem. The real emerging star arguably is computer graphics—look at *Men in Black* or *Twister.*

Another big draw: Simple emotion—witness *Good Will Hunting.*

Given these forces, the last remaining champions of the superstar system are those "satellite companies" that co-finance projects with the studios and hold on to overseas territories. These companies, such as New Regency, Beacon, and Mandalay, can afford to pay the big bucks to superstars because they get the foreign payoff. A prototypical example is Mandalay-Sony's *Seven Years in Tibet,* starring Brad Pitt, which registered under $40 million in the U.S. but did $100 million abroad, where Mandalay makes its big money.

To be sure, given the continued expansion of overseas box-office relative to the U.S., studios are becoming less willing to divide the pie the old-fashioned way, demanding instead a worldwide fifty-fifty revenue split.

In view of all this, why are the studios still making $20-million offers to top stars? To be brutally specific, after the disappointing performance of *Mad City* and *Primary Colors,* why does a long line of offers still await John Travolta?

"Chalk it up to bureaucratic self-protection," one studio president tells me. If a studio fails with a superstar slate, he says, that failure traditionally has been easier to explain away to stockholders than if it fails with unknowns.

The experience of Warner Bros. over the last year may have punctured that myth, however. That studio had the longest winning streak of any studio, yet 1997, its worst year in a very long time, was littered with superstar failures. And the rest of the industry took note.

Having said all this, of course, my director friend is still going to have to wait ten months to start his superstar movie. And he's grumpy about it. "I feel like the game is changing but I still have to play by the old rules," he says.

—*Variety*, April 20, 1998

.   .   .

One of the continuing anomalies of show business is how so many major stars managed to involve themselves in projects that seemed doomed from the outset. In the GQ *of January 1995, I tried to scrutinize the superstars' often haphazard decision-making processes.*

CAN ACTORS READ?

Some years ago, while cutting my teeth as what is euphemistically called a "production executive," I was placed in charge of a western that was to star a promising young actor named Robert Redford. Consistent with protocol, my first move was to call on the director, Silvio Narizzano, who had built a reputation in London turning out realistic kitchen-sink dramas, such as *Georgy Girl.*

As I talked with Narizzano, an alarm went off in my head. Though he may have understood urban angst, he was utterly unprepared for the rigors of a western. His ego was such that he hadn't even given much thought to the locations or cast.

I sought the advice of my colleagues as to our options: delaying the picture, replacing the director, et cetera. The consensus was to move ahead as planned. Narizzano was a bright young man, after all; perhaps this was his eccentric, seat-of-the-pants way of attacking the project. Redford, too, was a comer, riding high after good notices for *Barefoot in the Park.*

However, I had been warned that Redford was astute and immensely self-protective. Once he met the director, he might share my anxiety.

I didn't have to worry for long. After his meeting with Narizzano, Redford didn't exactly quit the picture. He simply vaporized. Gone without a trace. "That's Redford," said his agent with a shrug. "You know, an actor has certain instincts. He feels it in his gut. . . ."

Redford's vanishing act constituted my introduction to a major but little-discussed issue in show business—the "golden gut." With production and marketing costs spiraling, Hollywood today is more star-driven than ever. And the stars, mindful of their power, are more flighty and neurotic, quitting projects that are just about to start principal photography, flitting from film to film like confused butterflies in an overly lavish garden.

For illustration, one need look no farther than the still-ubiquitous Redford. Though he himself has become a skilled filmmaker—witness *Quiz Show*—Redford recently backed out of two high-profile movies to which he was committed: *Crisis in the Hot Zone*, with director Ridley Scott, and *An American President*, with Rob Reiner. He thus bade farewell to well over $20 million in pay for perhaps seven months' work.

Redford is hardly alone: Michael Douglas, Sharon Stone, and Jodie Foster, among others, also have abandoned major movies at the eleventh hour, presumably with the encouragement of their jittery agents.

What's going on here? Though countless tedious books and articles have been written about the executive decision-making process at movie studios, no one tries to analyze how actors make up their minds—a process that is vastly more exotic and, arguably, more important. When a star sidles up to a project, tens of millions of dollars change hands and armies of production people spring into action. The fact that Kevin Costner fancied the idea of putting on fake gills to play a subterranean survivalist in *Waterworld* meant that Universal would effectively commit more than $135 million to create and market an aquatic extravaganza. And studios keep waving scripts before Schwarzenegger, even though a yes from him could easily set one of them back a good $80 million in production costs alone.

If you want to guarantee a very brief conversation, try asking a star how he selects his roles. Usually there will be scratching and squirming and a mumbled reference to the script and the director. Then you'll elicit an admission: "Well, I get this feeling in my gut. . . ."

Yes, the gut again. The golden gut.

The problem with gutmanship, to be sure, is that the results are notoriously unreliable. Scrutinize the choices of top stars over the years, and you find yourself staring at a landscape littered with dashed expectations. Costner looked like a genius for deciding to do *Dances with Wolves*, but *Wyatt Earp* turned out to be one of the biggest bombs in Hollywood history. Julia Roberts seemed like she could do no wrong after *Pretty Woman*, but Disney's *I Love Trouble* proved to be aptly titled. Even the vaunted Schwarzenegger followed the megahit *Terminator 2* with the debacle called *The Last Action Hero*.

Then there's the Charlie Sheen story: Not exactly a rocket scientist, he overcame the stigma of the Brat Pack by linking up with such films as *Platoon* and *Wall Street*. But now, after flopping in *The Chase* and *Terminal Velocity*, Sheen's lost his heat.

Which brings us back to our original question: What factors go into an actor's decision to say yes? What makes that golden gut start tingling?

Before we grapple with that, it's important to mention one factor that doesn't go into the mix. When a star ponders a potential role, it's not exactly an intellectual exercise. Though no one, to my knowledge, has ever charted the IQs of movie stars, I would venture to say that they are not exactly on a level with those of Harvard Ph.D.s. Actors don't think in terms of Great Ideas. They like role-playing. They obsess over certain scenes. They fret about how they will look.

There are exceptions, of course. The late Burt Lancaster had a keen intelligence and often took on films because of their challenging points of view—*Judgment at Nuremberg*, for example. But examine the great star vehicles of the past and you find that the actors in question generally had to be dragged kicking and screaming to the starting gate. Neither Bogart nor Bergman wanted anything to do with *Casablanca*. Marlon Brando never said "I've got to play the Godfather," but I do remember his saying "I need the money." Jeanne Moreau landed some great roles, but she also turned down Mrs. Robinson in *The Graduate* and Nurse Ratched in *One Flew over the Cuckoo's Nest.*

It is my belief then that despite all the vague references to "artistic instincts," a star will cozy up to a prospective role if he or she receives satisfactory answers to at least one of the following:

1. How much will I get paid? Though most stars affect total naïveté about their compensation, they are, in fact, mind-bendingly competitive. Even someone as "cool" as Warren Beatty can, if pressed, recite the deals of every rival leading man down to the esoterica of shifting levels of gross—the formula for contingent compensation may fluctuate several times after breakeven. When neophyte Jim Carrey leapfrogged to $7 million on the strength of *Ace Ventura: Pet Detective* and *The Mask,* agents all over town heard from their clients.

2. Can I play against type, and how far can I go? Tom Hanks felt he was hitting the wall as a white-bread Mr. Nice Guy in movies like *Turner & Hooch,* so he did what every actor yearns to do—he hired a new agent and said, "Get me some shticky character roles." Usually, this sounds the death knell for a career, but Hanks and his new agency, Creative Artists, batted a thousand. First came *A League of Their Own* (Hanks was fat and flaky), then *Sleepless in Seattle* (Hanks was geeky and vulnerable), then *Philadelphia* (Hanks was skeletal and poignant), and then the pièce de résistance—*Forrest Gump.* In the space of two years, he had transformed himself from a blah, light comedian into a mythic figure and, along the way, managed to earn in excess of $50 million.

To appreciate the magnitude of Hanks's good fortune, one must consider the gifted Robert Downey Jr.'s flopping as Chaplin. Or Meryl Streep in *Death Becomes Her* and *The House of the Spirits.* Which brings us to our next question:

3. Will the role save my ass? Though many stars are self-destructive, some show remarkable survival instincts. After her success in *Out of Africa,* Streep became mired in such disappointing efforts as *Postcards from the Edge.* No shrinking violet, she decided to take a page from the survival manual of male superstars—she made a solid, old-fashioned action flick. *The River Wild* was a by-the-numbers hostage thriller, but the critics were lavish in their praise.

4. Can I show off my devastating powers as a sex symbol? If the actor doesn't have the chops to pull off character roles, as mentioned in No. 2, he may resort to this time-honored tactic. But while many women have built careers around pure sex appeal, this has been a dangerous road for leading men. Think of Mickey Rourke, only 42; the bank recently foreclosed on his home in the Hollywood Hills, and Cedars-Sinai admitted him for suicidal tendencies. I made *The Pope of Greenwich Village* with Mickey, back when he was in his promising tough-guy mode. He loved the accoutrements of stardom—zooming around Hollywood on his Harley, enticing bimbos like a Venus's-flytrap. Over time, Mickey enmeshed himself in a series of pseudoerotic laughers, like *9 1/2 Weeks* and *Wild Orchid,* and the offers began to dry up. "The one thing I'll never do is sell out," he used to assure me. "I'll never become a pretty-boy for hire."

Mickey, you'll never get the chance. Which brings us to our final question:

5. Do I have to carry the picture? Stars may have huge egos, but they (and their agents) also know how to hedge their bets. Hence, while demanding top billing, they are drawn to projects in which they can play off another major star and even attract a big-name director. If the movie goes down the drain,

at least the blame can be spread around. Having a best-selling author attached to the project also helps—despite his public disdain for Tom Clancy's work, Harrison Ford clearly has a comfort level with the Jack Ryan franchise.

To be sure, stars can pose all the right questions and still end up making a string of turkeys. That's why most actors, in the end, come to rely on luck, as well as their gut. Last summer's big sleeper, *Speed,* fulfilled few of the criteria posed here, yet it made Keanu Reeves a superstar. That's what's known as serious luck!

Indeed, in pondering his next career moves, Reeves, a rather nihilistic, freewheeling type, may simply roll the dice and skip the checklist.

I once produced a picture starring Patrick Swayze, and just as the director was lining up the first shot, the actor drew me aside, a troubled took on his face. "May I have a private talk with you?" he asked.

"Sure," I replied, my stomach tightening. Was Swayze going to propose a last-minute rewrite? Was he pulling out of the project? Retreating to his dressing room, he voiced his concern. "I've been worrying about the character I play," he said.

"What about him?" I asked.

"There's something wrong with his looks," he said. "I've been thinking about him, and, frankly, I think he should have a mustache."

I blinked. "A mustache? We're about to start principal photography."

"Facial hair would represent a new look for me. I haven't done it before."

"I appreciate that, Patrick," I replied. "But it's a little late in the game." We talked for several minutes. I tried to reassure him that facial hair would not be consistent with the background and motivations of the character he was playing.

Swayze, as usual, was a good guy and he relented. We started the picture. He did fine without facial hair.

And it was a useful reminder that things can get dicey when actors want to think as well as act.

—*GQ*, January 1995

.   .   .

Of all the Hollywood superstars, none has proven to be more shrewdly manipulative of the system than Warren Beatty. In the April 1996 GQ, *I tried to explicate the Beatty mystique.*

THE ACTOR AS PATRIARCH

There's a rule of thumb in Hollywood: Movies that are accorded the most lavish premieres yield the most paltry profits. A case in point is *The American President,* a movie that was both very expensive and immensely ingratiating, yet failed to produce the sort of blockbuster business required to justify the nearly $100 million spent on its production and marketing.

The premiere was a glitzy, star-studded Los Angeles gala that felt more like an inauguration than a movie opening, with hordes of gawkers jostling for glimpses of the guests and the two leading men, Michael Douglas and Warren Beatty.

Warren Beatty? Beatty, to be sure, wasn't cast in this movie and rarely even goes to premieres, but he was the most buzzed-about attraction at the party as he squired his wife, Annette Bening, through the crowds of her admirers, a look of utter confusion on his now craggy features. "This is the first time I've ever seen Warren look downright befuddled," noted one agent as he observed the spectacle. "Here's the man who always has to be the center of attention playing the reluctant consort."

Indeed, the casting of Warren Beatty in the role of "best supporting husband" struck many that evening as the ultimate third-act irony to Beatty's often bizarre career. For over three decades, Beatty has exhibited his mastery of several quite different and complex roles. He has been the priapic prince whose legendary liaisons involved virtually every female denizen of Southern California. He has also played the reluctant auteur, who, despite great promise, has managed to direct only four movies in three decades. He has played the sidelines politico, the confidant of Bobby Kennedy, the handler of Gary Hart, a sort of liberal-at-large who, for all his good intentions, has never managed to back a winner. Finally and most effectively, Beatty has played the role of the diffident superstar, the A-list actor who, at any given time, seems to be playing hard-to-get with every studio chief and producer in town—the actor who is always "interested" but will hardly ever commit.

In short, Warren Beatty has been an elusive creature of Hollywood who has made a way of life out of promising more than he delivers, a man charming yet tentative, arrogant yet self-doubting. And as he approaches the milestone of his sixtieth birthday, he is also a celebrity being forced into some unfamiliar territory. He is suddenly a husband and father, not a lover-at-large. He is married to a woman who is becoming a bigger star than he. Most daunting, as the utter failure of *Love Affair* (which Beatty produced as well as starred in opposite Bening) vividly demonstrated, he is no longer able to get away with playing the romantic lead.

The last fact must especially gnaw at him, because his longtime rival, Robert Redford, who is also approaching 60, still manages to play the heartthrob in movies like *Indecent Proposal*. Both Beatty and Redford scoff at the suggestion of a rivalry, but Hollywood is full of producers and agents who can attest otherwise. Beatty's friends are accustomed to hearing him put down virtually every Redford project, saying, "I read that script and turned it down." Indeed, the quickest way to blow off Beatty is to let it slip that Redford has seen the script first.

"Warren has to feel like he's seen every script, reviewed every deal, turned down every part," says one top agent. Not that Beatty's gamesmanship has always worked to his advantage. While he was, in fact, offered projects like *Butch Cassidy and the Sundance Kid* and *Indecent Proposal* before Redford, he clearly misjudged their potential. The Sundance Kid role in 1969 transformed Redford from a comer into a major star, and *Indecent Proposal* earned him millions.

While Redford's career took off in the 1970s, Beatty, after a couple of impressive star vehicles, found himself struggling through turkeys like *$* and *The Fortune*.

A comparison of the two men's filmographies reveals that only four of the twenty movies Beatty starred in over the course of thirty-five years could be described as hits, and only two of these *(Shampoo* and *Bonnie and Clyde)* were semiblockbusters. By contrast, eight of Redford's twenty-eight movies were hits, and several others were small but estimable films *(The Candidate, Downhill Racer)* which more than earned back their slender budgets.

Each has directed four films, and again one has to tip one's hat to Redford. All of his stints as auteur produced movies that were memorable in one way or another—*Ordinary People, The Milagro Beanfield War, A River Runs Through It,* and *Quiz Show*—though only the first fulfilled box-office expectations.

In contrast, Beatty's efforts have proved a mixed bag. *Heaven Can Wait* was respectable but forgettable; *Dick Tracy* was a triumph of style over content; *Love Affair* was clearly a misfire. Indeed, only his remarkable 1981 movie, *Reds,* stands out as a significant contribution to his craft.

In tone and subject matter, Beatty's adventures as a filmmaker seem all over the map, lacking a coherent style or point of view. Redford's work, on the other hand, betrays certain consistent traits: The films deal with family, morality, and the integrity of the environment. While Beatty's movies can be mischievous and capricious, Redford's tend to be rather austere and standoffish. As an actor and a producer, Beatty stirred the imagination of his audience with the hail of bullets in *Bonnie and Clyde* and the under-the-table blow job in *Shampoo.* One remembers Redford, the actor, as the righteous reporter in *All the President's Men* or the straight-as-an-arrow athlete in *Downhill Racer.*

At this moment in his life, Redford has taken on a mythic aura among an entire generation of young filmmakers as the Medici of the movies, the father of the Sundance Film Festival, which every year draws to Park City, Utah, a flock of scruffy directors, each of whom hopes to become the next Quentin Tarantino, Edward Burns, or Bryan Singer. As Redford said during a press conference at last year's event, "Most important to me is to press home new work and new visions."

As president of the Sundance Institute, Redford campaigns for global-warming policies, land-use legislation, mining reform, radioactive-waste disclosure, and the preservation and restoration of national parks. In 1992 he executive-produced and narrated *Incident at Oglala,* a feature documentary based on the highly controversial imprisonment of Native American Leonard Peltier. Redford is also a partner in the Showtime Networks' new twenty-four-hour Sundance Channel, and through the deep pockets of his partner, Disney, his Wildwood Productions seeks out material for him to direct. (Disney forked over a record-setting $3 million for *The Horse Whisperer,* a then-unpublished novel by first-time author Nicholas Evans.)

With all this action, Redford is nonetheless the sort of person who can take a stroll on a sunny day and not cast a shadow. No one quite knows where Redford lives or with whom or how he spends his spare time. Now and then he does interviews to promote his movies or his causes, but he is always an hour or so late without explanation, and immediately upon hearing the questions, he assumes a rueful expression, suggesting that he's sorry he agreed to show up in the first place.

"Hollywood is full of people who say they know Warren Beatty, but no one really knows him," says one showbiz attorney. "You find very few people who even lay claim to knowing Redford."

I have worked with both actors on various movies. I have had long conversations with Redford and have always found him polite, thoughtful, and utterly distanced. As one director puts it, "Redford is the most Presbyterian superstar in the history of Hollywood."

Needless to say, Warren Beatty is a helluva lot more fun, even under the most demanding of circumstances. When it's crunch time, he can also be a faithful ally. During my years as a studio executive, I was charged with the task of supervising a film called *The Parallax View,* which, in the final days of preproduction, was suddenly stalled by a writers' strike. Blocked from giving important suggestions on the screenplay, Beatty nonetheless worked hard with the director and the studio, hammering out his own script notes and never once resorting to movie-star tantrums. On *Love Affair,* by contrast, Beatty drove both the studio and his crew up the wall because of bouts of indecision. Indeed, it took an eleventh-hour intervention from Robert Daly, co-CEO of Warner Bros., to force Beatty to make his final editing decisions and thus avoid the unconscionable—missing the release date.

Having said this, I can fully empathize with the comments of John F. Kennedy Jr. who, upon completing an interview with Beatty a few months ago for his new magazine, *George,* wrote about his subject: "Every word that comes out of his mouth seems to be inspected, picked over, and held up to a light before he parts with it." I have talked with women who insist that, during moments of sexual congress, Beatty still chooses his words (and sounds) with the probity of a judge delivering a sentence.

Beatty's extraordinary caution would seem out of character for a man who has experienced such good fortune in his life. Strolling into town in 1961, he served a brief tour of duty in a supporting role on the TV series *The Many Loves of Dobie Gillis* before becoming an instant star with his first movie, *Splendor in the Grass.* Six years later, he fostered *Bonnie and Clyde,* which was not only a huge hit but also an "up yours" to the Hollywood establishment—Warner Bros. had so disdained the project that the studio gave him a big piece of the gross in lieu of an up-front salary.

Barely thirty, Beatty found himself at once a millionaire and a maverick—the leading man every studio wanted, as well as the libidinous loner who abjured the company of studio hierarchs. There was no actor within memory who commanded the mystique of Warren Beatty. He was handsome, smart, loved, and hated. The town was at his feet.

"To his friends, Warren was always known as 'the Pro,'" says producer Robert Evans, who found his way to Hollywood just a little earlier than Beatty. "The guy's brilliant—that's the only word for him. Through all his ups and downs, he kept himself number one on everyone's dance card."

Myriad legends surround the Pro, most of them involving his genius at manipulation. According to one, Beatty persuaded the always reluctant Barbra Streisand to commit to a project in the '70s, then kept delaying it so he could enlist her help in the presidential campaign of George McGovern. Another myth has it that Beatty has rarely if ever paid an agent's fee, promising instead that he would deliver other clients and projects to the various agents who have represented him. Beatty clearly encouraged the mythology surrounding his deal-making talents—he was one of the first stars of his generation to receive gross participation from the first dollar of receipts, much to the frustration of superstar rivals.

"Everyone realized that Jack Nicholson had more charisma, that Dustin Hoffman was a better actor, that Paul Newman was sexier, that Redford carried more box-office clout. But then you looked at every studio's wish list, and there sat Beatty," says a studio production chief.

With all his shrewdness, however, Beatty's career seemed increasingly clouded in the '80s by an emerging obsessiveness. "It was all about dalliance, not work," observes one Hollywood veteran who remembers Beatty's youthful days. "Whether it was women or film projects, Warren compulsively loved to flirt." There were endless meetings, plus an abundance of one-night stands.

Beatty's friend and mentor, the late Charlie Feldman, tried to elicit Beatty's help in making the transition from agent to producer and desperately courted him for *What's New, Pussycat?* Months went by before Beatty finally said no, thus breaking Feldman's spirit. On *Butch Cassidy*, George Roy Hill became so frustrated with Beatty's demands and procrastination that the irascible director told him to take a walk and went with Redford instead.

Beatty also dithered over material that he controlled. He procrastinated for years over *Reds* before finally doing battle with it in 1980. He's been obsessing over a bio-pic on Howard Hughes for almost two decades without ever committing to it.

The mind games took their subtle toll. During preproduction of *Bugsy*, director Barry Levinson told a reporter, "Warren did only two movies during the decade of the '80s, and it's hard to get back into it when you're out that long." Indeed, as Beatty's productivity diminished, his obsessiveness grew ever more problematic. He agonized endlessly about his deal, his script, about costars and supporting players, and especially about marketing and publicity. Jeffrey Katzenberg, then chairman of the Walt Disney studio, became so exasperated during the making of *Dick Tracy* that he wrote his famous twenty-eight-page memo, which stated: "The number of hours *[Dick Tracy]* required, the amount of anxiety it generated, and the amount of dollars that needed to be expended were disproportionate to the amount of success achieved."

When the memo was leaked to the press, resulting in a Beatty tantrum, Katzenberg tried to calm the waters, pointing out that his memo wasn't directed at Beatty but rather at the "blockbuster mentality" that had seized the industry.

Beatty's game-playing with the studios was minor compared with his gamesmanship with women. For three decades, Beatty has managed to keep a sort of giant scorecard in his mind that seems to encompass everyone of the opposite sex who has ever set foot in the industry. He has an imprint of their appearance, physical dimensions, and sexual propensities; he also has an astonishing array of phone numbers committed to memory.

I remember Beatty and a couple of other Hollywood Lotharios going through an elaborate exercise one afternoon. The two others would mention a name, and Beatty would rattle off her phone number. Of perhaps two hundred names, Beatty faltered only five or six times, all the while smiling smugly, as though he were explaining the precepts of Archimedes. "It's kind of fun to sleep with Warren," recalls one lissome starlet who claims to have done so on two or three occasions, "but you always feel like once the wienie goes up, the interest goes down. It's like a neon sign saying, 'Next case.'"

Beatty himself never talks about past conquests, but when bantering with John Kennedy Jr. he couldn't resist a few random observations. Acknowledging what he called this country's "high level of hypocrisy about sexual behavior," Beatty noted that sexuality was "akin to virtue" in the '60s and '70s. Today, however, "we [the public] are very entertained by us clowns whose sexuality has been paraded before the populace—to be ridiculed, to be chastised."

Given this country's strain of puritanism, Beatty dismissed the idea of ever running for public office, even though "I do have the advantage of having spent a vast number of years—more than three decades, actually—as a famous person who never once cheated on his wife."

"And?" Kennedy asked.

Beatty pondered the question briefly, then said, "I don't want to do it—I might get too interested in actually getting elected." And that would involve making a commitment of some sort—a practice Beatty has assiduously avoided.

Not that Redford would run for office, either, preferring instead to remain a distant icon. The difference is that while Redford is busily preparing to direct and star in *The Horse Whisperer,* is currently starring in *Up Close and Personal* with Michelle Pfeiffer, and recently signed to star in *Shooter,* Beatty is still on the sidelines, taking his meetings, pondering his options.

Beatty's career is rather like his conversation—there's always the suggestion of great things to come, the pregnant pauses hinting that a profound thought is about to be summoned up. Yet, at the moment of highest expectation, there is only silence— silence and that charming, whimsical smile that suggests, "I know something you don't know. I know how to get any beautiful woman I choose, I know how to keep famous directors begging, and I know how to reduce studio chiefs to tears of frustration."

You know all that, Warren, but try not to look over your shoulder, because there's a whole new generation of hot young stars, filmmakers, and Lotharios bearing down on you, eager to usurp your exalted place in the Hollywood firmament.

—*GQ,* April 1996

PART IV

DREAM FACTORIES

A couple of generations ago, the Hollywood studios were run by rough-and-tumble immigrants who were dreamers as well as entrepreneurs. Today's studios and TV networks run on business plans, not dreams. And, as I explained in the March 1999 GQ, their bureaucratization often leads to bizarre extremes.

TORTURES OF DEVELOPMENT HELL

Let me acknowledge up front that there's something intrinsically smarmy about this article. A persuasive case could be made that I should not be writing it, since it's based on information from documents I should never have seen. Further, I will be discussing projects that are works-in-progress and hence not ready to be held up to public scrutiny.

Having said all this, why am I proceeding with this nasty exercise? Well, for one thing, the documents are too amusing to ignore. They are also more revealing of Hollywood's mind-set than any public speeches or interviews. As such, they explain why the movie business finds itself in such a mess far more eloquently than would any weighty analysis that I could summon up.

The documents that I've contrived to obtain consist of the so-called "development lists" from the major studios. They trace all of the studios' projects from conception until production, listing the writers, filmmakers, and stars involved, along with brief summaries of the plot.

This information is sensitive because it presents each company's blueprint for the future. A weak development slate can spell disaster for a film studio. Mindful of their rivals' propensity for imitation (witness last summer's two asteroid pictures and the previous summer's two volcano movies) the studios guard their lists zealously.

Perhaps too zealously. For the fact remains that, given the studios' tendencies to think alike, the lists are surprisingly similar in tone and subject matter. Indeed, their executives would do well to worry less about the theft of ideas and more about the reasons behind this incestuous thinking.

Having said all this, let's cut to the chase. Based on a perusal of the studios' development lists, what sort of movies will we be seeing over the next two or three years?

If you believe the charts, the answer is: Fewer giant special-effects epics like *Armageddon,* more gross-out comedies like *There's Something About Mary,* lots more teen genre pictures like *Ever After* and *I Know What You Did Last Summer,* and an assortment of pricey sequels to big hits such as *Men in Black* II and *Dr. Dolittle* II but probably not *Godzilla* II.

Will they be any good? That, of course, is impossible to predict from plot outlines, but judging from titles and synopses, I can already list a few movies that I'm not exactly panting to see.

For one thing, I distrust any project that's described in development charts as a marriage between two old movies. New Line is developing something called "Wrecked," described as *"Clueless* meets *Alive."* I don't think so. It's also developing "Sentimental Maniacs," a wedding comedy described as *"Moonstruck* meets *The Big Chill."* Perhaps they shouldn't meet. Then there's an even more off-the-wall project entitled "Slapping Scarlett," which, according to the development chart, is "a teen comedy loosely inspired by *Gone with the Wind."* It may need a laugh track.

Often it isn't the so-called "log line," but rather the title itself that inspires skepticism. Would you see a movie entitled "Animal White House"? Or "Crime Cleaners"? How about "How to Marry a Black Man"? Then there's "My Baby's Mother." They may turn out to be great scripts, but the titles need the rewrite crew.

Disney in particular seems to hatch comedy ideas that sound a bit too aggressive. I'm taking a wait-and-see attitude toward "Dog Eat Dog," dealing with a young woman who hires her dog trainer to reprogram her pampered boyfriend.

I feel equally skeptical about a comedy called "Hairworld," which deals with a hair stylist who wins something called the Olympics of Hair, along with a new boyfriend. Sounds like a hairy premise.

I feel the same hesitancy over a script with the uncomfortable title "Bone in the Throat," described as a black comedy about two chefs who find themselves caught up with mobsters. I'm choked up already.

Before plunging deeper into development hell, let's pause a moment to examine the process. When a studio puts a project into development, the only "elements" usually consist of a writer and producer. In rare instances, a star also involves himself since some studios make what are called "vanity deals" intended to build loyalty toward their particular company. To be sure, scripts developed under the aegis of stars are the most accident-prone, since stars tend to gravitate toward the biggest deal and rarely display pride of authorship.

The development process can be triggered by several mechanisms. A writer may pitch an idea to a studio, usually confining his narrative to fifteen minutes, the normal executive attention span. If a writer is sufficiently fired up about his idea, he may even invest the time and effort to write the script "on spec," hoping to auction it to the highest bidder. Studios, of course, also buy the rights to hot novels or plays. Magazine or newspaper articles may also serve as grist—witness the recent $500,000 sale of a *New York Magazine* article about four brash young publicity women in Manhattan.

Spec scripts enjoyed their moment in the sun in the mid-'80s until the prices became too insane and the casualty rates too blatant. A prize example was *The Long Kiss Goodnight,* which brought a young screenwriter named Shane Black some $3.5 million and resulted in a turkey of a movie. By 1997, the "pitch" was making a comeback. Under this exercise, studio executives, rarely avid readers to begin with, must merely listen to someone telling them a story and then simply say yes or no. Indeed, the "pitch" has become so popular that some agents, upon reading a client's finished screenplay, advise them to hide the script and pitch the story. If a deal is made, the writer waits three or four months, then drags out his completed script and turns it in.

Given all the money changing hands, why has the process come to be known as "development hell"? The answer is that roughly ninety percent of all scripts end up on the junk heap. Before they're abandoned, however, most go through a torturous rewrite process that taxes both the talent and the sanity of all involved. It's not uncommon for a writer to turn in seven or eight drafts, each one eliciting a fusillade of "script notes" from the development staff. And with each successive draft, the script often gets worse rather than better.

Indeed, in a fleeting mood of masochism, I put myself through the exercise of reading both the first drafts and the final shooting scripts of several of the movies released during the summer of '98. In one case after another, whether the project was *Six Days, Seven Nights* or *Godzilla,* the initial screenplay struck me as being far more satisfying and better crafted than the final drafts that went before the cameras. The original screenplay called *There's Something About Mary,* which the Farrelly brothers turned into a major hit, had been knocking around studios for almost a decade, with "each draft becoming less and less funny," according to Peter Farrelly.

And who are the Mephistophelean figures presiding over development hell? They're bright young men and women armed with MBAs and other impressive educational credentials. Though called "creative executives," they are utterly uncreative, their life experience consisting mainly of watching videos and TV.

When I first joined the ranks of studio executives some years ago, no one was called a creative executive. Each company employed a story department inhabited by seasoned readers who had occupied their posts for many years. When I gave them a script to analyze, their responses would often be brilliantly derivative. "Hitchcock faced that problem in '41," one would say, "and here's the trick he used to solve it." Or "I remember how Willy Wyler, that old bastard, dealt with that same issue."

The habitués of story departments were a seasoned and salty lot who had done their homework and could help you out of a jam. Some present day executives also provide constructive suggestions, but talk with writers or producers locked in development hell and they report a pervasive pattern of frustration, if not agony. Each draft of a script is greeted with a detailed, multi-page document that is signed not by an individual, but simply by "The Creative Group." "In my entire career I have found maybe one or two legitimately helpful ideas buried in the dozens of script notes that I have received," comments one writer whose name adorns several successful movies. "All they are is bureaucratic obstacles."

Some important filmmakers have devised strategies for circumventing these obstacles. When Steven Spielberg agreed to direct *Saving Private Ryan,* a script developed at Paramount, his representatives made it clear that he simply had no interest in hearing anyone's theories about how to improve the script. Spielberg brought in his own rewrite men and crafted subsequent drafts as he saw fit. When Warren Beatty made *Bulworth* at Twentieth Century Fox last summer, the studio never saw a script and had no notion of the story until seeing the finished movie.

For those with less clout, the best tactic is to try to surround their projects with the proper buzz words to lend them an aura of commerciality. The inevitable result is a heavy dependence on story gimmicks. Glance down any studio development chart and the gimmicks hit you in the face. Without revealing too much in the way of stories or studios, here's a random sampling:

- When a blizzard forces cancellation of all flights, a young woman hires a cab to carry her home to her wedding, only to fall in love with the cab driver.

- When a gay man gets amnesia from being hit on the head by a disco ball, his father takes the opportunity to persuade him that he's really straight.

- A woman traces the roots of her long-lost wealthy family, only to discover she is really descended from a clan of wolves.

- When three men find themselves transformed into chipmunks, they decide to form a touring musical act.

- When two gorgeous bimbos turn up at their bachelor pad, two buddies discover that their visitors are actually aliens bent on obtaining DNA-laden sperm samples.

- A divorced man, desperate to regain his worldly goods, undergoes a makeover and remarries his ex-wife who doesn't recognize him.

- A petty thief mugs an old woman who turns out to be the mother of a Mafia capo and he is forced to serve as her bodyguard.

- A wife agrees to change places with her husband's mistress who, as luck would have it, is virtually identical to her except for a twenty-year age difference.

One key obstacle that will be faced by these "high-concept" scripts is that their characters will seem hollow, since they're all designed to neatly fit an arcane premise. Inevitably, therefore, the casualty rate will be high—unless, that is, they are tailored for the teen market. Having studied the nation's changing demographics, and the extraordinary success of youth-oriented movies like *Waterboy* starring Adam Sandler, studios at this moment are willing to greenlight scripts that would otherwise run into a wall of resistance.

Survey the development charts and you quickly discover the most popular teen theme: A group of nerds swallow a magic potion or otherwise orchestrate a makeover only to extract their revenge on the popular kids who had scorned them.

In some cases the revenge consists merely of social one-upmanship, but in others murder or mayhem ensues. One story focuses on Halloween night in an amusement park, where the revenge syndrome assumes a predictably dire toll. The names of these development projects tell it all: "Fear the Reaper," "Planet Deb," "The Pledge," "Slave Day," and, more persuasively, "Bitch, Bitch, Bitch."

If standards seem more relaxed with teen projects, they are stringent in the case of sci-fi movies. For while teen movies can be made on the cheap, a sci-fi movie, if approved, can trigger a $100-million spending spree. Special-effects feasibility studies often go hand in hand with story costs, so that a studio may sink some $20 million into development before it begins production.

Given the risks, the sci-fi stories presently in development strive relentlessly to find new ideas and premises. In preparation are movies involving mutant bats escaping from tunnels under Manhattan, stone gargoyles that spring to life at the moment of the millennium, Tripods using mind-control devices to control the earth, a bioengineered virus that seeps from a Manhattan construction site, menacing necronauts who travel through space, and mutant "X-Men" who possess supernatural powers.

At least two sci-fi epics that I've scouted out hopefully will find their way into production. One involves the kidnapping of Santa Claus into outer space; the other relates the story of a hacker who discovers that the Internet has developed its own consciousness and aims to destroy the human race. I'm not sure this qualifies as science fiction. I'd also lobby for a project at Universal called "Earth Dick," in which an alien race thinks it's found its hero to save the universe, only to discover he's merely an actor who plays an action hero on TV. Now, that's a high concept!

To hedge their bets, every studio also has assembled its own wish list of remakes. If a movie worked once, after all, why not dust it off and try again? Universal, which sought to resuscitate a shot-by-shot version of *Psycho* late last year, is gearing up *Beyond a Reasonable Doubt,* a 1956 Fritz Lang murder mystery; *The Birds,* the Hitchcock thriller from 1963; *Gambit,* a 1966 romantic comedy; *The Incredible Shrinking Man,* a remake of the 1957 comedy being tailored for Eddie Murphy; and *The Invisible Man,* a sci-fi fantasy dating back to 1933, about a chemist who can make himself vanish on command and sets out to conquer the world.

Having plowed through studio development lists, it's impossible not to come away from the experience with a built-in resistance to high concepts, gimmicky premises, and plastic characters. I plead guilty to these prejudices, but at the same time, I don't want to give the impression that the studios are devoid of intriguing story ideas. Indeed, I can cite several projects that, based on plot outlines alone, I would personally look forward to seeing on the big screen. Tom Hanks, working as a producer, is developing a story at Fox about a chaplain who rediscovers his humanity after surviving a siege in the Vietnam war. Renny Harlin is readying a script about a father-son journey to check out New England colleges, a welcome departure for Harlin. Jerry Bruckheimer is trying to create a movie at Disney about the Irish journalist who was murdered after chronicling the IRA's secret activities. I also hope Penny Marshall gets to make her piece about the Gulf War, and that Jonathan Demme has success with his movie about the agonies of the Brooklyn Dodgers in trying to integrate baseball. Since I'm a cat person, I'd even like to see "Nine Lives," a Universal development project about a nerdy guy who saves a cat from getting hit by a car and is rewarded when he finds that he himself now has nine lives.

There are, in fact, a lot of movies I'd like to see. I just hope their writers and producers don't perish in development hell before they see the light of day.

—*GQ*, March 1999

.   .   .

While nearly all major industries had managed to control inflation through the '90s, costs kept soaring in the movie and TV industries. In the June 1996 GQ, *I scrutinized the causes of this phenomenon as well as both the financial and artistic price. The article was published before the completion of history's priciest picture,* Titanic, *which cost over $200 million to produce and launch, but which also demonstrated that some "blockbusters" can indeed make a huge profit.*

WHO'S MINDING THE STORE?

Cutting my teeth in my first studio job some years ago, I decided to test my luck by pitching a rather unorthodox movie project. In that era, studio meetings were considerably less formal than they are today, and they were attended by a mere handful of functionaries, compared with the fifty or so who clamor to be heard at studios in '90s Hollywood. Despite the relaxed atmosphere, I remember being a bit timorous in my advocacy, and with good reason. As I recall, the meeting went something like this:

BART: I believe we should make this movie. It's . . . different, but I believe in it.

EXECUTIVE A: Different? What's the story line?

BART: It's what you might call a love story, only it involves an 80-year-old woman and a 17-year-old boy.

EXECUTIVE B (*wincing*): I'd say it's different! And the cast?

BART: No big stars. A young director—he's done one picture. There's music tied in too—a rock star, or at least I think he will become a star off this picture.

EXECUTIVE C (*mopping his brow*): So far I'm carried away. At least tell me that the old lady and the kid don't—

BART: Well, actually, there's a scene in which the woman and the boy . . . I mean, the audience won't see anything graphic. . . . Besides, the boy is gay and—

EXECUTIVE D: Look, can we move on? I mean, we've got three pictures shooting that are way over budget and—

BART: Look, this project will cost $3 million tops. There's comedy, there's empathy, and no downside risk.

EXECUTIVE A: Tell me, at least, that a really top writer wrote the script.

BART: Actually, it was written by a kid who cleans a neighbor's pool. He left the script on a pool chair and—

EXECUTIVE B (*exasperation setting in*): OK, OK. Three million bucks. We'll make it, providing we don't have to talk about it anymore and I don't have to see dailies.

BART: Seems fair to me.

EXECUTIVE D: Now, moving on to these other pictures . . .

The movie was made by Paramount. It was called *Harold and Maude,* and although not exactly an instant hit, the film became a cult classic and ultimately a financial success. It also made Cat Stevens a rock star and Hal Ashby a major director.

My purpose in citing this anecdote is simply to point out that a discussion of this sort could never happen in today's studio system. For one thing, a screenplay written by a pool cleaner would never work its way up the myriad layers of studio bureaucracy. The subject matter would be deemed unacceptable, the story line could never provide the basis for a theme-park ride or a tie-in with McDonald's, prospects in TV would be dim, et cetera.

Moreover, if any young executive seriously suggested that a studio picture could be made for $3 million in today's Hollywood, he'd be laughed off the lot. According to official industry figures, it now costs some $50 million to produce and market the typical studio picture—and these figures are on the low side. It's not at all uncommon these days for a studio to green-light projects with a negative cost of $60 million, then toss in another $25 million for prints and advertising. And I'm talking not about big-canvas action pictures or superstar vehicles but about what used to be called program pictures, with middle-of-the-road casting.

And the trend keeps spiraling upward: Twentieth Century Fox two years ago made a surprise hit called *Speed* for $35 million with two budding stars, Keanu Reeves and Sandra Bullock. This year's wannabe-*Speed, Broken Arrow* with John Travolta and Christian Slater, cost just under $60 million.

Now, if you're an ordinary moviegoer, at this point you might very well ask, Who cares? If the studios toss more money at movies, their largess will be reflected on the screen. The action scenes will be more exciting, the special effects more vivid.

Well, that's not exactly what's happening. Scrutinize the budgets of Hollywood's would-be blockbusters and you'll find that much, if not most, of the money seems to end up in people's pockets—people who don't exactly need the money—and not on the screen.

Arguably, an inverse relationship is developing between the quality of Hollywood films and their increasing cost. That is to say, as movies get more expensive, they also appear to lose their edge, if not their panache. And no one worries more about this phenomenon than the people who own the studios.

That's one reason, for the first time in more than fifty years, the so-called owners, like Rupert Murdoch of Fox, Sumner Redstone of Viacom (Paramount), Edgar Bronfman Jr. of MCA, and Ted Turner who owns three moviemaking entities, are all assuming a much more hands-on management style at their companies, rather than leaving the studios to the "hired guns." Not since the halcyon days of the studio system, when hard-bitten hierarchs like Jack Warner and Louis B. Mayer wrote the checks and also called the shots, have the proprietors actually run the candy store.

To understand their concern, examine this year's Oscar nominations. It wasn't that long ago that the five thousand members of the Academy of Motion Picture Arts and Sciences used the Oscars as an occasion to heap praise upon the best of the studio product—glossy Hollywood projects like *All About Eve* and *The Sting*. Many of this year's nominees reflected the degree to which stalwart Academy members are turning against orthodox Hollywood pictures—witness the success of such relatively low-budget films as *Sense and Sensibility, The Postman,* and *Babe*. And of the five directors nominated for Oscars, not one belonged to Hollywood's elite circle of filmmakers who make $5 million or more per picture; four of them don't even usually work in Hollywood.

The message? The soaring cost of making movies in Hollywood has eliminated the studios' willingness to take risks. It simply costs too much money to venture forth with a controversial subject or gamble on a new actor. Hemmed in by runaway budgets, the studios opt to play it safe. And it doesn't take a genius to detect that "safe" movies more often than not are boring movies.

But let's go back to the beginning: Why does it cost so much to make a movie these days? Ask that question around Hollywood and you get sharply divergent answers. Producers blame the unions. Unions blame the studios. Studios blame greedy stars and agents. Agents blame the structure of the marketplace. Superstars blame the Zeitgeist. The answer is that they're all to blame.

Star salaries have lost touch with reality. Within eighteen months, Jim Carrey's price soared from $450,000 to $20 million. George Clooney looks great on *ER*, but does that justify Warner Bros. paying him $28 million to commit to *Batman* (the deal theoretically spans three pictures)? If Julia Roberts is worth a $12-million paycheck, why did no one go to see *Mary Reilly*? Was Sylvester Stallone deserving of the $20 million he received for his role in the misfire *Assassins*?

The example set by studio executives is one of profligacy, not restraint. How can a studio chief ask his filmmakers to bring down costs when he is flying around in his corporate jet and maintaining four or five homes of a scale that makes Arnold Schwarzenegger's spread look like Watts? One studio chief just renewed his deal guaranteeing him $150 million over five years. Another was given a golden parachute totaling $50 million. Indeed, Sony in recent years appears to have turned out more golden parachutes than movies.

The studios have gone overboard with action pictures on the false assumption that they represent automatic hits with foreign audiences. True, MCA's $175 million fiasco, *Waterworld*, was bailed out overseas. (The film did $171 million abroad, compared with

$88 million in the United States.) But a careful examination of box-office data shows that foreign audiences are also drawn to comedies and intimate stories like *The Bridges of Madison County*. (It grossed $108 million outside the United States.) The Stallone and Schwarzenegger megamovies are no longer instant hits abroad.

Top-of-the-line directors are lavishing absurd amounts of money on their films in an effort to protect their franchises (and fees of $10 million per picture) and the studios are caving in to this excess. Some of the biggest disappointments of last year emanated from such pricey filmmakers as Sydney Pollack (who spent $75 million on a dud called *Sabrina*) and Richard Donner (who received $12 million to direct *Assassins*). The studios assented to overblown shooting schedules, their elaborate perks, and housing demands. The unions are demanding too much money. A movie set is one of the few places in the world where blue-collar laborers who haul cable or move props make well over $100,000 a year and talk about their investment portfolios and their condos in Hawaii. But the hard fact is that the below-the-line workers make proportionately less than they did a decade ago. And most of them regularly sneak in work on videos or nonunion productions, toiling for lower pay and no medical benefits, to maintain their living standards.

The big question hovering over the movie business today is simply, can the trend of runaway costs be reversed? In Hollywood there's an axiom that says "what goes up never comes down," but is there a way of changing this?

The answer is yes, but it would require a radical shift in Hollywood practices. And there's certainly no guarantee that the industry is up to the challenge. Here are some of the basic steps Hollywood would have to take:

1. Spend more money on movies and less on overhead. A little more than twenty years ago, a superbly successful but scarcely noticed palace coup occurred at Paramount. Outraged by soaring overhead and meager box-office, the key executives

supervising production, administration, and business affairs moved off the lot to a suite of offices in Beverly Hills. The entire executive entourage was reduced to six people. Stars were notified there would be no more perks. When you arrive at the airport, don't even expect a limo.

Coincidentally, a succession of films soon emerged from the studio that changed its fortunes—*The Godfather; Goodbye, Columbus; Paper Moon; Rosemary's Baby;* and so forth. The lesson: You don't need sixty people to decide which twenty movies will be made.

2. In their heyday, the Hollywood studios made money because they created big stars, nurtured their careers, and, most important, kept them under contract. Today each studio is out there bidding against its rivals. No one is under contract. And unlike record companies, few studios have stars under option so that if they "hit" in one picture the studio has a favorable price on the next project. There is no law or Screen Actors Guild agreement mandating against star contracts. To be sure, some stars would rebel, as Humphrey Bogart and Clark Gable did, spending years on suspension as a consequence. With contracts, agents and managers would haggle over new terms. But at least the studios would be back in the business of building stars, not just exploiting them.

3. In the same vein, more top stars must follow the lead of Bruce Willis and develop a two-tier system relative to their fees. Willis gets $20 million for action films of the *Die Hard* genre that made him famous. But he also regularly takes small and quirky roles for sharply reduced fees in films like *Pulp Fiction, 12 Monkeys,* and *Four Rooms.* As a result, he has helped bring about edgy, interesting movies that normally wouldn't have a prayer. And he's also furthered his career as an actor. How many stars have followed Willis's example? Pathetically few. But Sly Stallone seems bent on emulating this strategy, having changed course by accepting scale

wages (with significant back-end participation) for a $10-million Miramax film called *Cop Land*. Willis and Stallone share the same agent, Arnold Rifkin of the William Morris Agency.

4. The studios must accelerate research into the burgeoning world of special effects. Through the magic of morphing, it is possible to create the illusion of size and movement without sending out units to blow up real dams or detonate buildings. The effects-wizards are out there, but the studios are simply not utilizing their wizardry or spending enough to develop their exotic arsenals. For the first time since the invention of sound, the way in which Hollywood makes movies is undergoing a revolution. These changes must be accelerated to achieve economies of scale.

5. Last, the owners who are taking control of the day-to-day management of the studios must find a way to curb their appetites. One would expect that, since they write the checks, the "new Napoleons," as Howard Stringer, ex-president of CBS, calls them, would be more cost-conscious. In fact, they are so fiercely competitive with one another that they are bidding-up costs, not curbing them. If they do not exert a degree of self-control, the typical movie budget will start looking something like this: star salaries, $40 million; director, $10 million; marketing, $30 million; and production costs, $5 million.

Will the audience feel cheated? You bet—and with justification.

So Hollywood faces two opposing demands: The industry leaders must find a way to raise quality yet reduce costs, to create a bigger bang with fewer bucks.

None of that should seem daunting to an executive making $150 million over the next five years, with a $50-million golden parachute to look forward to in case things don't work out.

—*GQ*, June 1996

.　.　.

As the cost of moviemaking continued to rise, more and more pressure fell on the marketers and merchandisers. The studios, too, felt constrained to take on "marketing partners" such as fast-food chains and toy makers to share the burden, as this article in the March 1997 GQ related.

MOUNTING THE MEGAPICS

Hollywood has become a rather rude place. Even if you're an important player, it's often difficult to get your phone calls returned. Not long ago, I happened upon three young studio-development executives who were passing their lunch hour by putting together a semi-facetious list of people who would definitely receive callbacks. Tom Cruise was a unanimous selection. So was novelist Michael Crichton. So was David Green.

David Green? Who is he?

Green spearheaded, until recently, McDonald's movie-marketing tie-ins and hence tossed around tens of millions of dollars to help promote Hollywood blockbusters. As such, he became a hot item among studio moguls, as have his counterparts at toy companies and fast-food chains, and others who bring promotional dollars to the movie business.

Since the David Greens of the world have their phone calls returned promptly, they're not exactly naïve about their clout. Indeed, McDonald's is playing an ever-increasing role in determining movie ad campaigns and release dates of Hollywood's huge "event" pictures. There have even been cases when some of the burger guys have disapproved of a specific scene or proposed a different ending.

And what is the message that all this sends? In present-day Hollywood, movies have become merchandise to be mass-marketed to an international audience. And with the new generation of effects-laden event pictures costing as much as $150 million to $200 million to produce and distribute, it's a matter of survival to bring in partners at the production and marketing levels. And why not? Selling Big Macs isn't that much different from selling *Twister* or *Independence Day*, is it?

Well, yes and no. Many in Hollywood are nervous about the tail-wagging-the-dog influence of the marketing men. They wonder whether we're that far away from the time when marketers, not film-makers, will have the dominant voice in shaping new "product," as they do at, say, Procter & Gamble.

This may sound alarmist, but here's the reality: Never before have event pictures so dominated the agendas of the movie studios. Though studios like Rupert Murdoch's Twentieth Century Fox may argue that they offer a diverse program of movies, it's the megapics that command everyone's attention and dictate the allocation of resources.

Indeed, as release schedules are juggled and rejuggled, Fox may well find itself in the unenviable position of marketing three megapics within a three-month corridor—*Volcano*, the big disaster picture; *Speed 2: Cruise Control*, the sequel to the Keanu Reeves action hit (without Keanu); and *Alien Resurrection*, yet another *Alien* sequel.

These massive projects will be fighting for shelf space with disaster pictures like *Dante's Peak*, *The Flood*, and James Cameron's *Titanic*, which in turn must butt heads with such high-profile entries as *The Lost World: Jurassic Park*; *Air Force One*, starring Harrison Ford; the much hyped re-release of *Star Wars*; and, finally, the umpteenth coming of *Batman*.

Do these sound like big-time gambles? That they are—the biggest chips Hollywood has ever placed on the gaming table. And the studios are scared to death. After all, twenty years ago the downside on a prospective blockbuster was no more than $20 million; today companies face the specter of $100-million write-offs.

So why is anyone willing to take this sort of a gamble?

Ask a studio apparatchik and you'll get a by-the-numbers response. Hollywood commands a global audience, they will say, and it's the big event movies that travel best across language and cultural barriers. That's what Hollywood stands for, they'll tell you: It's all about showmanship.

On one level, they're absolutely right. Hollywood has always been a cathedral of glitz. The studio system was geared to stars and star vehicles. When the system worked best, however, it presented a diverse menu of shrewdly crafted commercial fare. Witness the ten Oscar nominees in 1943: *Casablanca, For Whom the Bell Tolls, Heaven Can Wait, The Human Comedy, In Which We Serve, Madame Curie, The More the Merrier, The Ox-Bow Incident, The Song of Bernadette,* and *Watch on the Rhine.*

With the advent of the '60s and '70s, Hollywood product acquired a fascinating edge: *Bonnie and Clyde, The Godfather, Shampoo,* and *Chinatown* were all commercial films that were eagerly embraced by overseas audiences despite (or because of) their sharpened, more contemporary point of view.

Ironically, the event pictures that changed Hollywood forever— *Jaws, Star Wars, ET: The Extraterrestrial*—were not really preordained to fit that category. Yet the mind-boggling largess reaped by these movies incalculably raised the expectations of the world's media barons. If a movie could make $500 million almost inadvertently, then why not do it intentionally? they reasoned. Go for the prize!

Suddenly, the Hollywood studios were being gobbled up by global giants like Murdoch's News Corporation, Viacom, and Seagram, companies with huge debt burdens and global-distribution platforms. These entities not only expected hits, but also positively depended on them for their survival.

Hence the new era of movies as merchandise began. The working hypothesis—or business plan, to use the argot of the business-school types—is simply to design an assembly line for instant hits. Hammer out a plot for an event picture, plug in the theme-park rides, the toys, the music, and all of the other ancillary goodies ahead of time (rather than waiting for them to happen by accident), then line up your financial and marketing partners to spread the risk.

Considered purely in terms of marketing, the plan sounded fine. When event movies like Warner Bros.' *Space Jam* and Disney's *101 Dalmatians* opened during the 1996 holiday season, for example, it was all but impossible for a moviegoer to avoid the myriad tie-in promotions, not to mention the blizzard of merchandise. Michael

Jordan had his name on everything from pillowcases to tattoos. McDonald's dispensed 101 different collectible Dalmatian pups to its diners. For *Toy Story,* Burger King even ran out of plastic toys, which were remarkably similar to those being sold in toy stores. Both MGM/UA and BMW were blissful about the results of their massive tie-in campaigns built around the opening of the James Bond movie *Goldeneye.* Car tie-ins had not been successful in Hollywood for more than a decade.

The aim of all this, of course, is to build awareness for new movies while adding pizzazz to the mundane task of chomping down a Big Mac. A fast-food partner can provide as much as $40 million in media buys to support a film, not to mention additional money it spends on premiums and assorted point-of-purchase material. These campaigns have helped marginal films turn into winners. In 1995 PepsiCo bailed out Paramount's lame adventure movie *Congo* by laying out millions for Taco Bell TV spots that looked more like commercials for the movie than for the restaurants.

Such bailouts are not always successful, however. Pizza Hut distributed millions of squirt guns to support *Flipper,* which nonetheless sank beneath the waves. McDonald's was unhappy when 1992's *Batman Returns* turned out to be a singularly dark, violent movie, since the company had invested millions in a Happy Meal tie-in program.

Tensions between the studios and their promotional partners also bubble to the surface when editing problems postpone the release of a movie. Columbia delayed the opening of *Radio Flyer* in 1991 but forgot to tell Dairy Queen, its marketing partner; the studio had to make a financial settlement. More often filmmakers are instructed to make their dates, irrespective of the cost or the problems involved. The results are obvious to the seasoned moviegoer: clumsy editing, mismatched scenes, and other glitches.

A friend worked twenty-hour days for more than two weeks last year as part of an emergency team editing a major event movie. "I'd be lying if I told you our work was anything but slipshod," he acknowledged to me. "I mean, Starbucks can take you just so far."

Nonetheless, given the stakes, marketing partners are inevitably exerting more and more influence over the film product and picking their bets earlier in the process. Burger King and Warner are exploring an alliance that would permit the chain to select movies while they're still in development. Indeed, producers may start pitching the burger people directly, because they realize it's a safe route to a green light from the studio. Last winter Disney's modestly budgeted $28-million film called *George of the Jungle* was inflated into a $55-million megapic because McDonald's decided that the Tarzan spoof was a good target for tie-ins. Having just closed an exclusive ten-year agreement with Disney, the Big Mac empire found itself locked out of the latest *Batman* and Spielberg movies, and hence fixated on *George*. The studio promptly hired a pricey special-effects company to create computerized creatures to spice up the live-action film—creatures that could also be used as premiums to keep the kids happy while they're stuffing their faces with fries.

George may conceivably end up being a better movie because of this, but one wonders about the long-term impact on other projects. Look back to the 1943 list of Oscar nominees: Would *Casablanca* have been a better movie with a special-effects budget? (Its producers used model airplanes for the climactic getaway scene and then had to find midgets to act as mechanics to keep things in scale.) Can you imagine *For Whom the Bell Tolls* with giant action scenes and special effects?

The harsh reality of moviemaking these days is simply this: As the effects get bigger, the characters seem to get smaller. *Twister* remains the ultimate example of plastic characters wandering around a lunatic landscape uttering inane dialogue as cows and automobiles blow past.

All of which underscores the central dilemma of event movies: Can quality filmmaking survive in a corporate structure that treats movies as merchandise? Can a filmmaker give life to his vision working on a huge canvas and hemmed in by studio bureaucrats and marketing mavens?

While it's too early to make a final judgment, it's appropriate to send up warning signs.

1. Subject matter: Since *Twister* and *Independence Day* will have a combined gross of more than $1.5 billion worldwide, it's inevitable that the '90s menu of event pictures will be dominated by disaster and sci-fi. Before investing a few billion more in volcanoes and floods, however, studio chiefs would do well to remember that Hollywood has already gone through several major cycles of disaster pictures, with the later films in the cycle usually coming close to self-parody.

   They should also remember that the most memorable sci-fi epics of our time, like *Star Wars, Close Encounters of the Third Kind,* and Stanley Kubrick's *2001: A Space Odyssey,* represented personal statements by their filmmakers, not some hamburger chain's idea of a surefire hit.

2. Budgets: As budgets soar past the $100-million level, studios become eager for the "protection" of star names yet are squeamish about cutting them in on fifteen to twenty percent of the gross receipts. The upshot: The stars of most event pictures of the next decade will be the special-effects wizards. Hence Hollywood may be guarding its profits at the risk of losing its traditional safety net—star power.

3. Quality: It doesn't really matter to a toothpaste manufacturer whether his product is superior to that of his competitor, but when the packaged-goods mentality is applied to movies, things get dicey. By and large, movies work when filmmakers are passionate about them. Movies don't work when everyone involved in the process regards them as product. This is especially true when the guys who sell burgers have a chance to comment on how a movie ends or whether it's too downbeat.

In short, I'm really glad that McDonald's David Green got his phone calls returned. I just hope his successor doesn't place too many of them.

—GQ, March 1997

PART V

SCRIBES

Everyone admits there can be no movie or TV show without a script. Yet the writers who crank out these scripts have always thought of themselves as the most oppressed, and undervalued, participants in the Hollywood food chain. In the March 1995 GQ, *I examined the ramifications of this dilemma.*

THE SCREENWRITER: DIALING FOR DOLLARS

Before I begin, let me admit the following:

I was working as an executive at Paramount Pictures when no less a writer than Truman Capote was hired to write a screenplay based on F. Scott Fitzgerald's *The Great Gatsby*. Capote so disdained the assignment that he instructed his secretary to type out the novel's dialogue word for word, then inserted some stage directions and scene numbers and demanded his full fee.

I was at MGM when the screenwriter Robert Towne persuaded the studio to pay him $250,000 a year without requiring him to write a word. The deal called for the gifted but terminally blocked (that is, languid) Towne to meet with stars like Barbra Streisand and Goldie Hawn and cajole them into making their pictures at the studio. (He couldn't—and they didn't.)

I was at Lorimar when a screenwriter renowned for his fervent pitches sold one story idea to my studio and another to Warner, only to get the two mixed up. When he turned in the wrong script to each studio and both became angry, he protested, "So I forgot what I pitched! That can happen to anyone!"

The point of these tales is simply that writers can be whiners. They can be con men. They can be a pain in the ass. I volunteer all this up front because most pieces about the plight of screenwriters sentimentalize them. We are asked to think of them as victims, despite their outrageous wage scales and self-indulgent lifestyles.

Is this school of thought correct? Are times really that tough on Hollywood's front lines? Let me answer by describing a curious ritual that is reenacted every Friday at around 7:00 P.M. and that serves as a metaphor for Hollywood's conflicted attitude toward writers.

At that hour each week, assorted studio and network executives, agents, and managers all over town emerge from their warrens and head for their BMWs and Land Rovers. Though they've been liberated from their weekday routines, they are rather grim-faced, even surly. The reason is that their briefcases are absolutely bulging with scripts, treatments, and reader reports—formidable stacks of paper that make up the weekend's homework.

Bear in mind, if there's one thing Hollywood's young hotshots do not want to do on a weekend, it is read. Screening pictures, networking, partying, working out with a trainer—now, those are desirable activities. But asking these aggressive, hyperactive individuals to read perhaps twenty hours of material constitutes a form of torture.

Having both observed and participated in this Friday-night ritual, I'm convinced it's an important clue to understanding Hollywood's love-hate relationship with writers. The movie and TV industries have an unrelenting appetite for raw material. They need writers; they chew them up and spit them out. Hence their functionaries eagerly court writers; they fawn over them and lavish obscene sums of money on those deemed to be hot. And they also absolutely detest them. Writers, after all, take up too much time. Their egos must be massaged. Worst of all, they keep writing things that someone has to read, consequently screwing up weekends— the ultimate transgression.

But what actually transpires on these ritualistic weekends? Do all those scripts in all those bulging briefcases really get read and assessed? And, if so, to what effect?

Not long ago, I was visiting with the top man at one of the studios—a studio that had just released two or three back-to-back flops. "What really pisses me off about those pictures," he fretted, "was that I know none of my key people actually read the damned scripts. Everybody's an 'executive' who's too important to read. They expect the next level down to do the grunt work, and that level expects their underlings to do it."

How are sound judgments to be made, he asked, if no one bothers to read the original material? To this executive and to others in Hollywood, "material" is a magic, if exasperating, word these days. The major studios are keenly aware that this is not exactly a golden moment in the history of the movie industry. Few truly memorable films are coming off the assembly line. Oscar voters this year have had to scramble as never before to come up with even a marginally respectable list of contenders.

One solution to this shortfall, the studios believe, is to assume a more aggressive posture in the literary marketplace. After all, if you need an infusion of new ideas, who else to turn to but the idea men?

And, presto, writers are back in vogue. At least superstar writers are. The studios are ferociously courting best-selling novelists such as Michael Crichton and John Grisham, who can deliver "important" pictures that can be packaged with major stars. The movie rights to certain books are being gobbled up even before a publishing deal is closed, as with Howard Blum's *Gangland* (about mobster John Gotti) and Nicholas Evans's *The Horse Whisperer.*

Evans, a onetime journalist and a neophyte novelist, had an especially wild ride. His unfinished manuscript deals with a girl injured in a riding accident who believes her recovery is tied to the well-being of the horse. The tale instantly registered as a potential feel-good blockbuster. After an intense round of bidding, Hollywood Pictures, a unit of the Walt Disney studios, handed over $3 million for the film rights. Not wasting any time, Evans's agents promptly transferred the action to their book deal, eliciting a bid of $3.15 million from Dell Publishing—a $6-million coup for a novel that isn't even finished yet!

The spec-script market has been gripped by a similar fever, and the fabled gonzo screenwriter Joe Eszterhas was among the first to cash in. The former Rolling Stone journalist has set up two projects in recent months that could ultimately yield him $7.5 million—a spec script entitled "Foreplay" and a four-and-a-half-page treatment called "One-Night Stand." Both are in the sex/thriller mode of *Basic Instinct,* for which he received a neat $3 million. Meanwhile, Shane Black, who wrote *Lethal Weapon* and who auctioned *The Last Boy Scout* for $1.75 million, hit a $4-million jackpot with a rather violent action script called *The Long Kiss Goodnight.*

Faced with the need to pay big money for spec scripts, the studios have quietly been cutting back in other areas. Several are curtailing their regular development budget (Disney's has been chopped in half) and reducing the discretionary funds that permit producers to develop their projects at will.

The net result: While the superstar writers are reaping huge rewards, money is drying up for kids trying to break into the business and for the workmanlike pros. "This is an extraordinarily difficult time for the mid-market writer," notes Ronda Gomez, one of the town's veteran literary agents. "They see big-name writers making all that money, but the solid professionals who have made a very good living in this business for many years are feeling the squeeze."

Predictably, the discrepancy between the big bucks and the big squeeze has caused a certain degree of trauma in the writing community. Even in the best of times, writers like to complain—especially the affluent ones. Talk to any group of screenwriters and they'll tell you horror stories about how they've been spurned, mistreated, and misunderstood. Many writers, to be sure, like pain. It fuels their anger; it bolsters their sense of isolation. And that keeps them writing.

The reality is that in Hollywood, now as in the '30s, the writer is essentially a cog in the machine—an expendable contributor. The common presumption in the movie industry is that a project keeps improving as new writers are added to the mix. Hence three writers toiled on the script of Universal's big-budget extravaganza *Waterworld* (which will end up costing between $130 million and $160 million, depending on whom you believe) before the star, Kevin Costner, took a whack at it even as the cameras were rolling. A record thirty-five were enlisted to pitch in on *The Flintstones.*

The problem with hiring multiple writers is that it usually doesn't work. When I was a production executive, I always made a point of reading my way through the company's most expensive projects, the ones that had moved from writer to writer, from draft to draft. I discovered that, with only a handful of exceptions, the movies didn't keep getting better; they kept getting worse.

My conclusions were, to be sure, highly subjective. There are no hard-and-fast criteria by which you can evaluate a screenplay. But in my judgment, the scripts had been sapped of their power and passion as they wound their way through the process. The movies weren't being developed, they were being dismantled.

"There's something terribly seductive about rewrites," says Paul Attanasio, a former *Washington Post* film critic who, since switching his base to Hollywood, has been credited with the screenplays for *Quiz Show* and *Disclosure.* "It's usually a panic situation. You come in as the gunslinger, the potential hero. And the producers usually explain the dismissal of the previous writer with some hydraulic metaphor. 'He went dry,' they'll explain. Or, 'He's played out.' Then they'll tell you, 'All we need is a dialogue polish.'

"The trouble is that the whole idea is ridiculous," he continues. "Dialogue isn't just a flavoring; it's an organic part of the script that grows out of the characters. If you change the dialogue, you're also changing the characters, so the idea of a dialogue polish per se is silly. The whole rewrite process trivializes what writers really do."

Despite the big bucks involved in "body-and-fender" work, these days most successful young writers, like Attanasio, prefer to write original scripts. Indeed, more and more sharp young agents bill themselves as specialists in this arcane trade, which is akin to drilling for oil: Some scripts may never sell; some may bring in a million dollars or more. Producers employ energetic young "trackers" whose main job is to stay wired to the promising spec scripts coming into the market.

Though spec scripts are often of the gimmicky action genre designed to exploit the market, there are some impressive exceptions. "By and large, the best screenplays tend to be written relatively early in a writer's career and derive from his own personal experience," observes Ken Lipper, an investment banker and former deputy mayor of New York City who came to the movie business relatively late in life, when he was hired by Oliver Stone as chief technical adviser on *Wall Street.* He recently wrote *City Hall* for Al Pacino. In the process of prepping for his new career, Lipper studied the oeuvres of many top screenwriters, which he found to be a depressing experience. "The typical writer does some superb original work, writing with passion and power about his own distilled experience," he says. "He's then hired over and over again to adapt and modify someone else's work, and the quality of his own writing starts to ebb."

Lipper's conclusion: "If I were running a studio, I'd prefer to hire twenty young writers to do original work, rather than spend a million dollars for someone who's taking it on as a job."

Writers may argue endlessly about how to beat the system, but they tend to agree on one issue: The method by which their work is assessed and their career evaluated is downright demeaning.

The fate of most writers rests with conscientious young apparatchiks employed by the studios, by agents, or by producers and directors under various titles—creative executive, development head, or, more candidly, reader. They plow through the avalanche of material that engulfs Hollywood, sifting out the good from the bad and preparing reports for their bosses.

These reports may involve simple synopses or perhaps complex grading systems that assign different values to "dialogue," "originality of premise," and the like. Some marginally dyslexic producers even instruct aides to put their summaries on a cassette so they can listen in their car as they roll through town.

The drawback to this system is not that the readers are stupid or irresponsible. Rather, they are simply overworked and inexperienced.

They read so many novels and scripts that their judgment is as blurry as their eyesight. And though most are graduates of film or business schools, their life experience is limited. "They judge movies in terms of other movies," says one veteran producer. "Their whole mind-set is self-referential. They'll read a script and tell you, 'It's *Forrest Gump* meets *Beverly Hills Cop.*' They know absolutely nothing about what happened prior to 1980."

It's a devastating experience for a writer, who may have been responsible for three or four outstanding movies, to realize that the fate of his latest creation has fallen into the hands of a few twentysomethings who will probably meet over coffee and trash his favorite lines.

Then again, he may get that magic phone call that propels his work into a bidding war and a possible million-dollar payoff.

"I once had a career. Now I have a lottery," observes one old friend who has turned out some wonderful scripts in his time. "If I'd wanted to live like this, I would have spent my life in Vegas."

Come to think of it, Truman Capote may have had a point.

—*GQ*, March 1995

. . .

When a movie turns out to be a hit, the director takes the bow. When it's a flop, the writer is often the one who takes the blame. That, at least, is the common cry emanating from Hollywood's writing community, whose members claim they don't get enough credit—not even on the screen. Their complaint was examined in an August 3, 1998, column in Variety.

WRITERS ON THE WARPATH

As the level of angst continues to build over the so-called "possessory credit," David Zucker deserves a pat on the back. On his new film, *BASEketball,* the credits read: "A Universal Pictures Release of a David Zucker Game."

If Zucker had followed the lead of most of his colleagues, he would have called it "A Film by David Zucker" or "A David Zucker

Film." In summers past, directors of the big, frivolous movies didn't bother to flaunt the possessory credit, but now the tensions have heightened, as the credits on the new releases indicate. Despite the armies of skilled artisans laboring on these movies, *Armageddon* is "A Michael Bay Film" and *Lethal Weapon 4* is "A Richard Donner Film."

And screenwriters, among others, are increasingly indignant about it. An ad hoc committee representing the most celebrated and highest-paid writers has been meeting regularly to come up with a strategy to combat the directors' credit grab. Their aim is a return to the old "directed by" credit, which implicitly leaves the writers a little room for self-respect. And they're making their position known to the top studio executives in no uncertain terms. Among the writers believed to be active in the cause are Frank Pierson, Paul Attanasio, Aaron Sorkin, and Shane Black, among others.

Anyone reading the latest issue of *DGA Magazine,* published by the Directors Guild of America, has to empathize with the writers' viewpoint. In a series of interviews with directors of the big summer movies, one after another advances arguments favoring the possessory credit—arguments that by implication discount the contribution of writers.

There's the "I was there every day" argument, epitomized by Michael Bay. "We had like seven or eight writers on *Armageddon,* and they're gonna say that they're more responsible for the movie than me?" he asked. "I haven't had a day off in a year and a half. I'd love to see a writer that didn't have a day off in a year and a half."

In his interview, Bay didn't mention a writer named Michael Hensleigh who pondered, wrote, and rewrote the story of *Armageddon* over a span of six years before he approached Bay about jointly presenting the project to Joe Roth at Disney.

Then there's the "vision thing" propounded by Forest Whitaker. Explaining why he wanted his credit on *Hope Floats* to read "A Forest Whitaker Film," he says, "That credit to me means that it's from that point of view or vision. . . . It's like saying 'the storyteller is . . .' 'A Film by Forest Whitaker' is more about the complete spirit of the film instead of 'directed by,' which feels more technical to me."

A screenwriter might argue that, technically, Whitaker's actors read lines and, technically, those lines were written by a writer.

Finally, there's the "I am the boss" argument advanced by Randa Haines, who directed *Dance With Me*. The possessory credit is appropriate, says Haines, because she "is involved so intimately in every single decision that is made. . . . All these things are set by the director in collaboration with the people you have chosen."

If these "collaborators" are so important, one might argue, why assign a credit that diminishes their role? Indeed, this is the argument advanced by the lone holdout on the possessory credit issue, Martin Campbell, who directed *The Mask of Zorro*. Campbell declined to take a "film by" credit "Because I believe everybody contributes to the film, right down to the guy who opens the stage in the morning. If my name goes on, I think the other hundred and fifty crew should go on as well. . . . I feel everybody's contribution is valuable."

Campbell's magnanimity may be explained by the fact that he's a New Zealander who got his start in London and lives in Provence. Hence he's immune to the Hollywood quest for immortality.

The position of his DGA colleagues, however, seems to be hardening, and so is that of the top writers. Indeed, they're talking to attorneys about their future strategy. Among their possible moves:

Top writers could give a preferential deal to a studio that pledges to banish the possessory credit. A "writers' company" could even be formed to reward that studio with a flow of important projects.

The most prestigious writers could simply decline to write for directors who demand the possessory credit, favoring instead the Martin Campbells of the world.

Many writers agree that the least productive path would be to try to force a settlement via the Writers Guild. The WGA's impotence was further demonstrated last week when the membership voted down a referendum endorsing a list of strategic goals, one of which embodied what the guild ambiguously terms "creative rights."

The vote principally seemed to be a shot at Brian Walton, the WGA's embattled executive director—the referendum would have extended the early termination clause in his contract by one year.

Though the guild itself may be somewhat immobilized, top screenwriters working in the industry refuse to be inhibited in their quest. David Zucker may call his new movie "a game by David Zucker," but to writers, the possessory credit issue is not an exercise in game playing. It strikes at the heart of their craft and their self-worth.

—*Variety*, August 3, 1998

·   ·   ·

In an era of moviemaking when special effects all but drown out the dialogue, the writer's job is undergoing a major change, as I discussed in a May 28, 1996, Variety *column. The column was written, too, before the release of* Titanic, *the most successful "effects" movie of all time, whose dialogue was nonetheless attacked by many critics as banal and even irrelevant.*

SCRIBES ON A MISSION IMPOSSIBLE

MEMO TO: The Writers Guild

Having been catapulted through the first two entries in the summer blockbuster derby, I have come to realize that some serious rethinking must be done about your writing awards. The categories have clearly fallen behind the times.

Now, let me say at the start that I rather enjoyed both *Twister* and *Mission: Impossible,* having succumbed to the Morph Mania that characterizes the new generation of techno-thrillers. I'm even looking forward to *The Phantom, Independence Day,* and all the other megamillion-dollar popcorn epics that are about to explode from the pipeline.

However, I am also aware that movies of this genre have to be evaluated in an entirely different way. Audiences want a theme-park ride, after all. That means the effects are the stars. Old-fashioned things like character development, empathy, or even story logic don't really matter anymore. Which brings us to the question of writing awards. How can you compare the script of *Fargo* with that of *Twister*? It doesn't make any goddamn sense.

It's time for a new category—call it "Best-Written Theme-Park Ride." Or "Best Deconstructionist Action Script." Or even "Best Non-Writing for a Special-Effects Movie." The time has come to think to the future.

It's interesting to see how film critics deal with this dilemma. Richard Schickel, for example, in his review of *Mission: Impossible* in *Time* magazine, argued that "they don't construct thrillers anymore, they deconstruct them. It's as if they were making a musical that was all production numbers, no book."

While Schickel accepts all this as "postmodernism for the masses," he acknowledges that he's old-fashioned enough to miss "those little throwaway scenes where people hint at loves, hates, beliefs, disbe-liefs—what Hollywood's wise old hacks call 'rooting interest.'"

Well, sure. The bottom line is that, much as audiences may be buffeted by the action sequences in *Mission: Impossible,* most people really can't figure out what's going on. I even talked to one of its scriptwriters who conceded he still loses his way in the narrative.

In *Twister,* by contrast, it's very clear what is going on: The pro-tagonists are a bunch of lunatics who keep hurling themselves into the "suck zones" of tornadoes, which keep recurring with mind-numbing regularity—once every ten minutes, it seems.

There are even a few "throwaway scenes" of dubious subtlety. Bill Paxton brings his new fiancée to "tornado central" where, while chasing twisters, he hopes to persuade his ex-wife to sign the divorce papers. Still other "throwaway scenes" develop the heavies who try to race the good guys to each new funnel, only to lose their way. The bad guys finally get blown away—literally—but it's never quite clear why they're bad guys in the first place.

Not surprisingly, the personal stories in *Mission: Impossible* and *Twister* do not exactly elicit the emotional nuances of, say, *Jules and Jim.* Indeed, one can't help but wonder why Tom Cruise, who coproduced *Mission: Impossible* under his deal with Paramount, didn't give himself something more to do as an actor—or, for that matter, at least a better haircut.

One must assume that Cruise, as a producer, understands that the characters are really there to serve the effects, not the other way around. It turns out that earlier drafts—by Robert Towne, Steven Zaillian *(Schindler's List),* and David Koepp *(Jurassic Park)*—actually included the semblance of a love story involving Cruise and Emmanuelle Beart, the lovely French actress. In the editing process, however, those subplots were surrendered before the tyranny of pacing. The action must keep pounding along, it was decreed, and characters must not get in the way. As a result, the Beart character is left hanging there, like a curious artifact of a past movie epoch.

"This is a transitional period in moviemaking," reflects one of the movie's writers. "Audiences are looking for a high-tech fun ride, not for an emotional jolt. My hope is that there also will be room in Hollywood for the emotional movies."

Well, maybe. But meanwhile, folks, I think we should do something to honor those writers who labor in the wilderness of effects movies. Consider their plight: They know their work will go through many writers, many drafts, and many committees. They know that, in the end, the wizards manning the computers carry a lot more weight than the wretched writers, who are sort of anachronisms whom no one can figure out how to replace as yet.

Hence my proposal: The exact name of the award is up for grabs, but maybe we should face the issue dead on and call it "Best Screenplay by an Acknowledged Anachronism." That would sum it up just fine.

—*Variety,* May 28, 1996

.   .   .

While writers may be perennial complainers, there's one aspect of their work they can't complain about. Writers' fees have soared in present-day Hollywood, as I discussed in a February 3, 1997, column in Variety.

PEACE THROUGH PROFLIGACY

If there's one precept that sums up Hollywood in the '90s, it is that living well is the best revenge. At a time when corporate America is obsessively downsizing and cost-cutting, Hollywood has launched itself on a sybaritic odyssey. Albeit only a privileged few are along for the ride.

Hollywood's decisionmakers simply don't buy the notion that "less is more." Faced with the choice between spending lots of money versus spending little, they opt for lots. They feel more secure making big movies rather than small ones and hiring big stars rather than middle-range ones, whether for TV or film.

In short, they have come to embody a whole new mind-set that the Harvard Business School would do well to scrutinize: Peace of mind through profligacy.

I was discussing this condition the other day with a friend of mine who is a top producer of movies and who was bemoaning the script-development process. A number of his high-profile projects are in the rewrite stage, and in each instance the work is being done by writers earning between $100,000 and $150,000 a week. The amount of money going out each week leaves him weak-kneed. "Studio executives only feel comfortable with top-of-the-line writers," he reports, "and the stars also want star writers on their projects. So if you want a go picture, you follow the rules."

And the rules he finds downright amazing. A whole new writers' elite has been created—people who make $1 million a year and more, thanks to the new rules. And why not? If the studio chiefs are bent on green-lighting $100-million pictures rather than $10-million ones, why shouldn't they prefer spending $150,000 a week on a writer rather than a puny $15,000?

My producer friend assured me he had fully adapted to this modus operandi, but that certain ramifications of the "new rules" left him perplexed. In dealing with the new elite of writers, for example, these questions had presented themselves:

1. What do you say to a $150,000-a-week writer who takes three-hour lunches? This may seem like a mundane issue, but over a period of a month, he might have run up a $100,000-bill masticating when he could have been hammering the plot into shape. Do you tell him to eat faster? Or go on a fast?

2. What do you do when a writer says he's blocked? I once sent a "blocked" writer to Maui for a week's R&R, but I was paying him a mere $25,000 for the entire rewrite, not $150,000 a week. If someone was effectively paying me $30,000 a day, or $15,000 for a single morning, I think I might get writer's block too, and Maui wouldn't help.

3. What happens if your high-priced writer is burdened with domestic problems? I once had a writer working for me who, like clockwork, would shut down every Thursday because he was feuding with his wife. Are $150,000-a-week writers too rich to have personal lives? If they get depressed because of a family quarrel, do they deduct money on the back end?

4. Who's liable for computer glitches? Given the wonders of technology, computers regularly eat scenes or otherwise manifest arcane viruses that disrupt the writing process. If a writer is having trouble licking a scene, he usually protests, "The scene was great, but it disappeared into the system." At these prices, do you have a computer dweeb at a writer's elbow for just such an exigency? This would seem to be a minor investment to save a $150,000 scene, especially if it's about to go before the cameras.

5. What happens if the rewrite sucks? "If one $150,000-a-week writer lets you down, you quickly bring in a $175,000-a-week writer for a repair job," advised my producer friend. "You don't want to let the project go down the drain." It's not at all uncommon, he acknowledged, for a script to go from an 'eight' to a 'six' because of a mediocre rewrite. You may end up

spending a total of $5 million on rewrites, but it's still modest compared with the $15 million you may have to pay your star.

Besides, if a script costs a lot of money, it's got to be better—that's simple logic. The higher the cost, the better your odds for success. The "new rules," remember?

—*Variety*, February 3, 1997

. . .

On August 8, 1994, I scrutinized the work of perhaps the "hottest" of Hollywood's "hot" young writers, who had made a killing on spec scripts that featured an astonishingly high body count. Not long after publication of the Variety *column, Shane Black hit something of a cold streak when his "hot" scripts landed at the box office with a dull thud.*

GROSS AND GRISLY

MEMO TO: Shane Black

I've got to hand it to you, Shane, you know how to beat the system. Not just beat it, nuke it. Other writers may thrash around in development hell, but along you come with your mayhem machine—that's probably what you call your computer—and, pow, a $4-million spec script emerges before you can blink an eye.

No one can remember a deal quite like it, Shane, nor a script like it either. I've been talking to people around town who've read the script and, based on my survey, the breakdown is something like this: About one third of those who read the script vowed to quit the business forever; another third made firm offers; the final third simply threw up. So you see, Shane, your writing not only makes you a lot of money, but it also gets people talking.

But that's part of your problem. When you galvanize this sort of attention, you're no longer just a writer, you become an "industry figure." And I think you should start thinking about that before things get out of control.

(Let me pause here to explain a few points to the uninitiated. Shane Black is a 32-year-old writer who first achieved prominence by selling an action script called *The Last Boy Scout* for $1.75 million—it was not exactly an artistic triumph. He later did a key rewrite on *Last Action Hero,* which didn't win kudos either. His new spec script, *The Long Kiss Goodnight,* was auctioned last week to New Line for a record $4 million and reportedly will be filmed by the husband-and-wife team of Geena Davis and director Renny Harlin.)

And that brings us back to you, Shane. At the end of your new script, you promise a sequel built around the same characters, which I assume you'll want to sell for at least $6 million. Therefore, this would be an appropriate time to deal with a few pressing issues.

There is, for one thing, the issue of violence. As readers of this column can testify, I am not exactly a crusader against violence in the cinema, but you may turn me into one. It's not just a question of body count, Shane—in your scripts, most victims are eviscerated, detonated, or vaporized so that there are not sufficient body parts left to count anyway.

Clearly, you relish the minutiae of death, which accounts for that tasty little scene where the guy gets shot through the head in a diner, his brain splattering onto the grill "where it sizzles along with burnt hamburger." Nice stuff, that. Also the moment where a deer comes crashing through the windshield of a speeding car and the poor beast gets wedged there, thrashing around, cracking the skull of a passenger and gouging our heroine until she shoots him. There's also the scene where she sticks a hypodermic needle into a bad guy's eye.

Apart from the random mayhem, a lot of children seem to be standing around witnessing the bloodshed, and even getting blasted away during it—I'm glad you're fond of children, Shane.

To be sure, you introduce a "fresh" character into all of this, a woman named Charly Baltimore who makes the Terminator look like a wuss. Charly not only has amnesia but also a lot of pent-up anger, not to mention a long list of enemies, and that's why she utters aphorisms like, "Life is pain, get used to it." She also urges men to "Hit me . . . it makes me go into my thing." "My thing" obviously turns you on, Shane, since you describe it in such excruciating detail.

Another "thing" you dwell on—vomit. "The building vomits flame" on page 47, "the earth vomits upward" on page 106, and myriad guns vomit regularly throughout the screenplay. Maybe that's why many of your readers are left heaving, Shane.

Then there's the issue of scatological dialogue. Obviously, you have a weakness for down-and-dirty characters. That's why a character dressed like Santa Claus, riding in a sleigh filled with children, shouts "I got a prostate the size of a fucking melon—half my life a doctor's hand is up my ass. I should marry the fucker."

Which brings me back to the "role model" issue. Young writers out there will imitate you, Shane. What you have done in *The Long Kiss Goodnight* is to carry everything to its logical extreme. Your computer has spawned the grossest dialogue, grisliest killings, most sadistic torture scenes, and most mean-spirited heavies. In doing so, you have not only exploited the system but you have also laid it to waste. You've left nothing for the wannabe Shane Blacks to try to top.

By making a woman your instrument of mass destruction, to be sure, you have opened up new opportunities for actresses. But let's see if even Geena agrees to do her shtick. I mean, it's really a great moment for an actress when, drowning in a freezing pool, she reaches into the underpants of a bloated blue corpse to steal his concealed pistol which she uses to blast the villain (she "does" the job kneecap by kneecap, just to make it more fun).

What am I telling you, Shane? First, you have some remarkable gifts. Your dialogue crackles (if it doesn't explode). Your scripts have tremendous energy. You have an ability to command both attention and money.

But cool it, kid. Your weapons are out of control. If the French have established a "language police" to protect their native tongue against vulgarization, then Hollywood may have to come up with its own language police to protect against Shane Blackisms.

In the scene you wrote for the Oval Office, an adviser tells the president, "Colonel Baltimore is the single deadliest individual I've ever encountered. She . . . scares me."

You scare *me,* Shane. Before *The Long Kiss Goodnight* is finished, you may scare New Line. My God, the earth may even vomit upward.

—*Variety,* August 8, 1994

.   .   .

Among the veteran screenwriters, jaunty, freewheeling Joe Eszterhas, a one-time journalist at Rolling Stone, *managed to turn out "big-bucks" screenplays with the greatest consistency and also fired his agents with even greater regularity. I described Eszterhas's modus operandi in* Variety *in May 15, 1995, along with some unsolicited recommendations about his future career. Following the column, Eszterhas, too, hit a cold streak as movies like* Showgirls *and* Burn Hollywood Burn *flopped at the box office.*

THE SECRET AGENT: JOE ESZTERHAS

MEMO TO: Joe Eszterhas

SUBJECT: Career aims

If my addition is correct, you stand to earn somewhere between $6 million and $10 million as a writer this year, and those are pretty good wages by any standard, Joe. But nonetheless, this column has some blunt advice:

You're doing it all wrong, Joe. It's time to go back to square one.

What brought this to a head were the reports of you out there last week, shuttling between ICM and CAA, auditioning new agents. It was all a bit unseemly. After all, only four years ago you blew off CAA, and then put out the story about CAA's "foot soldiers" threatening to stomp on your body on Wilshire Boulevard— the metaphor was always a bit murky—and now here you are, giving them a chance to put you into turnaround yet again.

That pointed up the basic error of your ways, Joe. You think you need an agent, when in actual fact you should become one.

The way I see it, the Joe Eszterhas Agency could become a real kick-ass player in today's largely dysfunctional agency field. Indeed, it might be the only agency that could satisfy even your own lofty expectations.

Let's be frank about one thing, Joe—you have an obsession about the Big Bucks. Barely a week goes by without the details of some new Eszterhas scheme finding its way into the press—selling the four-page treatment of *One Night Stand* to New Line for $4 million was the most recent example. Earlier, there was that $3 million for *Basic Instinct*.

Now, I've read *One Night Stand*, Joe, and I can tell you that you'll never find an agent who can make deals like that back-to-back. Nor could any agent bail you out of the kind of situation you had at Columbia, when you turned in two pages of rewrite on *Gangland*, the film about John Gotti, and your agent demanded payment for a full rewrite. Word is you collected $2.75 million, despite the unpleasantness.

You don't like doing rewrites, Joe. Indeed, you've got to face the possibility that maybe you don't like writing at all at this point in your capitalistic career.

Hence the Joe Eszterhas Agency, a company that will not simply make deals for writers but could bring the whole agency business into the twenty-first century. Consider the following:

Since many writers, directors, and other artists today must pay an agent, a manager, a business manager, and a publicist, the Joe Eszterhas Agency could be the first full-service agency. With your prowess at promotion, Joe, you could sign up the best and the brightest with the promise that, for a mere fifteen percent commission, you'd take care of all their needs—gonzo dealmaking, publicity, investments, the works!

The Joe Eszterhas Agency also could do the following:

Script recycling. Too many writers are knocking their heads against the wall, trying constantly to come up with new material. On the other hand, Joe, you have demonstrated how, with shrewd recycling, plots and characters can be reconfigured and re-marketed. *Spy* magazine even charted the specifics of your recycling program, project by project. Again, this is a leadership role for you, Joe.

Foreign sales. Many of your most important deals have involved producers who pre-sell foreign territories based on your name, so it seems appropriate you teach your craft to other writers. Why should a spec script be offered only to Hollywood producers when foreign distributors and other wheeler-dealers might, given the opportunity, come up with a better price?

Ego reinforcement. The biggest problem in Hollywood is self-esteem. Most people get down on themselves. You're the obvious exception, of course, as we are reminded every week on some national TV show that reiterates your accomplishments. Writers need an inspirational leader, Joe—someone who can convince them they're smart, original, and even capable of making a buck.

This brings us to possibly the most important service the Joe Eszterhas Agency could provide: You could represent not just writers and other working stiffs, but a whole other class of people as well.

The way things are working out in town these days, Joe, there are many agents who frankly need a good agent to represent them. The evidence is right there in front of you: Clients are peeling off with alarming regularity. Morale is low. Clusters of hot young agents keep defecting from major agencies, only to form new pockets of angst. The business is a mess, Joe.

Hence, rather than talking to ICM about whether they might still represent you, you should volunteer to represent them. I know guys over there who would delight in the prospect of you marching into Jeff Berg's office to demand better perks and salaries on their behalf. Berg himself might even ask your help in convincing Mel Gibson to do a few more *Lethal Weapon*s and back off this directing gig, which is costing ICM big money in commissions. You might even help Arnold Schwarzenegger finally decide on a script!

Think of what you could do for the telcos, Joe. Think of Howard Stringer, stranded in his phone booth, with that truncated new logo—Tele-TV. It looks like a TV repair service, Joe—they clearly need assistance from you. You also could help Rupert Murdoch figure out what to do with all those MCI billions—I mean, how many long-distance phone calls can even Rupert make?

The world of business needs you, Joe. It's time to abandon the childlike trade of screenwriting. You know the old dictum—the smart poker player knows when to get up from the table. Besides, if you stay too long, someone ultimately may see you crossing Wilshire Boulevard, and, well, I don't want to remind you about what might happen.

—*Variety*, May 15, 1995

. . .

Hollywood's most successful screenwriter, Michael Crichton, has always managed to stand above the fray, making his millions but almost never getting his name in the paper. After publication of this Variety *column on March 1, 1993, Crichton's record became even more enviable. Twister, which he wrote with his wife, Anne-Marie Martin, was a megahit. So was the sequel to* Jurassic Park, *called* The Lost World. *And the TV show Crichton created,* ER, *continued to be a huge success, with NBC ultimately paying $13 million per episode to renew the series in 1998.*

CALM IN THE EYE OF A SHOWBIZ STORM

This town is all but overflowing with hungry-eyed filmmakers armed with projects that, in their minds, are ready to go before the cameras. Yet the studios say "no"—studios that are admittedly facing a serious shortfall of product. The reason for this anomaly? Either the wannabes lack talent, or fresh ideas can no longer penetrate the decision-making bureaucracy.

Given this dilemma, the career of Michael Crichton stands out as a fascinating aberration. Towering, cerebral, marvelously eccentric, the six-foot-nine-inch Crichton is responsible for two upcoming megapix, *Jurassic Park* and *Rising Sun,* representing a combined investment of well over $100 million. Hence the doctor-turned-director-turned-novelist is at once at the center of

Hollywood power, yet utterly removed from it. He is the king of "high concept," yet has never pitched an idea or asked a studio exec, "What's selling today?" He has mastered "the process" while demonstrating disdain for it.

Jurassic Park and *Rising Sun* were both cutting-edge novels and now, transformed into very expensive movies by directors Steven Spielberg and Phil Kaufman, their success or failure will have a major impact on the fate of Universal and Twentieth Century Fox, which are releasing them. As for Crichton, he has long since moved on to other projects and fresh ideas. His newly completed novel, *Exposure* (he's going to change the title), is already the subject of multimillion-dollar bidding.

Though Crichton has directed six pictures, his present modus operandi is straightforward. He writes the novel (he's written thirteen) and, if asked, will do a first-draft screenplay, structuring the story as a film. But when a director starts whining about character nuance or story polishes, Crichton ambles off into the night. He's been through all this too many times, heard too many directors and studio execs complain that endings lacked punch or characters lacked empathy. "*Citizen Kane* didn't have particularly sympathetic characters," Crichton observes. "Somehow the film seemed to work OK."

It was just twenty years ago, at age 30, that the eager Harvard-educated physician came to town to direct his first film, *Westworld,* at the old MGM of Jim Aubrey. The film was typical Crichton, steeped in riveting ideas, but the directing was not exactly up to David Lean standards. The pattern continued with projects like *Coma, The Great Train Robbery,* and *Runaway.* Whatever their limitations, they represented the work of a superb storyteller and an eclectic mind, two qualities not exactly in oversupply in Hollywood.

But Crichton became increasingly impatient both with himself and with the process. He seemed more comfortable in the solitude of his study than amid the frenzy of a movie set. The books rolled out. The money rolled in.

Crichton was prompted to write the provocative *Rising Sun* after returning from Asia to find Los Angeles (starting with its airport) tumbling into Third World status. It was a thriller with an edge; some found it hostile toward Japanese, especially Japanese businessmen. Others just found it compelling.

It was an open secret at Fox that the relationship between Crichton and director Phil Kaufman was far from smooth. Kaufman is the sort of man who can give a didactic ten-minute lecture about the color of his carpet. Crichton did his draft but has yet to see the finished product, which stars Sean Connery and Wesley Snipes.

The making of *Jurassic Park,* by contrast, was the sort of adventure that fascinates Crichton—an exercise in technological filmmaking at which Steven Spielberg is a master. The fate of the dinosaur epic carries even greater impact now in light of last week's changes in the top echelon of Matsushita, the giant Japanese company that acquired MCA. The new honchos reportedly are less enthusiastic about show biz than their predecessors.

Hence Michael Crichton, author of the biting bestseller critiquing Japanese business, now finds himself playing an important, if indirect, role in determining the fate of a major Japanese venture.

Though cool-headed and gracious, Crichton himself is feeling the pressure these days. His once-quiet office is now bursting with activity; his part-time secretary has been supplanted by two full-timers. Though he's trying to do some writing, he feels almost as if he's back on a movie set.

Would Crichton ever direct again? He admits to mixed feelings about this prospect. He knows he's having a great run and is reluctant to disturb the rhythm. He also senses that this is a "dull period" for Hollywood filmmaking—"a period of remakes and recycled ideas." Though he has kept himself out of the power circle and has few, if any, Hollywood friends, producers continue to drop by his office to pitch ideas—especially sci-fi ideas.

"Some of the ideas are interesting," he reflects, "but people in this town have a tendency to confuse foreground with background. They'll finish their pitch and I find myself asking, "Great, but where's the story?"

In his younger years, Crichton himself was occasionally criticized on these grounds, getting caught up in the "great idea" but missing the story. That cannot be said any longer. At 50, Crichton has slowed his pace and become more contemplative and self-critical. He lives a writer's life in great style, sharing one of Santa Monica's grand houses with his wife and four-year-old daughter. While people in Boston or New York often recognize him as he wanders into bookstores, that rarely happens in Los Angeles, where people only recognize stars or directors.

But that doesn't bother Michael Crichton, a man who manages to stand at the epicenter while, at the same time, hovering to one side, observing the frantic activity and outright panic with the perfect detachment that only a seasoned novelist can possess.

—*Variety*, March 1, 1993

·   ·   ·

No writer ever came closer to figuring out the system than did a slight, bearded ex-attorney named Ron Bass, whom I discussed in the October 1998 GQ. *After the article was published, two films that Bass helped write,* Stepmom *and* What Dreams May Come, *were both criticized on the grounds that they were maudlin—a rap that Bass strongly resented. But as even his critics point out, Bass was still laughing all the way to the bank.*

THE SCREENWRITING MACHINE

I was working as a studio suit several years ago when I first encoutered Ron Bass. At the time, he was a showbusiness attorney, a short, shaggy, unprepossessing man who spoke in a numb monotone as he efficiently but unimaginatively dealt with the nuts-and-bolts issues of his clients' careers. My deliberations with him consisted of the customary detritus of showbusiness negotiations—salary, back-end participation, perks. Bass pursued his agenda with a quiet relentlessness, even as he conducted virtually identical colloquies at other studios involving other clients. But then he was a boring man who, I felt, was extravagantly overpaid for doing boring work.

What I didn't understand at the time was that Ron Bass was a maniac, albeit a brilliantly surreptitious one. The dull-voiced attorney before me was a sort of audio-animatronic puppet who had been juiced up and set in motion hours earlier. The real Ron Bass was someone else entirely—an overmotivated zealot who set his alarm clock for 3:00 A.M. so he could complete a full day's work at his real profession before his alter ego started lawyering.

A few years ago, Ron Bass came out of the closet, so to speak. The monotonal attorney vanished. The lunatic who awoke at 3:00 A.M. every day took over full-time.

These days Ron Bass is at the top of his game, but to say his game is screenwriting is misleading. If success were measured purely in monetary terms, Bass is probably the most successful writer Hollywood has ever seen. He writes, on average, eight screenplays a year and gets producer or executive-producer credit (and fees) on many of them. He has a mind-bendingly rich deal at Sony Pictures under which it is virtually impossible for him to make less than $10 million a year in return for writing new scripts, patching up existing ones, and serving as mentor-at-large to other writers and production executives.

In so doing, Bass has essentially reinvented the way a screenwriter interacts with the Hollywood community. Far from being just another literary body-and-fender man who can be hired and fired at will, he, rather than the director, is the auteur. Certain of his deals (such as the one for *My Best Friend's Wedding*) specify that he cannot be rewritten without his consent (although he enthusiastically agreed when Julia Roberts rewrote her toast at the end of the movie, insisting Bass's lines didn't work for her). On other films, such as the $85-million Robin Williams project, *What Dreams May Come,* he works side by side with the director, in this case a New Zealander named Vincent Ward. And despite Bass's demanding style, directors have lined up to work with him. Steven Spielberg, for example, asked Bass to adapt the bestseller *Memoirs of a Geisha,* on which Bass is presently working. While most high-profile Hollywood writers specialize in a particular genre, such as action or comedy, Bass's body of work defies typecasting. He has written suspense films, like *Sleeping With the Enemy;* dramas, like *Rain Man;* ethnic niche pictures, like *The Joy Luck Club;* women's movies, like *Waiting to Exhale;* problem dramas, like *Dangerous Minds;* action movies, like the upcoming *Die Hard 4;* and, of course, romantic comedies, like *My Best Friend's Wedding.* "I want always to be exploring new subjects and new settings," he insists. "That's one reason I worked so hard to get to be doing what I am doing."

To help pursue these eclectic projects, Bass employs a staff of eight and pays them himself—rather well, he says. They are a disparate lot: One is a combination assistant–story editor; one is a researcher-screenwriter, one a physical-production specialist. He calls them "my core creative team" and says he could not function without them. One team member is Bass's sister Diane Bass, a psychiatric social worker who was "invaluable" as a consultant on *Rain Man,* he points out. Another, David Field, is a veteran screenwriter who once served as co-head of production at United Artists (he bore some of the blame for green-lighting the famous debacle *Heaven's Gate*). Field has helped Bass with about ten of his scripts, according to Bass.

With Bass's success have come gossip and criticism, much of it directed at his team. Says one Sony executive, "Wherever he goes, he has these acolytes following him around to record his every word as though it were gospel. He may be prattling away at a meeting with a director and some production executives, and you see these women, sitting there, taking it all down for posterity on laptops."

Bass is deeply offended by the suggestion, which surfaced around the time of *My Best Friend's Wedding,* that his team may have contributed more than research and ideas to his screenplay. He insists fervently that he does all the writing on all his scripts. "I may circulate a draft to my team and ask for comments," he says. "When I block out the outline for a new script, I solicit suggestions. I certainly need help on research. Since I write on a pad in longhand, I require the help of someone who can read my writing and type my scripts. But no one writes a word except me."

Aides accompany him to story meetings, he says, because a lot of good ideas are exchanged at these meetings. "I have always been surprised that people can toss ideas back and forth, and yet no one seems to be taking notes. The assumption, I suppose, is that everyone remembers everything. Well, if I'm talking for forty-five minutes and my imagination is percolating, I want to know these ideas are being recorded, even though it may irritate some people."

One reason Bass wants this assurance is that, at any given time, he may be at work on three or four different projects—again, a marked departure from the way nearly all other writers work. "I don't want downtime between projects," Bass explains. "On a typical day, I may work six hours on my present script, then spend eight more hours outlining and blocking scenes for my next one. By the time I finish one project, I have a jump start into my next."

Bass's near-fanatical drive to maximize efficiency may arouse suspicion among rival writers, but, again, Bass feels it's all perfectly normal. "Look, this is what I do for a living, and I want to be not only good at it but also productive," he says. "I don't get out of bed to start work at three in the morning anymore, like I used to when I was lawyering, but I still get up at 4:00 A.M. to ensure I have a full day. That may include writing after dinner. With the help of my creative team, I can write eight screenplays a year without fear of burnout. I would be disappointed in myself if I were less productive."

Perhaps this is because he's seen what has happened to many former clients—the curtain suddenly falls; the demand for one's work vanishes. In a way, Bass seems to have a premonition that this will happen to him someday, and so he is determined to set down as many tales as possible before his moment in the sun fades.

His ferocious fecundity is impossible to appreciate unless one has worked with other writers. As a studio executive, I worked with gifted writers like Robert Towne, who would come into my office, shrug, and say, "Sorry, I've got writer's block. I can't deliver." I have worked with superb craftsmen like Alvin Sargent who, in a good year, would write a single screenplay—it would be a wonderful screenplay, to be sure, but getting it was like pulling teeth.

Bass simply can't comprehend this level of performance. To him writing is a sort of compulsion; he seems positively fixated by the written word, infatuated with his flow of ideas.

Yet his writing habits are nothing if not eccentric. Having trodden humbly to his law office for seventeen years, Bass seems downright threatened by any office today. Sony offered to turn over a suite of offices to him and his team, as the company does for all in-house writers, but Bass declined. (His two-person production team, however, does have an office on the Sony lot.) Instead, he wanders around Los Angeles with his pad and pencil, turning up in parks, coffee shops, and the homes of team members.

On a recent morning, I corner him at the home of a blonde aide named Jane Rusconi who lives in Sullivan Canyon. Rusconi, a Yale-educated screenwriter and researcher (she worked with Oliver Stone on *JFK*), seems entirely comfortable with her boss sitting at a wooden table in her backyard, sipping coffee and scratching on his pad. Nearby, Rusconi's and Bass's horses stand in their stalls, awaiting their morning sojourn. The canyon, which is tucked away near Pacific Palisades in West Los Angeles, is a funky headquarters for equestrians. During the five-minute drive along Old Ranch Road off Sunset Boulevard, I passed six people ambling along on horseback.

But Ron Bass is not here to ride; he's here to work. "I like to work outside, if it's not raining or not too cold," he explains matter-of-factly. "I mean, it's just me and my pad, so I can drift around and get the work done."

At first glance, Bass seems unlikely casting for the role of movie millionaire. Slightly hunched, his round face fringed with a graying beard, he wears a sport shirt and cords and talks in calm, lawyerly cadences. He is as passionate about his stories as he is about his work habits, but he still expresses himself as though he were outlining a deal memo.

Before starting a new project, he goes through a ritual of blocking every scene, naming every character and capturing their "voices." His outlines are so specific that scenes are numbered and placed in a three-act structure. Bass adheres to the practice of some screenwriting gurus of not writing dialogue during these initial stages. Some writers need to play with dialogue to get the feel of their characters. To Bass, however, this can be a trap—the writer may fall in love with his dialogue and lose sight of structure and character arc. To the disciplined practitioner, dialogue comes after the building blocks are set firmly in place.

Once all this has occurred, Bass seeks the advice of not only his amanuenses but also studio executives and his director, if one is involved at this stage of the project. While most writers are prickly when the studio is mentioned, Bass insists he greatly enjoys "talking story" with his two principal contacts at Sony—John Calley, the studio chief, and Gareth Wigan, a co–vice chairman of Columbia TriStar. "They are professionals," he declares. "They have excellent story minds."

The typical script notes dispatched by middle-management studio executives, however, get Bass as riled up as any other writer. "It's not just the individuals who are wrong; the entire system is wrong," he says. "These production executives with their MBAs want to become your bosses. The way it should work is that the studio should lend you people during the development process. They wouldn't work for the studio chief; they'd work for the project, and hence you could talk to them, argue with them."

Though Bass may criticize some general studio practices, try eliciting a specific criticism of a specific individual and, unlike virtually any other writer who ever worked in Hollywood, he becomes furtive and self-protective. In part it's a holdover from his hear-no-evil, see-no-evil lawyering days; in part it reflects the fact that, as he puts it, "I'm the most insecure, nervous person around." Ask him about the practices of showbiz lawyers and he defends them stead-fastly. Long a partner of Barry Hirsch, a successful attorney whose extraordinarily aggressive methods are widely criticized in Hollywood, Bass holds Hirsch up as a model of decorum.

And though many feel the studios have been caught up in a fever to create effects-laden blockbusters, Bass insists this is a shining moment in Hollywood history. It's appropriate that Sony occupies the old MGM lot, he argues, because Sony is the best-run company since the MGM of Irving Thalberg and Louis B. Mayer.

Anyone making as much money as Ron Bass has a right to be cloyingly content, I suppose—provided that saccharine quality doesn't contaminate his work. Indeed, some argue that sentimentality is the biggest weakness of Bass's scripts. "Every character is a little too nice, and everything has to be tied up in a sweet little bundle," says a director of one Bass script. (Interestingly, Bass was replaced by Richard LaGravenese on *The Bridges of Madison County*—a rather treacly story to begin with.)

All that notwithstanding, one has to admire a man who has run the gauntlet and emerged with such a sunny attitude. He labored for years at a career for which he had zero passion. Yet today Ron Bass is the ultimate happy camper: a man doing exactly what he feels he was born to do—tell stories.

—*GQ*, October 1998

.   .   .

While Hollywood is willing to pay millions for a hot new property, in October 1993 I wrote in Variety *about some studios that had quietly decided to search their vaults for material which had been acquired years earlier but was ultimately abandoned for one reason or another. Participants in the search said it was a fascinating experience—but one that resulted in zero new movies.*

SCRIPT ARCHAEOLOGISTS MAY UNEARTH FILM GEMS

Everyone hits the wall a few times a year. I remember one dismal Friday in February some years ago, back in the days when I held down a posh studio job. Then, as now, weekend diversion for studio functionaries consisted of going through a dozen or so brain-numbing screenplays, many of them submitted by producers who had deals on the lot.

Peering at the pile that awaited me that weekend, I freaked. Hurling all of them into the closet, I abruptly summoned the story editor. I was up-to-here with action and coming-of-age scripts, I said. What I needed to see that weekend was a sort of highlight reel of screenwriting. I wanted to pore over scripts by F. Scott Fitzgerald, Truman Capote, Ben Hecht, Dalton Trumbo—the best scripts by the best writers that had not been made into films.

An hour later, two dazed emissaries from the story department appeared in my office bearing an armful of very dusty scripts, brown around the edges. "You really want to read these?" the story editor asked.

"I need nourishment," I gasped.

The old guy smiled. "You're in for a treat," he confided.

He was right. That weekend, I was introduced to superbly weird characters, brilliant dialogue, astonishing narratives—and some pretty awful story structures. I could see why most of the scripts, remarkable as they were, had never been made. But I was also reminded of something I'd almost begun to forget—that there was a difference, as Truman Capote liked to put it, between writing and typewriting.

All of this came to mind the other day when I learned that a couple of studios had decided, in effect, to emulate what I had done that weekend, except on an organized basis. Exasperated by the soaring prices of spec scripts, by the stratospheric demands made by "hot" screenwriters, and by the generally dismal level of screenwriting, these studios had embarked upon a sort of archaeological dig to find long-abandoned material from their story vaults. As a result, bright young execs found themselves sifting through stacks of decades-old projects in an effort to discover some long-forgotten gem.

The launching of these treasure hunts is extraordinary in a town that has long spurned its own history. Many hotshot development mavens have never heard of the writers whose work they're being asked to reexamine. They can tell you what Shane Black ate for breakfast but go blank if you mention Michael Wilson. They can recite Jeff Boam's credits but think Waldo Salt was a steak tenderizer.

John Calley, the man charged with resuscitating United Artists, is one exec who supports these probes into the cinematic past. Having just hired 29-year-old Jeff Kleeman from Francis Coppola's staff at Zoetrope, Calley plans to send him digging through some long-abandoned UA scripts written by those two masters Dalton Trumbo and Michael Wilson, and is convinced he'll find a viable project.

Calley had also hoped to revive Andre Malraux's *Man's Fate*, but discovered to his dismay that MGM/UA sold the underlying rights some years back. "There are some great projects that were stalled by extraordinary circumstances," Calley notes. "A star pulled out at the eleventh hour or a company ran out of money. But when you read the basic material, you cannot help but be amazed by the quality of writing compared with much of what is being written today."

Warner is another company that is actively looking to its past and has even brought in shrewd industry veteran Barry Beckerman to supervise the activity. Two of Warner's biggest hits last year were based on screenplays that had moldered in the vaults for some time—*The Bodyguard* for seventeen years and *Unforgiven* for twelve. It was Warner exec VP Bob Guralnick who, with Kevin Costner, unearthed *Bodyguard*, a film that has since passed $400,000,000 worldwide, and the experience persuaded him that "we are sitting on a gold mine of unproduced properties."

Among the works being scrutinized now are those by Budd Schulberg, Arthur Miller, Frederic Raphael, Larry Gelbart, and Larry McMurtry. But the digging doesn't always come easy. Beckerman and Guralnick spent weeks trying to unearth a fabled Nunnally Johnson original called *The Frontiersman*, which at one time was slated to be Jack Warner's first independent production. The script, which had vanished from Warner's story department, finally was located in a long-forgotten Warner archive at the Burbank Public Library.

One question still unanswered: Will today's hot stars and directors be willing to commit to scripts written a decade ago?

Beckerman, for one, believes the "classic" scripts will carry the day. "It comes down to this: The writing is so much better than what's being turned out today that there's no comparison. There are great parts to play."

If his theory is correct, many more people will, as I did that dismal Friday in February, sneak a few old screenplays into their weekend reading bags, without feeling guilty about it. "I've just got Kevin Costner to commit to a brand new—er, old—script by F. Scott Fitzgerald," some bright young development exec may pipe up sometime soon.

That would be a meeting-stopper.

—Variety, October 11, 1993

.   .   .

Veteran screenwriter William Goldman decided on an unusual maneuver to illustrate the process of writing and selling a spec script for his new book. After this column was published in Variety *in July 1999, Goldman's script was put out to the studios. On its first round of submissions, the unfinished work elicited not a single offer.*

GOLDMAN PLOTS AN ADVENTURE
IN THE SPEC TRADE

Spec scripts hit the market on a daily basis, but when CAA sends out a screenplay called "The Big A" this week, it will carry with it some extraordinary baggage. In fact, I cannot remember any screenplay submission remotely like this one.

Placing "The Big A" up for auction, writer William Goldman is essentially putting his ego on the line—an extraordinary move in a very self-protective town.

"The Big A," you see, is an unfinished script. It has no third act. It will be submitted to studio chiefs on condition that they must not only read it, but must also put forth their critiques in writing.

Their responses, in turn, will be published together with the screenplay in Goldman's forthcoming book, a sequel to his hugely successful *Adventures in the Screen Trade*.

The purpose of the exercise is to create a book that realistically depicts the excruciating process of writing and marketing a screenplay. Hence, along with the incomplete script and studio responses, Goldman will include the candid critiques of six prominent screenwriters who also read Goldman's script.

Two of them, John Patrick Shanley and Tony Gilroy, advised Goldman to toss out his story and start over, even proposing new story lines. The others, Callie Khouri, Scott Frank, and the Farrelly brothers, Peter and Bobby, liked Goldman's narrative, but offered a blizzard of suggestions to improve it.

A grizzled veteran of the movie wars, Goldman is orchestrating this exercise in ego-bashing with a certain pained delight. Even as he explains the process, his expression is that of a patient passing a kidney stone.

As one of Hollywood's highest-paid writers, Goldman hasn't actually auctioned a screenplay in thirty years—not since *Butch Cassidy and the Sundance Kid*, an auction that changed the way scripts are sold in Hollywood.

Since that event, Goldman has written or co-written an extraordinary range of movies, such as *Marathon Man, Misery, The Princess Bride*, and *The General's Daughter*. But to many moviegoers, film students, and random cinéastes, Goldman's most memorable contribution may have been his book *Adventures in the Screen Trade*, a shrewd, sardonic glimpse at the business of writing and making films.

His new book, *Which Lie Did I Tell?*, will be published in March by Pantheon. When the paperback edition comes out next year, it will contain the final blow-by-blow on the sale of the screenplay, replete with comments from studio executives explaining why they bid on the script or why they passed.

Goldman acknowledges the possibility that Hollywood executives might turn out to be more self-protective than he, declining to comment on the script or perhaps demanding that their comments be "off the record."

Certainly, the task of evaluating a Goldman script carries some special responsibilities. As arguably this country's best-known screenwriter, he's also the man who coined the vaguely threatening line, "Nobody knows anything," referring to his colleagues' inability to predict how a film will perform. Goldman also once quoted an executive as saying, "This is the worst script I've ever read—unless Tom Cruise wants to do it."

Given this hardheaded outlook, Goldman is uncertain how his new script will be received. The story involves a detective, his wealthy ex-wife, and his two young children who show a propensity to follow his career path.

Besides having no third act, the script regularly pauses for some random Goldmanisms. At the end of one scene, the writer acknowledges his fond wish that he could have come up with a better idea. From time to time, he examines his various plot options before plunging into the next scene.

The reader, therefore, becomes a participant in the writing process, sharing Goldman's procrastination and anxiety, and ultimately in the selling process as well.

And, at the end of it all, he may even come to share Goldman's conviction that "nobody knows anything"!

—Variety, July 19, 1999

PART VI

FILMMAKERS

A changing of the guard has been taking place in the ranks of Hollywood filmmakers. Those directors trained a generation ago in theater or live television are being supplanted by a new generation that graduated from videos and commercials. In the April 1997 GQ, *I examined the styles and backgrounds of these directors. Fourteen months after publication of this piece, one of the principal young filmmakers cited, Michael Bay, was responsible for the biggest summer hit of 1998,* Armageddon, *a film many critics said was edited like a souped-up video.*

THE YOUNG AND THE RESTLESS

Firing someone is never a lot of laughs, but if you wish to embark on a truly existential experience, try firing a film director. During my seventeen-year career as an executive at three studios, it was my dubious privilege to fire twelve directors. Not surprisingly, none went quietly. I vividly recall the protestations of one auteur—it would be unkind to cite his name—who was shooting a complex period picture on a distant location. Two weeks into principal photography, it had become clear that the work was going badly. He'd fallen way behind schedule and was completing half a day's work for every scheduled day. His star was threatening to walk, claiming the director had no grasp of the material. The dailies seemed scattered and uninspired. My colleagues and I agreed on the inevitable solution: Replace the director.

A decision like this isn't made lightly. When a director is dismissed, the production almost always has to shut down while his replacement supervises script changes, visits the locations, and so forth.

And then there's the Sturm und Drang of the actual dismissal. On this occasion, I arrived on location and asked for a meeting at the end of the day's shooting. The director didn't show. I called him at his residence. His assistant, or perhaps his girlfriend, curtly told me he was unavailable and hung up on me. The following morning, I arrived on the set at 8:00 A.M. for the final shoot-out. I approached the director after the first take of the day and, in a manner I felt was suitably compassionate, informed him that he was off the picture. "Get off my set," he promptly replied.

"Actually, I'd appreciate it if you would get off the set," I responded.

"My set," shouted the auteur, "and I'm calling the security guards to throw you off."

Realizing that we could spend the entire day ordering each other off the set, I walked away from this confrontation to have a quick word with the assistant director and the production manager. "Shut it down and send everyone home," I quietly advised.

"What if the guy still refuses to leave?"

"It'll get very lonely out here with no actors and no crew," I reminded them.

I cite this incident to underscore the degree to which directors today feel their sense of empowerment. There's never been a time when directors exercised as much control or earned as much money as they do in today's profligate, turbocharged filmmaking environment. Directing has become not so much a profession as a franchise. Success brings millions of dollars a year in income and the chance to choose and control one's projects. And only if there are monumental screwups will some studio dispatch a "suit" to the set to send a director packing.

Having said all this, I also see a changing of the guard taking place in the community of filmmakers. An entire generation of directors, such as Sydney Pollack, Sidney Lumet, and Norman Jewison, who came of age artistically in the anything-goes '60s and cut their teeth in theater or live TV, is passing from the scene. Rarely has there been more opportunity for neophyte filmmakers to get their first shot—especially aggressive young émigrés from the worlds of music videos and TV commercials. Actors and actresses whose aspirations to become auteurs would have been ignored a generation ago are suddenly being allowed to direct independently financed features or made-for-cable movies. What was once an elitist fraternity is not so exclusive anymore.

The results constitute both good news and bad news. Some promising talent is emerging from the pack—witness David Fincher *(Seven)* and Michael Bay *(The Rock)*. At the same time, some positively dreadful examples of self-parody are also on display—mindless movies reflecting the worst excesses of vidiocy, and thespian-helmed cable movies in which the actors positively chew the scenery.

All of which raises intriguing questions: Where do mainstream Hollywood directors come from? From what sort of backdrop does talent emerge?

When you're involved in the studio decision-making process, you quickly learn that everyone feels he or she has the makings of a director. Everyone has a unique story to tell and knows how to aim that camera.

If it's that easy to craft a film, why are so many dreadful movies made each year? In fact, directing a film is a mind-bendingly difficult discipline. And despite having worked with scores of directors over the years, I do not have an easy answer as to where good directors come from.

All I know is that I never wanted to be a director, which set me apart as something of a freak. My reasoning was admittedly idiosyncratic. Directors don't operate in a vacuum. The realpolitik of the movie business is that directors need stars. Stars also need directors, of course. They need to bully and intimidate them. When you are directing a star, you must be ready to answer questions like, What was my character's relationship with his father? Was he popular in junior high school? Does he have facial hair? Is he well-endowed? And having explained all that, you must be prepared to have the star come forth with his own answers to all those questions—ideas that will cause weeks of rewrite.

Though I never aspired to be a director, there is no shortage of those who get a chance, and most who do usually fall on their faces.

The survival rate in the directing profession is astonishingly low. And it's difficult to forecast the winners and the losers.

In the old days of the studio system, directing-talent tended to float to the top of the reservoir of resident artisans. Many were already working as assistant directors or as directors of short subjects, waiting for their break. Howard Hawks received the summons one morning when a director turned up too drunk to work. Henry Hathaway was a prop man on a western when the director was injured and the desperate producer told young Hathaway to take the reins. Contract writers also used their proximity to the action as a career wedge—hence the rise of Preston Sturges, Billy Wilder, and Joseph Mankiewicz.

By the '50s and '60s, live TV provided the best training ground for filmmakers such as Arthur Penn and John Frankenheimer. A decade later, the film schools produced an astonishing bumper crop of directors, including Francis Ford Coppola, George Lucas, Martin Scorsese, and Steven Spielberg. I met Coppola not long after he graduated from UCLA's film school. He sheepishly admitted to me that he'd worked his way through college shooting what were then called "nudies"—tame soft-core movies that wouldn't stretch the R rating today. By the time he was in his mid-twenties, he'd already become one of the town's most prized body-and-fender men; working round the clock, he could refashion a troubled script in one weekend.

Over the years, top filmmakers have managed to find all sorts of ways to get noticed. Hal Ashby *(Coming Home)* had been an outstanding film editor; as a director, he edited his best pictures in his head as he shot them. Jan De Bont *(Speed)* was a top cameraman.

And Paul Newman was . . . well, Paul Newman. As with other major stars (Robert Redford, Warren Beatty, Kevin Costner, Tom Hanks), Newman's involvement with directing has seemed more like a flirtation than a career. His directorial debut was in 1968 with *Rachel, Rachel,* after which he made four more films and then seemingly stopped with *The Glass Menagerie* in 1987. Beatty made a big mark with *Reds*, but he has directed only two movies in sixteen years. Certainly the most prolific of the star-directors has been Clint Eastwood, who's been responsible for eighteen films since 1971. Tom Hanks was sufficiently depressed by the limp response to *That Thing You Do* that he doubts he'll do a reprise. We'll see whether there will be second efforts from Al Pacino *(Looking for Richard)*, Johnny Depp *(The Brave)*, or even Madonna (she says she will direct a movie called *Going Down*).

To be sure, stars have a big advantage in getting their pictures made—they have the ultimate leverage. Warner didn't want to blow its relationship with Mel Gibson, so when he fixated on a curious project called *The Man Without a Face*, the studio flashed its green light. Studios were fretful about his second movie too, an expensive costume picture called *Braveheart*, but that one paid off handsomely.

Indeed, Gibson's success, not to mention the honors heaped on Eastwood, seems to have promoted an extraordinary zeal among colleagues in the acting fraternity to take on the mantle of director. This has not come as good news to their agents, who watch their commissions wither as clients assume auteurlike pretensions. Studio chiefs, too, have mixed feelings. It's already tough to elicit a commitment from a star—projects often sit around for a year or two awaiting the "availability" of a bankable player. And once a star decides to direct a movie, he may be out of action for yet another year.

Artistic reservations also come into play. "Many actors can visualize a scene, but they can't see the whole narrative," explains one studio production head. "They'll zero in on a character, the way an actor is supposed to do, but they'll forget about the overview. Actors scare me when they say they want to direct." Arguably, Barbra Streisand the director has become obsessed with Streisand the actress (see *The Mirror Has Two Faces*).

While studios may show reluctance, the ever-eager cable-TV companies have positively panted to give actors their first break. A key reason is that the cable programmers are always star-starved. Important performers feel it's a step backward to appear in a made-for-cable project, a sign that top-line movie work is no longer available to them.

To help solve this dilemma, Showtime went so far as to develop an entire program of star-driven half-hour shows, called *Directed By*, to showcase neophyte actor-auteurs. Last season spotlighted Christian Slater, Richard Dreyfuss, and Christine Lahti, each of whom, in turn, managed to elicit the support of name performers who wouldn't normally be interested in working for Showtime. Lahti recruited Danny Aiello to play a wealthy widower who becomes enamored of a hip call girl, played by Lahti. Dreyfuss rounded up William Petersen, Carrie Fisher, and Anne Archer to help him relate the story of a successful architect eager to rekindle a spark with a former lover.

Whether on Showtime or elsewhere, actors have received mixed notices for their directing efforts. The émigrés from the worlds of videos and commercials seem to be making a more effective transition to theatrical features.

In pitching themselves, newcomers such as Alex Proyas *(The Crow)* and Marco Brambilla *(Demolition Man)* emphasize that they are better suited technologically for the effects-laden movies of the moment. They know what scenes to let their computers direct. Moreover, they're schooled to accommodate the fleeting attention span of today's channel surfers. They can deliver pace—lightning pace. Michael Bay's Levi Strauss commercial collapses the history of a couple from first glance to first Levi's to first child into less than thirty seconds.

"Hollywood follows what's hot," says F. Gary Gray, the 27-year-old music-video director who made *Friday* for New Line Cinema, a film that cost $3 million and grossed $30 million. "It's a kind of bandwagon thing. They go where the heat is."

Often a commercial is an advertisement for its director as well as the product. The Nissan spot depicting GI Joe using his sports car to seduce Barbie away from Ken elicited six feature-film offers for Kinka Usher and Mark Gustafson, the codirectors.

All this works in the best interests of companies like Propaganda Films, which both produces movies and represents directors of commercials and videos. Propaganda's stable includes Michael Bay, David Fincher, and Simon West who's directing *Con Air* for Disney, thanks to his Pepsi commercial depicting a small boy sucking himself into a soda bottle.

The big question remains whether someone schooled in selling a product can also tell a story and illuminate a character. Video directors have left a trail of failed movies behind them, going back to Julien Temple's *Absolute Beginners* and Steve Barron's *Electric Dreams*.

"It boils down to a question of sensibility," says one veteran producer who himself is a failed director. "Sure, you can find someone who can point a camera, who can yell 'Action,' who can condense a three-minute dialogue scene into thirty seconds, but can he evoke emotion?"

In short, are they artists? The great directors of the past were certainly quirky and idiosyncratic, and they were artists in their fashion. Some, like Billy Wilder, were brilliant and well-read. Some, like Sam Peckinpah, prided themselves on their tough talk, not their erudition. Some, like Francis Ford Coppola, were brilliant talkers. Others were amazingly inarticulate.

I once produced a movie directed by Franklin Schaffner, who made superb films such as *Patton* and *Papillon*. I marveled at the calm, quiet way he handled his incendiary star, George C. Scott. Toward the end of the shooting schedule, Schaffner was frustrated by one difficult scene and tried more than fifteen takes with his actors. Finally, he walked over to Scott and took him aside, and the two disappeared for several minutes. When they returned, the next take was positively brilliant.

Later I asked Scott what the director had said to him. "He didn't say a goddamn thing," the feisty actor replied. "He just stood there, and we both smoked awhile, and then he said, 'Why don't we try it once more, only better?' So we did."

Franklin Schaffner died in 1989. We could use some more like him.

—*GQ*, April 1997

.   .   .

No generation of filmmakers experienced anything like the flameout of the '60s directors, most of whom by the '90s seemed mythic but barely remembered. In a Variety *column on June 15, 1998, I tried to summon up the reasons for their rapid demise, in the context of Peter Biskind's book about that period.*

SELF-DESTRUCTION AS AN ART FORM

MEMO TO: Peter Biskind

No book in recent times has attracted more attention in Hollywood than *Easy Riders, Raging Bulls*, Peter, and you should be immensely pleased by that response. Talking to those who've plowed through the book, however, I find readers to be polarized along generational lines. Readers under thirty-five ask, "Is that really the way it was?" Those over thirty-five tend to reflect, "That's not really the way it was."

The key reason why your book is being read with such fascination, Peter, relates to the central question you posed: Why did the brilliant young filmmakers who burst on the scene in the late '60s and '70s self-destruct seemingly at the height of their power? As the jacket of your book baldly states it, "The sex-drugs-and-rock'n'roll generation saved Hollywood." True. But having saved it, why couldn't they save themselves?

The filmmakers in question are such as Peter Bogdanovich, Billy Friedkin, Hal Ashby, Bob Rafelson, Dennis Hopper, Roman Polanski, and Francis Coppola. All soared to amazing heights in terms of both achievement and ego—we're talking here about *The Godfather, Taxi Driver, Coming Home, Nashville*, and, of course, *Easy Rider* and *Raging Bull*.

By and large, however, by the time the filmmakers of that generation reached their forties, their best work was behind them. Some died young, a few went into exile, and others kept on working, not as trendsetters but as run-of-the-mill commercial directors.

There were exceptions to the rule, to be sure—the two most remarkable being Steven Spielberg and George Lucas. Neither was caught up in the drugs-and-rock'n'roll subculture of the '70s. While their confreres were anguishing over radical approaches to the cinema, Spielberg and Lucas stumbled onto a radical idea of their own. In *Jaws* and *Star Wars*, they laid the groundwork for the "blockbuster" mentality of the '80s and '90s.

But as your book vividly reminds us, Peter, most of the trailblazers of that era seemed to stumble as soon as they learned to walk. You discuss their problems in exhaustive detail: the betrayals, the debaucheries. Indeed, you lay it on thick.

OK, so Bert Schneider, producer of *Easy Rider*, carried "radical chic" so far that when a friend died and her body was cremated, he held a wake for her at which bereaved guests snorted the ashes like they were snorting coke.

OK, so just before the '70 Oscars, Dennis Hopper was so full of himself that when he ran into old-school director George Cukor at a dinner party, he poked a finger into the old man's chest and roared, "We're going to bury you. We're gonna take over. You're finished."

OK, so Lucas and Coppola were so cheap, they quarreled bitterly over the distribution of profits on *American Graffiti*. "Francis was questioning my honesty," Lucas complained.

One thing you never seem to run out of is ugly incidents, Peter. Every time a filmmaker of that era turned his movie over to a studio, the response was instant hostility. Colleagues even disparaged one another's work. All of Lucas's alleged friends told him his cut of *Star Wars* was appalling. And when Coppola showed *The Conversation* to his partners in the Directors Company (a company set up to support one another's work), Friedkin said, "It was like watching paint dry."

And here's where I think you missed the boat, Peter. Of course, there was a lot of meanness and backbiting in that era, just as there is today. But the one element of that period you almost completely miss is the pervasive sense of excitement—yes, of joy. It was almost impossible to go to the movies, or to put on some music, without being all but overwhelmed by new ideas and new sounds. The entertainment business of old had died; what replaced it was down-right thrilling. And for the people caught up in creating it, life was a nonstop, ecstatic party.

Sure, Vietnam cast a pall over our political life. As a result of the Pill, recreational sex was playing havoc with Eisenhower-era family values. Drug use was flagrant and often self-destructive.

But even the drug culture, as it existed in the '60s, is widely misunderstood today, Peter, and your book doesn't help. Curiously, drugs contributed to the optimism of the period. Writers, painters, filmmakers, and musicians believed that by smoking dope or dropping acid they could actually surpass the boundaries of their talent.

Sometimes the results were both ludicrous and punitive, but arguably the outpouring of revolutionary music and art stemmed at least in part from the optimism and even self-delusion generated by drugs.

Of course, in the end, the whole epoch collapsed upon itself in a haze of greed and egomania, and this you vividly portray, Peter. In film, as you remind us, the iconoclastic antiheroes of the '70s were reborn as Sly and Arnold, the steroidal superheroes of Reagan America. *Bonnie and Clyde* and *Harold and Maude* were succeeded by tent-pole movies with their asteroids and volcanoes. Hollywood went corporate.

That's when the fun stopped, Peter. Your book forgets to say that.

—*Variety,* June 15, 1998

.   .   .

While most of the '60s directors had faded from the scene, two proud survivors of that extraordinary epoch, George Lucas and Francis Coppola, were still very much in evidence, as I discussed in Variety *on July 27, 1998.*

"GEORGE AND FRANCIS SHOW" RETURNS

If you glanced at the newspapers last week, you may have shared my sense of déjà vu. By God, the George-and-Francis show was back in town.

There was George Lucas with his neatly trimmed white goatee, a bit portly at 55 and as taciturn as ever, making one of his rare public appearances in Los Angeles for the twenty-fifth-anniversary screening of *American Graffiti*. Even as he spun anecdotes about that seminal movie, one could tell his mind was elsewhere—namely, on the task of winding up his next *Star Wars* film, which embodies yet another bold advance in the technology of filmmaking.

And then there was Francis Coppola, the gumutlich Godfather at age 59, back from visiting his daughter, Sophia, on location of a movie she is directing, and buzzing about new entrepreneurial adventures for his beloved, if battle-scarred, Zoetrope company. Surely, the $80-million judgment from his suit against Warner Bros., on the movie *Pinocchio*, further incentivized him in launching projects.

Lucas and Coppola aren't about to work in tandem again, as they did a quarter of a century ago when their collaboration yielded movies like *Graffiti*, *THX-1138* (which Lucas directed), *The Conversation* (which Coppola directed), or even *Apocalypse Now* (which Lucas almost directed but Coppola ultimately directed).

Together and separately, both still fill a remarkable niche in show business, yet seem to have deftly exchanged roles. At the outset Coppola was the innovator, the unflappably persuasive talker who rammed Lucas's first two projects past balky studios and then went on to set up entities like the Directors Co. at Paramount. Lucas, in that period, was shy and soft-spoken. He had the great ideas but seemed ill-equipped to sell them.

In recent years, of course, it's Lucas who has emerged as the billionaire businessman whose company, ILM, has recorded remarkable growth. "One of my goals has been to establish ILM as completely self-sufficient and profitable outside of the *Star Wars* movies," Lucas remarked the other day. In other words, at a time when Lucas is creating yet another *Star Wars* empire, the empire that *Star Wars* originally created has achieved its own maturity.

Despite his extraordinary success, talking with Lucas is still like meeting with a small-town banker to whom one owes money. He is impeccably polite and implacably distanced, as though fearing that you might ask an inappropriate question or perhaps even request a loan.

Given this mind-set, it was all the more amazing that *American Graffiti* emerged as such a sunny, upbeat movie—a film that helped propel the careers of Richard Dreyfuss, Harrison Ford, and a former child star named Ron Howard.

The making of *Graffiti* was a study in pain. Despite the fierce advocacy of Coppola, who was the producer, *Graffiti*'s budget was a slender $750,000. The shooting schedule was twenty-seven nights and one day. The cast and crew were relatively inexperienced, and, to make things worse, the company was tossed off its original location, San Rafael, after only one night because a bar owner objected to the noise.

When executives at Universal saw the first preview in San Francisco, their response was, to put it mildly, unenthusiastic. "Unreleasable," barked one top production executive. "Not even a TV movie," said another.

Lucas and Coppola kept screening the movie, hoping to pick up support from random Universal executives or to find a buyer at another studio. To each screening they invited secretaries, interns, Teamsters, and anyone else wandering by, and finally word drifted back to the senior suits that audiences seemed to love the movie.

Finally released in August 1973, *Graffiti* did unspectacular business at first, but kept building, week after week, until it emerged as that year's major sleeper.

For the twenty-fifth-anniversary screening, Lucas had the pleasure of resurrecting a few scenes that had been cut by Universal, including a delightful moment when Harrison Ford sings "Some Enchanted Evening" to his date. Indeed, George Lucas got the last laugh.

Today, of course, Lucas is completely autonomous in both his filmmaking and his techie activities. While other filmmakers work feverishly to meet release dates laid down by studios, Lucas sets his own agenda and delivers his projects when he is good and ready.

These days he is dividing his time between writing a new *Star Wars* prequel and completing postproduction on the earlier one. The next *Star Wars* pic will be released in May, with subsequent entries at three-year intervals.

And each will embody its own unique technology. The next *Star Wars* will have four times the number of digital shots as *Titanic*. Indeed, many of its characters will be digitally created, and there will be few actual sets.

The live-action characters will essentially inhabit a universe of digital animation. As Lucas acknowledges, "We had to create a new technology to tell our story. It simply didn't exist a couple of years ago."

But when he finally gets around to showing his cut, George Lucas will not have to worry about whether some production executive "gets it." Like his friend Coppola, he is too busy inventing the future to spend much time reinventing his past.

—Variety, July 27, 1998

.   .   .

Though Francis Coppola's biggest hits were released by studios, he nonetheless harbored the independent director's instinctive disdain for Hollywood "suits," as his litigation against Warner Bros. illustrated. On June 29, 1998, I discussed the implications of that lawsuit in Variety.

THE GODFATHER'S VENDETTA

Since everyone knows that the only people who win lawsuits are the lawyers, why do they keep suing?

For insight into this question, look no further than the *Francis Coppola v. Warner Bros.* suit, which went to the jury June 25.

No one who has read the testimony would suggest that this case illuminates any profound points of law. Rather, it illustrates the sheer nastiness of doing business in Hollywood. It has elements of blood feud, vendetta, and other "Godfathery" nuances.

As I reviewed the proceedings recently, I tried to put myself in the position of the typical government postal worker who finds himself glumly doing jury duty, trying to figure out why these rich people are beating up on each other.

Here are some of the issues the postal worker had to confront in this case:

Coppola, a rich and fabled director, makes a producing deal at Warner Bros. to develop a movie based on the children's classic *Pinocchio*. He envisions a story in which a teacher and a group of children are escaping Nazism during World War II and, even as they are on the run, the teacher reads from the famous old story. The film would incorporate live action, animation, music, and special effects.

Sounds like a worthy movie, the postal worker tells himself. Let's hear more.

Coppola makes a deal at Warner Bros. to produce the film. He doesn't sign it though. The unsigned deal sits on his lawyer's desk for over a year.

Interesting custom in Hollywood, the postal worker concludes. People go to the trouble of making deals, but they're too rich to bother signing them.

Coppola approves the hiring of a writer, Frank Galati, develops his script and submits that script to Warner Bros. He also asks for a directing deal comparable to the one he had at Columbia, where he had just completed a version of *Dracula*. He wants $5 million against fifteen percent of the gross.

Warner Bros. reads the script and the deal and is unhappy with both. OK, says the postal worker, a studio has a right to say no. They probably enjoy it.

Coppola becomes impatient. In a burst of creative energy, he writes his own script to *Pinocchio*. But since Warner Bros. wouldn't make his directing deal, he decides to take it to a more hospitable environment—namely, back to Columbia. Columbia says yes.

I can understand his logic, reasons the postal worker. If one place doesn't like you, try another. I wish the same applied to post offices.

Columbia forges ahead and closes a deal. Trouble is, they want the underlying rights. Warner Bros. again says no. They hold the rights and want something for giving them up.

Coppola says, you're blocking my movie. We didn't even have a deal.

Warner says, we had a deal. You just didn't sign it.

Coppola says, you're being mean-spirited. The only reason you're trying to block me is that Bob Daly (the Warner Bros. co-CEO) doesn't like me.

The postal worker says, wait a minute. This is getting mean. Everyone's arguing about deals—how about making movies? In my line of work, I've got mail to sort. I don't want to waste my time debating whether every stamp is sufficiently licked.

Coppola gives it one more try. Look, I even have the co-financing in place at Columbia. A French company named Chargeurs wants to do *Pinocchio*. At Columbia I have a deal, I have the money, all I need is the rights.

Warner Bros. says, sorry, fella. We may even go ahead some day and try to develop another script.

Coppola says, you're standing in the way of art. I want $22 million in damages.

The postal worker says these people are all whacko. I mean, if Coppola wanted to switch his project from Warner to Columbia, why didn't he submit his draft to Warner, get them to say no, and then clear the rights?

If I had to work with people like these, he concludes, I think I'd go postal.

The final indignity: The French who wanted to finance *Pinocchio* ended up putting their money into *Showgirls* instead. Then they went postal.

—*Variety*, June 29, 1998

. . .

Yet another product of the '60s, Terrence Malick, unexpectedly returned to the scene in 1998 with The Thin Red Line, *ending an absence of twenty years. In the December 21, 1998,* Variety, *I examined the idiosyncratic behavior of this maverick filmmaker.*

THE SILENT TREATMENT

While all the stars and star directors are busily chatting up their new movies this holiday season, the filmmaker who's eliciting by far the most attention stalwartly refuses to utter a word.

Everyone wants to write about Terrence Malick, a man who clearly prefers the sounds of silence. The New York Film Critics last week even bestowed their best-director award on him as if to celebrate his invisibility. Reporters requesting an interview don't even get a turndown. "Mr. Malick . . . I mean . . . well, everyone knows about Mr. Malick," the flustered flack will reply.

"What's with this guy?" one young reporter asked me. "Has he died and they're covering it up?"

Well, let me make a confession. I know Terry Malick. I dine with him. I chat with him. Once I even made a movie with him.

Given this background, I can offer several reasonably informed theories as to why Terry Malick won't talk. To be sure, I can't vouch for their validity because, when I asked him that question directly not long ago, he either couldn't or wouldn't give me an answer. That only served to bolster my theories.

So here's why Terry won't talk:

1. He thinks auteurs sound fatuous and defensive when they try to explain themselves and their work.

2. He has an exaggerated sense of privacy. He doesn't want to be asked questions like Why haven't you made a movie for twenty years? because, to his way of thinking, that's nobody's business. Besides, he doesn't know the answer.

3. He's not a very good talker. Sure, like any Harvard man or Rhodes scholar, Terry uses the language masterfully, but his ideas are so abstract that his answers to queries tend to get lost in an epistemological fog.

In short, one reason Terry Malick can't devise a linear plot is that he cannot even devise a linear sentence. As evidence, try to figure out the plot of *The Thin Red Line.* Or, for that matter, *Badlands* and *Days of Heaven,* his two earlier movies.

I once bought a script Terry wrote called *Deadhead Miles.* It was a brilliant piece of writing and actors lined up to play the roles, as with *The Thin Red Line.* Prior to the start of principal photography, however, I sat down with Terry and said, "This is a terrific screenplay, but the story line is fuzzy. How about giving our audience a little help?"

Terry gave me a bemused squint, one that he often wears, and shook his head. "I thought the plot was right there," he replied.

"Fine, then sit down and explain it to me."

Terry Malick talked for ten minutes. By the time he had finished, I was even more confused. Now, not only did I not understand his script, but I also didn't even understand his understanding of his script.

It wasn't just that he talked in abstractions: Terry Malick, I realized, was a living abstraction.

All this is readily apparent in *The Thin Red Line.* Plot lines start and vaporize. Characters blend into one another. Voice-over perorations march off in opposite directions. Visual images are constantly at odds with physical action.

I thought David Ansen put it nicely in *Newsweek* last week. What Malick had delivered was not so much a movie as a cinematic poem, he wrote. Malick's work had "a quality of meditation, at once closely observed and yet seen from afar."

OK, that sounds like an intelligent theory. Abstract, mind you, but so is the movie. And so is its silent moviemaker.

—*Variety*, December 21, 1998

.   .   .

Of all the filmmakers who came of age in the late '60s and early '70s, none surpassed the virtuoso talent and durability of Steven Spielberg. Both as director and producer, Spielberg's reputation, and wealth, has kept expanding. After this profile was published in the September '98 GQ, Saving Private Ryan *continued to pile up awards and remarkable grosses, thus rivaling* Armageddon *as the number-one film box-office performer of 1998.*

STEVEN SPIELBERG: THE AUTEUR AS BILLIONAIRE

Why has Steven Spielberg remained so important as a director, a mogul, and a cultural force long after his arguably more talented '70s counterparts burned out or faded away?

In his ferocious book entitled *Easy Riders, Raging Bulls,* Peter Biskind describes the brilliance and self-destructiveness of that band of filmmakers who became superstars in the late '60s and '70s only to burn out before hitting middle age. "The sex, drugs, and rock'n'roll generation saved Hollywood," Biskind tells us, but was ultimately unable to save itself. Directors like Peter Bogdanovich, William Friedkin, Hal Ashby, Bob Rafelson, Dennis Hopper, Roman Polanski, and even Francis Ford Coppola soared to great heights in terms of both achievement and ego yet were unable to sustain their momentum. Bogdanovich is quoted as saying, "I felt that by the mid-'70s, I'd blown it, Friedkin had blown it, Altman went into eclipse, Francis went crazy. Everybody kind of blew it in various shapes and sizes." To which Biskind adds, "Of that group only Steven Spielberg cruised through the next decade, going from blockbuster to blockbuster."

To be sure, Spielberg was slightly younger than the others and was never a captive to the drug scene. The movies that catapulted him to stardom, like *Jaws* and *Close Encounters of the Third Kind*, though superbly crafted, never embraced the artistic heresies of *Bonnie and Clyde, Taxi Driver, Nashville,* or *The Godfather.* Nonetheless, Spielberg's life and career were closely intertwined with the filmmakers of that period, and his durability—and fecundity—have astonished even his jaded contemporaries.

This past year has been a formidable demonstration of the range of his output. As a director, he's made back-to-back movies— *Amistad* and *Saving Private Ryan.* He also supervised the development and production of such major summer movies as *Deep Impact, The Mask of Zorro,* and *Small Soldiers.* Meanwhile, DreamWorks, of which he is a partner, has marshaled an impressive array of movies, TV shows, cartoons, video games, and other products.

Indeed, at a time when most members of his generation are scratching for gigs, the 51-year-old Spielberg has reinvented himself as a multinational corporation, with hundreds of millions of dollars in annual income and billions in assets. To some he is the savior of Hollywood—the miracle worker who pumps out mind-bendingly successful entertainment like *Jurassic Park* and *Men in Black.* To others he is the man most responsible for the trashing of Hollywood. By creating *Jaws* and the *Indiana Jones* movies, they argue, Spielberg invented the modern blockbuster and, worse yet, led the Rupert Murdochs, Sumner Redstones, and Michael Eisners of the world to believe that "tent-pole" movies could be produced on an assembly line. (The catch: It had to be Spielberg's assembly line.)

But there is no disputing Spielberg's unique niche. At a time when the studios were becoming increasingly fretful about the excesses of their erratic young auteurs, Spielberg contrived to blend impeccably into the big-bucks culture of the '80s. The Hollywood of *Easy Rider*s and *Raging Bull*s was reborn as the Hollywood of Sly and Arnold, the steroid superheroes of Reagan America. And there, at the center of it all, was Steven!

Talking to Spielberg today is like having conversations with two individuals living entirely disparate lives. He'll start out discussing his next directing project with passion and specificity, from the casting to the locations to the nurturing of the screenplay. Before beginning *Saving Private Ryan,* Spielberg told me excitedly about his plans to make it like "a very expensive independent movie": to shoot fast with handheld cameras, to build his cast around young actors such as Matt Damon and Edward Burns, and to put them through a semi-sadistic preproduction boot camp to test their mettle. As he was describing all this, I could sense his mounting excitement to get on with the film. Yet right in the middle of this speech, Spielberg suddenly segued from filmmaker mode to studio-production-chief mode, redirecting his passion toward the trailer for *Zorro* and the distribution pattern for *Small Soldiers.* When I talked with him early this summer, he was preoccupied by the fact that *Saving Private Ryan* was not being released until the end of July. "I've always released my pictures in the June 11 to 19 corridor," he said, words tumbling out and colliding in mid-sentence. "Then I saw how *The Fugitive* or *Air Force One* performed as late-summer releases, and I realized I'd been wrong in limiting myself. I should make use of the whole summer, even into September. If I deliver a good movie, the audience will be there for it."

And make use of it he did. Spielberg's personal summer slate this year surpassed that of three major studios, which was no accident. Look at the past few summers—that prime time for movies that accounts for almost forty percent of the year's box-office returns—and you recognize an astonishing degree of box-office domination: *Jurassic Park;* its sequel, *Jurassic Park: The Lost World; Men in Black; Twister;* and so forth.

Despite his frenetic drive, there is a humaneness about the way Spielberg the filmmaker deals with actors, writers, and crew. "Steven is not a tyrant or a yeller and screamer," says one longtime associate. "He is a decent man who wants to work in a decent setting."

Spielberg the one-man conglomerate can border on the ruthless, however. In his public utterances, he is a stalwart defender of the writer's contribution, but when he discusses movies he's producing, the writers seem more like replacement parts, to be hired and fired at will. It's not unusual for six or more writers to work on a project at Amblin, Spielberg's personal company, or at DreamWorks. A prime example is *The Mask of Zorro*, one of Spielberg's favorite projects, on which he received an executive-producer credit. In development for some six years at TriStar (under the Amblin banner), *Zorro* went through several drafts by Ted Elliott and Terry Rossio, John Eskow, and, finally, David S. Ward, an Oscar winner for *The Sting*. The project also wended its way through three directors, the final one being Martin Campbell, a New Zealander who directed the James Bond movie *Goldeneye*. Campbell had replaced Robert Rodriguez, a brilliant young independent filmmaker *(From Dusk Till Dawn)*, who had supplanted Mikael Salomon, the Danish cinematographer-turned-director.

The overarching question is, Why does he do it? Here's a man who could, like Stanley Kubrick, afford to meander from movie to movie, dawdling over casting, poking slowly around potential locations. He could play with his seven children or design new video games ("Whenever I go to visit him in the morning, he is playing with a video game, like some grown-up kid who's always coveting his new toy," says one associate). Or he could, if he wanted, simply devote his time to philanthropy—he is already remarkably generous in helping chronically ill children, for example. In short, having directed eighteen movies and made billions of dollars, he could simply kick back and do nothing. But he can't. "He's one of these people who are energized by having too much to do," says a colleague. "It's like he has this conviction that creativity comes out of chaos." Other associates have different theories: "It's a mistake to intellectualize about Steven," says one. "He's just plain insecure. No matter how many hits he has, he's still the nervous Jew who thinks it may all be taken away from him." The premature demise of many of his contemporaries may have reinforced this insecurity.

Spielberg's early professional traumas may have also played a part. Biskind's book reminded me of Spielberg's humiliation over losing control of the *Jaws* shoot in 1974, when his filming schedule ballooned from fifty-five days to one hundred and fifty-nine. The young director was convinced his career was ruined. Before returning from the Martha's Vineyard, Massachusetts, location to Los Angeles, he spent a sleepless night in a Boston hotel room, experiencing what he admitted was "a full-blown anxiety attack, sweating, heart palpitations. . . . I was too afraid to reach for the phone. I was a complete wreck." Spielberg was convinced the town would turn on him, just as it had turned against Coppola for his crazed self-indulgence on *Apocalypse Now*. And for a brief moment his fear proved valid. The word was that the young director was too inexperienced and undisciplined for such a complex production. The hallucinatory box-office results soon put those criticisms to rest.

Spielberg's own rationale for his seemingly chaotic work habits is much more straightforward. "I've been doing this long enough to know how I work best," he says. "When I focus on one project to the exclusion of all else, I lose my objectivity. I become completely lost in it. I live it and sleep it, and I lose my perspective. I fall in love with every scene that I shoot. I think something is wonderful when it isn't."

The solution, he has found, is to force himself to maintain perspective by reading other scripts, meeting with colleagues about projects, and otherwise diverting his monomaniacal tendencies. "I'm careful not to get overcommitted," he emphasizes. "After all these years, I know how much I can responsibly take on."

That workload could defeat almost anyone. Yet colleagues give him nothing but high marks for his attentiveness and contributions. A Sony studio executive recalls a disappointing draft of *Zorro* arriving during the Christmas holidays: "Frankly, I was depressed. I could see this project disintegrating before my eyes. Suddenly, my fax machine at home started humming, and here were three pages of extensive notes from Spielberg about how to fix the script. I couldn't believe it—on Christmas!"

Associates at DreamWorks, too, insist that when Spielberg is sent a script with an enthusiastic recommendation, his response is immediate. Bob Cooper, DreamWorks' new production chief, recently told his boss (who was working on *Private Ryan* at the time) that he was excited about a particular screenplay, warning Spielberg that it was an edgy, low-budget project that certainly did not fit the blockbuster mold. To Cooper's delight, Spielberg called early the following morning, voicing his vigorous support. "And he was in the middle of directing his movie," Cooper recalls.

Mindful of the need to expand the DreamWorks slate, Spielberg has been quietly building up the company's production staff and acquiring rights to more books and screenplays. The addition of Cooper, who formerly headed production at TriStar and HBO, was a key step in that endeavor. Prior to that, Spielberg was relying on his small coterie at Amblin—principally the talented, steadfastly calm husband-and-wife team of Walter Parkes and Laurie MacDonald—to supervise his wide-ranging projects.

Spielberg created Amblin fifteen years ago as his own personal "loan out" company, only to see it burgeon into a sort of Microsoft of production entities. Aside from such bread-and-butter winners as *The Flintstones, Casper,* and, of course, *Men in Black* (which grossed more than $600 million worldwide), Amblin owns a big piece of the TV hit *ER,* animated TV shows, such as *Animaniacs* and *Freakazoid,* plus toys and interactive projects.

Amblin alone would be enough to occupy a normal mortal, but as a partner in DreamWorks, Spielberg is also eager to build that four-year-old company to its potential. Critics of Spielberg tend to point to DreamWorks as a reflection of Spielberg's lack of focus.

Indeed, an aura of grandiosity accompanied the press conference that launched the company: posturing that was later to haunt it. The three founders—Spielberg, David Geffen, and Jeffrey Katzenberg, who had recently left Disney—referred to their entity as "our new country," suggesting that it would change the landscape of the entertainment industry.

While the company has done reasonably well for a start-up, its impact has been less than remarkable. Its TV slate has had its ups and downs (Michael J. Fox's *Spin City* was its only hit), and movies such as *Mouse Hunt* and *Peacemaker*, while successful, were essentially indistinct from the product of any other major studio. *Deep Impact*, the first DreamWorks megahit (a coproduction with Paramount), was a solid, if undistinguished, special-effects movie. Construction of the long-awaited studio facility, which was to be the centerpiece of the new company, has not yet begun. *The Prince of Egypt*, DreamWorks' second major animation effort, has been the subject of some shrewdly engineered ballyhoo, but the project is still unfinished (and scheduled for year-end release).

All of which underscores the central debate about the Spielberg mystique: Is he using his vast power and money simply to attain more power and money? Has his impact on pop culture been positive or negative?

An unpretentious man, Spielberg meticulously avoids posturing as some sort of pop-culture guru. He is a filmmaker; that's what he loves to do. In an essay in *Time* nominating Spielberg as the century's "most influential" filmmaker, film critic Roger Ebert points out that Spielberg's most important contribution has been in mobilizing "A-level craftsmanship" to recreate "old-style B-movie stories." Hence the *Indiana Jones* movies and even *ET: The Extraterrestrial*.

When he's tried to explore more serious themes, as in *The Color Purple* and *Amistad*, his success has been limited, critically and commercially. One exception was the remarkable *Schindler's List*, a modern classic that was extraordinarily successful in both arenas. Another is the superbly crafted *Saving Private Ryan*.

At their best, Spielberg's movies, whether directed or produced by him, remain singular examples of quality control—technically virtuosic lessons in the art of filmmaking. And as special effects have commanded a growing role, Spielberg, predictably, has been in the vanguard with *Twister* and *Deep Impact*. As examples of sheer skill, the movies are brilliant; as examples of storytelling, however, they are shallow.

It's hard to know where Spielberg will go from here. Having proved his durability, not to mention his adaptability, he might try, through DreamWorks, to foster a cinematic resurgence such as the one that overtook Hollywood when he started out in the '70s. Or he might choose to focus on his grandiose entertainments and special-effects extravaganzas. (He's already agreed to do a third *Jurassic Park*.)

In either case, he will certainly rival Bill Gates someday as the nation's richest icon. That in itself is no small achievement.

—*GQ*, September 1998

. . .

While an emerging generation of filmmakers was gleaning much of the attention in '90s Hollywood, the community paused to pay homage to a brilliant old pro, Billy Wilder, who celebrated his ninetieth birthday. I saluted Wilder on April 22, 1996, in Variety.

HOLLYWOOD'S WILDER MOMENTS

MEMO TO: Billy Wilder

Since you're about to celebrate your ninetieth birthday, Billy, I just wanted to tell you I wish there was a way of turning back the clock some sixty years. What a great shot in the arm it would be for Hollywood if a youthful Billy Wilder hit town armed with your talent and mean-spirited wit.

You and I both know, Billy, that Hollywood has no sense of its past. Even now some young agent is probably asking a colleague, "Who's Billy Wilder—was he the old guy who made the first *Sabrina*?" That's what it has come to—Hollywood is recycling your old stories without even knowing their source and, to add insult to injury, they're choosing the wrong movies. Having messed up *Sabrina*, there's talk now of remaking *Love in the Afternoon*, which would be an equally bad idea, and we all know what happened to *Sunset Boulevard*. If the studios want to plunder the Billy Wilder library, how about picking *One, Two, Three* or *Ace in the Hole*, or even that classic *The Apartment*, all of which embody attitudes and story lines that seem even more pertinent today.

That's why, rather than try to remake Wilder, I wish we could simply reinvent you. I've been reading a new biography called *Wilder Times* by Kevin Lally, Billy, and it reminded me that, back in the '40s and '50s when you were doing your best work, you managed somehow to give Hollywood an entirely different presence. It was you and your fellow filmmakers, like Alfred Hitchcock, who were creating the "buzz" in town, not the agents or studio functionaries. People were quoting your witticisms, not some CAA deal memo.

Your salon was the social hub, as well, as guests listened in fascination to Marlene Dietrich's stories of her Berlin days and her affairs with both men and women.

A vivid dinner guest, Dietrich could also be tough to handle on the set. You fought fiercely during the making of *Witness for the Prosecution,* Lally informs us, with the actress claiming that you threw all the good lines at her costar, Charles Laughton. You freely admitted your unstinting admiration of Laughton, Billy, even praising his obsessive preparation. "You can tell how good an actor is by looking at his script," you once observed. "If he's no good, the script will be neat as a pin. Charles Laughton's was so filthy it looked like a herring had been wrapped in it."

Your achievements seem all the more remarkable, Billy, when one considers that you arrived in the U.S. in 1934 with no money, no connections, and a rather marginal grasp of the language. Surely it was your sense of being the outsider that drove you to push the boundaries of moviemaking. It took an outsider's defiance to build a comedy around a guilt-free French hooker, as in *Irma La Douce,* or to invent a farce about the anal corporate mentality, as in *The Apartment,* or even to make a corrupt American army captain the ostensible hero of *A Foreign Affair.* Even when you put aside parody and farce, who else would have had the guts to make a serious movie about a drunk, as in *The Lost Weekend.*

Hollywood heaped rewards upon you when your films made money—three Oscars alone in 1961. Your gallows humor began to get you in trouble as '50s America grew affluent and numb. *Kiss Me Stupid* was a sort of Restoration comedy that dared to advance the notion that a little adultery might be good for a marriage, but it stirred anger rather than accolades.

Oddly enough, even that film holds up pretty well today, though in retrospect, when Peter Sellers suffered his heart attack four weeks into the shoot, you probably should have abandoned the project rather than stick in a badly miscast Ray Walston. A Peter Sellers farce needs Peter Sellers.

What all that taught you, however, was that edgy movies about adultery, politics, prostitution, and corporate hypocrisy were no longer the flavor of the day. Having been an outsider to start, Billy, you seemed to adapt remarkably well to yet again assuming that status. You continued to hurl barbs at the power structure: "The entire movie industry is in intensive care," you once said. You patiently explained to those who asked that you weren't interested in directing movies about kids or cops, protesting, "I can't shoot car crashes." The time will inevitably come, you explained, when studios will show interest yet again in the content of a picture, in the exploration of character. You're still waiting.

I came upon you during your brief tenure as a consultant to United Artists in 1986. Jerry Weintraub, then chief of UA, had brought you in to view finished cuts and advise on improving them. After seeing his first picture, you told Weintraub, "This picture is a big pile of shit. Perhaps I could tell you how to make it into a smaller pile, but it will still be shit." You and Weintraub soon parted company.

More recently, I came upon you at the Los Angeles opening of the musical version of *Sunset Boulevard*, when you were holding court for Nancy Reagan and other socialites. Everyone was being very civil and polite until one woman asked you, "Billy, why does the show open with this . . . this monkey?"

The Billy Wilder of old immediately took hold. "Don't you understand, the Glenn Close character was fucking the monkey before Joe Gillis came along? That's the story." Nancy Reagan looked like she was about to pass out, while the other socialites managed a forced laugh. You quickly turned your attention to other guests. That incident reminded me that we still need you, Billy, we need you more than ever. I realize you are content to stay home with your Picassos, Matisses, and Renoirs, but I wish you were back behind the camera.

In his book, Lally tells about the time you were stopped outside Spago by a young autograph hound who handed you a pen and demanded you sign three times.

"Why three?" you asked.

"Because with three Wilders I can trade for one Spielberg," the kid responded.

Well, Billy, I think Steven would join me in saying that the fair trade would still be one-for-one.

—Variety, April 22, 1996

.   .   .

On the producing side, another talented old pro, 81-year-old David Brown, was still one of the most active members of his fraternity, as I related in Variety *on January 5, 1998.*

STILL THE MASTER MAESTRO

Before all of us forget our New Year's resolutions, I'd like to own up to one of mine. I resolved to try to be more like David Brown.

Diligent and hard-working, David Brown can get as frustrated as any of us by the snail-like pace of studio and network decision-making. But unlike everyone else, he is all but unflappable. And though he's keenly aware of the foibles of his fellow man, I have never been able to elicit from him a nasty word about any of those around him.

All of which may help explain why, at the age of 81, David Brown remains one of the most productive showmen in the business. While others of his generation have long since settled for the sidelines, Brown this year produced Paramount's successful *Kiss the Girls.* Another Brown megapic, *Deep Impact,* is the studio's big summer release. He and Scott Rudin are preparing a movie based on the bestseller *Angela's Ashes,* and he is mobilizing a musical version of *Sweet Smell of Success* for Broadway, working with John Guare and Marvin Hamlisch.

If you ask David why he's working harder now than he did twenty or thirty years ago, he looks genuinely puzzled, as if to say, "Why not?"

"I'm enjoying myself more than ever," he explains matter-of-factly. "Besides, I'm so absurdly past retirement age that I'm not a threat to anyone anymore."

Though David Brown never talks about his age and certainly doesn't act it, his extraordinary history in the business is clearly a great resource to him. Take the idea for *Deep Impact*: Brown recalled pitching a *War of the Worlds*–type concept to Barry Diller two decades ago when Diller first surfaced as president of Paramount. A script by Anthony Burgess didn't gel and the project was sidetracked, but years later Brown revived the notion, this time in partnership with Steven Spielberg. The upshot: a joint Paramount-DreamWorks production for which both companies have high hopes.

As with *Deep Impact,* Brown firmly believes everything is worth a second try. Or third. He recently optioned John O'Hara's *Appointment in Samarra* for the third time and also has decided to take another stab at John Dos Passos' extraordinary epic, *USA,* which he sees as a movie for the millennium.

But make no mistake—David Brown dwells very much in the present. He's hip to all the studio gossip and can tick off the names of the hot writers or actors of the moment. A look at the work he has been involved with in recent times demonstrates he's hardly an antiques collector. The movies include the likes of *The Player* and *A Few Good Men,* while his TV efforts include the HBO series *Women & Men,* as well as a four-hour mini based on Dominick Dunne's *A Season in Purgatory.*

"Indeed, it's typical of David Brown that, until recently, he was responsible for conjuring up the shrewdly salacious cover lines that adorned *Cosmopolitan.* Hence, once a month, he would take time out from a script or budget meeting to write lines like "Get serious about your orgasms" or "How to trap a rich boy-toy."

Brown makes no bones about the secret to his resilience. "It's my nature to forgive and forget," he reflects. "Otherwise there's just too much baggage to cart around with you. It starts to get in your way."

As with any showbiz career, Brown has had his share of roller-coaster rides. He was a magazine editor when he first hit Hollywood in 1951 (he served as managing editor of *Cosmopolitan* in the pre–Helen Gurley Brown days—Helen later becoming his wife). Brown ultimately became a top executive for Darryl Zanuck and later a partner to his son, Richard. But he still remembers the time when he and Dick were effectively pitched out of Fox. "We were condemned to Siberia," he recalls. "We couldn't even eat in the Fox commissary. We'd go to the Valley for lunch."

He and Dick went on to share an astonishingly successful partnership, producing such films as *Jaws, Cocoon,* and *Driving Miss Daisy.* Over the years, their company migrated from studio to studio, in keeping with changing regimes and political climates, and now they're linked yet again on several projects.

"It's all just part of the business," Brown shrugs. "You don't take these things personally. Irving Lazar would be my best friend when I was in power, but I could never get him on the phone between studio gigs." Again, Brown got the last laugh: he's developing a Broadway play about the legendary, but deceased, Swifty.

Brown doesn't care for everything he sees on the showbiz scene. Like most other people, he resents the echelons of studio management that delay decision-making. "They all have their business degrees and give you their story notes." He misses some of the colorful old-time talent and literary agents. "Many were terrific storytellers," he recalls. "They were simply more fun. They weren't bloodless, but you often emerged bloodied after negotiating with them."

But while you may extract an occasional line of regret from him on some topic, he suddenly catches a second wind and launches into an enthusiastic account of a new play or movie. He still shuttles between Los Angeles and New York to attend screenings or meetings. "I love Los Angeles, even though I don't drive anymore," he says. "But when I hit New York, I feel like a great idea may strike me at any minute. I see those tall buildings and I know, 'Something good can happen to me today.'"

And it usually does.

—*Variety*, January 5, 1998

.　　.　　.

While David Brown was legendary for his durability, other Hollywood producers were finding their craft to be increasingly demanding, if not downright discouraging, as I related in the October '97 GQ.

PRODUCERS: FADING PATRIARCHS

Last spring I was invited to teach a graduate course at UCLA on the arcane craft of producing movies. When I turned up for my first session, I was surprised to find a lecture hall packed with some three hundred seemingly serious and dedicated souls, eager to learn how to flourish in what they regarded as a fascinating profession.

They were soon to receive a reality check, however. I had invited one or two established producers to join me at each session to talk about the satisfactions and vicissitudes of their profession—and asked them to be totally candid.

They were. One after the other, week after week, my guests presented a daunting picture of frustration, artistic compromise, and betrayal. Far from encouraging the students to take the plunge into producing, the guests seemed determined to throw cold water on their ambitions.

After hearing this fusillade, the class was understandably perplexed. At a time when movies are becoming glitzier and more expensive, why are producers complaining that their role has been diminished? Aren't they supposedly the ones who are managing these megamovies?

The answer, of course, is yes and no. Though technically the producer is still in charge, his role in the scheme of things has been significantly downsized from what it was in the heyday of the studio system. Arguably, that's one reason movies are in such a mess. The very people who should be running the show have been marginalized by the Hollywood power brokers.

A quick glance at the credits of most movies provides ample evidence of the producer's plight. *Face/Off* had nine people billed as producers. All sorts of characters, ranging from the star's manager or masseur to relatives of studio executives to ex-wives, have been jumping aboard the bandwagon, demanding not only credit but also money and random perks. The situation has become so embarrassing that a group of top producers recently established the Producers' Credit Board to fight off the onslaught of fringe players. "What's happening now is that the producer credit can be bought," says Kathleen Kennedy, who coproduced such films as *Schindler's List* and *ET: The Extraterrestrial*. "That process completely erodes respect for the credit."

Lately, the order of the credits has also been rearranged to diminish the producer's standing. At the start of a film, the credits used to appear in this order: "written by," then "produced by," and finally, and most prestigiously, "directed by." Now the writer's credit often intrudes between the producer's and the director's, thus shoving the producer into a less favorable position. The producing fraternity has filed protests but to no avail.

The change in credit order is indicative of the change in practice: Increasingly, studio executives ignore the producer and deal only with the director on important issues. Whether in preproduction or during the shoot, the producer is becoming a minor cog in the process.

If such indignities had been heaped on producers of previous generations, the studio gates would still be shuddering. The Samuel Goldwyns, David O. Selznicks, Mike Todds, and Hal Wallises were a positively ferocious breed, insistent on maintaining their power and perks.

Their entire modus operandi differed sharply from that of today's producers. Goldwyn, for example, usually bought his own material and financed development. He even bankrolled many of his films. The directors were mere hired hands. They shot the movie and then went away while the producer presided over the editing, the sound mixing, and the marketing. More often than not, today's producers function like hired hands. The studio buys material for them and foots the bill to hire the writers.

I was once on a soundstage with Hal Wallis when his director, having completed a scene, dropped by to suggest how it might be intercut with an earlier segment of the story. Wallis stared at the director as though he were a student who'd just tried to instruct his teacher and did not deign to reply. Indeed, unless you were Elvis Presley or John Wayne, talking to Wallis was a less than heartwarming experience. He had cold, hard eyes and an imperious manner that all but shouted, "Don't fuck with me!"

And no one did.

I've always counted myself fortunate that during my seventeen-year stint in the movie business only two of those years were spent as a working producer. My small independent company had the financial resources to acquire and develop projects and, even more important, to make firm offers to stars and directors. I could assemble packages—script, budget, star, and filmmaker—to present to the studios and elicit a quick yes or no. I therefore avoided the endless meetings in which echelons of studio executives could second-guess my ideas about cast and script.

Despite these advantages, I found it an excruciating process. Piecing together a package was akin to water torture. If a star committed to do your script, no director was available who satisfied the star's demands. If a director committed, no star was available within the director's time frame. Stars and directors have slots of availability, and if you miss one moment of opportunity you might have to wait a couple of years for the next one.

Even if I defied the Fates and managed to assemble a viable package, I quickly discovered that film packages were about as stable as the San Andreas Fault. Someone was always changing his mind or getting a better offer. I remember once bringing a director to a meeting with an agent to sew up the details of a deal for a major star. I thought the meeting had gone well, until the agent asked if he could have a moment alone with the director. I went into the reception room, and when the director next appeared, he was ashen.

"What happened?" I asked.

"He stuck his knee in my groin and said, 'Look, asshole, if you want my star, you're going to have to sign with me too.'"

"That's grossly unprofessional," I replied. "What did you say?"

"I panicked. I said OK."

The star in question did end up committing to the movie, but two weeks before principal photography, he had a demand. It seemed he had a favorite writer, and the script could use "one last touch-up." The cost, ostensibly, would be a mere $200,000.

I knew two things about this writer: He was adept at both developing writer's block and cozying up to stars. Furthermore, upon rereading my project, he estimated he would need about six weeks to do the so-called touch-up, even though we were supposed to start shooting in two.

Producers can become desperate at times like this. I flew the writer to Hawaii and checked him into a lavish hotel suite—that was the good news. The bad news was that I took away all his clothes, down to his boxers, and posted a 350-pound Samoan outside the door. He could not leave, I informed him, until he had turned in a draft. And if he developed one of his famous blocks, he might as well resign himself to spending the rest of the year there.

Denuded but challenged, the writer was inspired into a flurry of activity. He turned in his rewrite in six days, got dressed, and went home. It was a rare moment of producer's revenge.

Speaking before my UCLA class, the various producers described a similar array of war stories—pitched battles with agents, managers, studio bureaucrats, and so forth. But if the struggles over scripts and casting were intense, they were nothing compared with the warfare that ensued during the actual shooting schedule.

During the heyday of the studio system, the companies looked to their producers to control costs and keep the artists in line. It was not unusual for an illustrious director to be dismissed during principal photography and a substitute instantly marched into the fray.

Today the balance of power has shifted dramatically. Despite the fact that the cost of making movies has increased exponentially, it's the directors who have the muscle, not the producers. Hence, when someone like James Cameron decides to make *Titanic* for an astounding $200 million, the studio has no one to turn to—at least no one who has any leverage.

The primary cause of this power shift can be traced to the dreaded Michael Ovitz and his Creative Artists Agency. Thanks to CAA's zeal for dealmaking and mythmaking, directors' salaries soared from less than $1 million to as high as $10 million per picture. And along with money came perks—control over cast and material, approval of producers, and even of the final cut of the movie. By packaging its star clients with its directors, CAA was abruptly taking control of the money and the machinery of filmmaking away from the producer (CAA disdained representing producers) and giving it to the so-called auteurs.

Theoretically, all this could have resulted in superior movies— after all, the power should be in the hands of the artist. Well, maybe that's true in France, but not necessarily in Hollywood, where many of our directors are "shooters" rather than artistes—that is to say, they're skilled technicians who came out of commercials or videos. Give them a good script and they can deliver a well-crafted movie, but these are not people who, by and large, have either the knowledge or the passion to deliver memorable movies that move or inform a global audience.

There are exceptions, to be sure. Steven Spielberg, while capable of delivering finely wrought commercial fare like the *Indiana Jones* series, also nurtured *Schindler's List.* Other directors have not proved as versatile. As often as not, it's the producing fraternity in Hollywood that has demonstrated the ability to find and foster the more intriguing projects that might advance the medium.

All of which brings us back to the producers who spoke at UCLA. Despite their litany of complaints, they were still making a living as working producers—a very good living in some cases. What was their secret to survival?

Scrutinize the list of successful Hollywood producers today and you'll discover several distinct genres:

The Producer As Pitchman

Genial, fast-talking Robert Kosberg vastly prefers pitching stories to making movies. He's at his best spinning tales for avid studio executives in the hope that they'll finance the ideas as scripts and then as movies. His successes include *12 Monkeys* and *Man's Best Friend.* Hollywood's youthful development troops have grown to like Kosberg and his pitches. They're always funny and well-staged—and if the studio says yes, that means the executives aren't burdened with having to read and evaluate a script. They also understand that Kosberg is interested in the pitch, not the picture—when the movie goes into production, he knows better than to insert himself into the process.

The Star Toady

As canny as he is quirky, Jonathan Krane, one of the myriad producers on *Face/Off,* has managed to negotiate important credits for himself on many pictures, primarily because of his ability to control talent. A shrewd and experienced manager, Krane has most recently helped steer the revival of John Travolta, who over the past two decades has managed to go from stardom to obscurity to exalted $20-million-a-movie status. This is no small feat, considering Travolta is one of the most demanding actors when it comes to pay and perks and is also a stalwart Scientologist, with all that that commitment demands. Nonetheless, the dogged Krane has helped pick some excellent vehicles for Travolta, securing for himself executive-producer credits along the way, thus adding more money and prestige to his considerable management fees.

The Bulldozer

"There are ways to derail Scott Rudin, but you have to ask yourself, Is it worth the angst and pain?" So says one candid executive at Paramount, where Rudin has his production deal. Wide-bodied, hyperactive, and perpetually youthful, the fiercely aggressive Rudin has become a major player on Broadway (the revival of *A Funny Thing Happened on the Way to the Forum*) as well as in Hollywood *(Ransom)*, and his success stems from both his superior taste in material and his fervid pursuit of the projects he targets. Those who regularly deal with Rudin are steeled to his threats and tantrums, but at the same time they grudgingly respect the magnitude of his personal commitment.

The Scrivener

Once a top-ranking showbusiness attorney, bearded, soft-spoken Ron Bass quietly set about to write himself into a new way of life. His screenplays encompass a remarkable range of mood and subject matter—*Rain Man, The Joy Luck Club, My Best Friend's Wedding.* Presently ensconced at Sony with a lavish producing deal, Bass is both a never-ending font of story ideas and a streamlined rewrite machine, but more important, he is also fascinated by the broader facets of filmmaking, such as casting and editing. Though his instincts as a writer make him a stubborn, opinionated adversary, Bass's background as an attorney serves him well in his occasional role as mediator. Other writers both fear and venerate him. Some resent him for being so prolific; others complain that his success has made him annoyingly upbeat and mawkish. In any case, Bass gets it done, which is a trait that studios respect.

The Negotiator

A decade ago, Arnold Kopelson wrote himself off as a failed, middle-aged lawyer. But the death of his first wife, combined with a series of disastrous investments, set Kopelson on a new course: reinventing himself as a showman. A succession of megamovies, such as *The Fugitive* and *Eraser,* earned him one of the richest producer deals in town at Twentieth Century Fox, where he, like his stars, earns a percentage of the gross of each movie in which he is involved. "Arnold is the most relentless negotiator and also the most decent human being in the business," says one Fox executive. "Only he could have negotiated his own deal here." Kopelson employs his intense negotiating skills in making deals for material and talent, but his relentlessness is cushioned by an almost child-like enthusiasm for his movies and the talent he mobilizes. "What sets him apart is that he's a teddy bear," says a top agent. "You have to love him even though he drives you crazy."

The Diplomat

While most successful producers work the studios, Arnon Milchan, the Henry Kissinger of filmmakers, has built his power base on a globe-spanning alliance made up of the octopus-like Rupert Murdoch, Australian billionaire Kerry Packer, German media mogul Leo Kirch, and the giant Samsung Corporation of South Korea. Wielding global clout, Milchan has spawned such movies as *Tin Cup* and *A Time to Kill* by reminding Hollywood that if a studio doesn't do things his way, he can go ahead and shape his own destiny. The Israeli-born Milchan understands the nuances of Hollywood better than perhaps any other foreign producer, yet he also possesses a keen knowledge of what will play around the world. Given that the market outside the United States now accounts for well over fifty percent of all movie revenue, Milchan's command of the foreign market and his gift for complex intercontinental dealmaking have earned him a unique place in the Hollywood firmament.

The Rock

After spending years in the shadow of the late Don Simpson, his volatile, self-destructive partner, Jerry Bruckheimer, a quiet man with an even temperament, has carved out an important niche for himself with high-powered action fare—witness *Con Air* and *The Rock*. In an industry of high-strung screamers, the soft-spoken yet determined Bruckheimer is respected for his get-it-done qualities both on the story end and in physical production. During the pair's glory years coproducing *Top Gun* and *Beverly Hills Cop*, Simpson got credit for picking the scripts and stars, while Bruckheimer focused on production and business. But as Simpson sank ever deeper into the demimonde of drugs and hookers, Bruckheimer resolutely pulled away from their alliance and schooled himself in the creative areas of filmmaking. "The Simpson separation was a wrenching challenge," one major agent says. "Jerry handled it with class and dignity. He never knocked Simpson, even at a time when his excesses were making them both look bad." Now on his own, Bruckheimer has established himself as a major producing talent based at the Disney studio and is also pushing into television and other facets of show business.

That these and other producers manage to succeed at their craft by no means implies that they don't share the complaints of their colleagues. Even the most prolific of them recite a litany of charges against the system—the studios are too hung up on big-budget event pictures and won't take chances on new stars and new directors; studio executives fawn over hot directors and circumvent the authority of producers; agents representing top stars and directors abuse their authority and demand too big a piece of the pie; and so forth.

It all boils down to this: None of the present-day producers feels the system allows them the latitude to establish a wide-ranging body of work that reflects quality and integrity. In short, none has been able to come close to achieving the mythical status of a

Goldwyn or a Selznick. None has displayed the daring of a Mike Todd or the flair of a Cecil B. DeMille.

On the other hand, the Todds, Goldwyns, and DeMilles may not have fared any better than their successors in today's Hollywood. If the script of *Gone with the Wind* were around now, it might still be locked in development hell.

Oh, and about the students in my course? I surveyed a good number of them after the last session. Most insisted they still planned on a career in producing. After what they had heard, they deserved an A for determination.

—*GQ*, October 1997

.   .   .

Some of the younger directors in Hollywood in 1998 found rather odd ways to pay tribute to their favorite movies of the past, as evidenced in this column published on November 2, 1998, in Variety. *Soon after this piece appeared, Van Sant's remake of* Psycho *opened in theaters to meager results.*

PUTTING OUR POP CULTURE ON REWIND

MEMO TO: Gus Van Sant

I've been noticing those eerie billboards around town hyping your new movie, *Psycho*. Of course, they don't mention the movie. Rather they show a hand pressed against a shower curtain. "Check in. Unpack. Relax. Take a shower." We're supposed to make the connection. It's all very cool.

Also left unsaid is the fact that this is not so much a new movie as a shot-by-shot re-creation of the 1960 movie. The cast has changed, to be sure. Anne Heche sits in for Janet Leigh and Vince Vaughn for Anthony Perkins.

To be honest, Gus, while I think the billboards are cool, I can't decide about the movie. I realize everything is being recycled these days, but a re-creation? Shot by shot?

No, I'm not going to intellectualize about why pop culture has put us on rewind rather than fast forward. We've long since resigned ourselves to watching movies that are really old TV shows. And there's certainly nothing wrong per se about remakes. Francis Coppola recycled *Dracula* six years ago, so why shouldn't Universal next year have a go at *Frankenstein*?

I'm a bit more skeptical, however, about the notion of Warner Books tampering with the Bogart-and-Bergman myth in its new book called *As Time Goes By*, a sort of *Casablanca* prequel. This sounds not so much like repackaging our past, but rather plundering it.

It's one thing to look to the past for inspiration, Gus, but you're taking the process a step further. Implicit in your exercise is the admission that we cannot, in fact, improve on previous work, so let's just reconstitute it.

You may be starting a whole new wave, or old wave as the case may be. On TV, we may soon find re-creations of *The Honeymooners* or *All in the Family*. In film, think about a scene-by-scene playback of *Jules and Jim*. Even *Last Tango in Paris* would prove engrossing. Would a shot-by-shot reworking of *Birth of a Nation* prove as compelling as *Saving Private Ryan*? I doubt it.

There'd be problems with this exercise, Gus, and perhaps you're encountering some of them already. The rhythms of pop entertainment have changed. Things move faster today. Thirty years ago the typical dialogue scene in a film script ran six to eight pages. Today it's hard to find one that runs more than one. Words are out. Effects are in.

I wonder how you will deal with that in *Psycho*, Gus. When that film originally opened, as Patrick Goldstein reminds us in the *Los Angeles Times*, some major critics knocked the movie as "slow-paced." How would today's MTV-hyped teen respond?

To be sure, Hitchcock outsmarted the critics. Despite bad reviews, *Psycho* was a big hit—his biggest.

It could happen again. But if it does, Gus, don't you wonder whether the studios' dependence on recycled ideas might become downright obsessive? Will everyone start pitching the past?

Those of us who've become hooked on DVDs, Gus, already are hooked on old movies. If you look at the DVD version of *Bonnie and Clyde,* the color and sound are so vivid that the movie looks like it was made this year. Technology already has reconnected us with the classics in the most felicitous way possible. Hence, when we go to the movies or turn on our TV, it would be nice to see a new idea, not revisit an old one.

All this notwithstanding, Gus, I'm rooting for your success. It's a brave exercise. And who knows, twenty years from now someone may be re-creating *Good Will Hunting,* scene by scene.

—*Variety,* November 2, 1998

.   .   .

While Gus Van Sant re-created Psycho *shot by shot, Martin Brest completely reinvented another old movie, called* Death Takes a Holiday, *extending its running-time from a compact seventy-eight minutes to slightly over three hours. This movie also bombed, despite the casting of Brad Pitt. I questioned the merit of these protracted running-times in a November 1998 column in* Daily Variety.

MEET JOE SLACK

This is the time of year when two things happen to movies: They start getting better and they start getting longer.

The "better" part I understand. The Oscar hopefuls start lining up on the runway. Distributors believe that late November is the ideal time to let their contenders start strutting their stuff.

It's the "longer" part I don't get. No one likes movies that approach three hours in length. Exhibitors hate them, so do studios, and, for that matter, so do most moviegoers.

Unless, of course, the movie happens to be brilliant. Few begrudged David Lean his three hours and forty-two minutes on *Lawrence of Arabia.* There weren't many walkouts during the three hours and fourteen minutes running-time of *Titanic,* despite all its cornball dialogue.

But then you run into a film like *Meet Joe Black* and you wonder, "What were they thinking?" Here's a movie with a premise that works, provided you don't have time to think about it. That's the rub: You have precisely three hours and one second to think about it, which is remarkable considering it's based on a movie called *Death Takes a Holiday* which clocked in at seventy-eight minutes. *Meet Joe Black* is a film that seems intent on wearing out its welcome.

"*Titanic* was the culprit," claims the chief of one major studio, who doesn't want his name used. "When it comes to the crunch every director tells you about *Titanic*. They say it proved longer is better. They're wrong."

The *Titanic* syndrome started making itself felt in summer. Robert Redford is a taut man who talks in terse sentences, but his movie *The Horse Whisperer* was flabby by a good twenty minutes. *The Mask of Zorro* should have been tighter, and though it may be sacrilege to criticize *There's Something About Mary*, at one hundred and eighteen minutes it had plenty of sags.

To be sure, running-time is often illusory. When a movie isn't working it always seems longer—witness *Midnight in the Garden of Good and Evil*. *Godzilla* was only two hours and eighteen minutes, but it felt like three hours. Conversely, I didn't notice anyone checking their watches during *Saving Private Ryan*.

I've heard directors plead their case that "longer is better" in scores of meetings. Their arguments usually break down as follows:

"The mood of my movie requires careful pacing." That was basically the Martin Brest argument on *Meet Joe Black*. The weighty exchanges about life and death could not survive an *Armageddon*-like tempo, the director argued. On the other hand, how many weighty exchanges can an audience endure?

"My movie is politically important and needs time to breathe." This was the argument used to support the three-hour running-time of Oliver Stone's *Nixon* three years ago. The problem arises only if the movie turns out to be both important and numbingly tedious. A short, important movie is better than a long one.

"My movie is based on a famous novel and its readers would rebel if anything were cut." This was the rationale behind *Midnight in the Garden of Good and Evil.* The movie was interminable and most readers would have applauded cuts.

"It's my movie and if you don't like it you can go fuck yourself." This is genial James Cameron's approach, an argument that is surprisingly effective provided the director is armed with final cut. It worked for Cameron. It has proven self-destructive for many others.

The irony in all this is that film editors today have almost all migrated to electronic editing. They are thus empowered to implement suggested cuts and modifications from their directors with amazing swiftness and efficiency. The technology is in place. What a shame no one's telling them to cut anything.

—*Variety,* November 16, 1998

.   .   .

Though the movie-going audience seemed to rebel against overly long movies in 1998, it eagerly embraced the three-hour Titanic, *a fact that seemed to startle even its filmmaker, hot-tempered, egocentric James Cameron. Given Cameron's heavy-handed profligacy, I couldn't resist writing the hypothetical scenario published in the March 30, 1998,* Daily Variety—*an article the filmmaker made it quite clear he did not appreciate.*

AN AUDIENCE WITH THE KING

Peering into the future, we can imagine not one, not two, but four studios under the thumb of James Cameron and his newest opus. This column doesn't usually compete for "scoops," but the following story was too juicy to pass up since it concerns the Man of the Hour, James Cameron.

Two days after his *Titanic* won eleven Oscars, I've learned that Cameron has quietly closed a deal on his next picture, *Spider-Man.* A source close to Cameron explained that this project was selected in part because four companies claim partial ownership of the basic material. Under his deal, Cameron therefore has invited all four to co-finance his film since, the source said, "having only two studios backing him, as with *Titanic,* has proven too restrictive." *Titanic* was co-funded only by Twentieth Century Fox and Paramount.

Though the project is still in its infancy, it's been learned that a production executive has already been selected by the four companies to represent them on *Spider-Man,* and an initial creative meeting with Cameron has been held. While the production executive asked me not to disclose his name, he filled in these details about the initial meeting.

"Mr. Cameron decided we'd rent the old Chasen's for a quiet drink," the executive said. "Mr. Cameron arrived five minutes late and shook my hand. Since I had never met him before, I asked how I might address him during this and subsequent meetings. He replied, 'I think that should be obvious. You may call me King of the World. Or simply King, once we get to know each other.'

"I then asked him whether his staff had prepared any initial budget figures relative to *Spider-Man.* He froze me with a steely look, then reminded me that he never started business meetings without first holding a minute of silent prayer in memory of the victims of the *Titanic.* I realized the appropriateness of this gesture, but it was then, I'm afraid, I made my first faux pas."

"What was that?" I asked.

"Well, I said to him, 'Could we also have a moment of prayer for the companies putting up the money for your next movie?' I meant this as a joke—friends tell me I have a good sense of humor."

"How did Cameron react?"

"He was cool. He said simply, 'I plan to have you replaced with another production executive.'"

"And did that end the meeting?"

"No. I decided to grovel a bit. I said, 'King, I would appreciate a second chance. This represents a big opportunity for me. It would be a great honor to work for the man who made the most expensive—I mean, the most successful—movie of all time.'"

"And was he placated?"

"At least he moved on to the next item of business. He stated that since he had written, directed, produced, edited, and composed the music for *Titanic,* he wanted that made clear in the credits of his next picture. There would be no other names. It would just state, 'A Film by James Cameron.'"

"The guilds would have something to say about that," I suggested.

"I just nodded and took notes. Next, he moved on to his deal. Since the biggest movie star in the world has now reached the $25-million level, he's decided to demand $30 million up-front, against thirty percent of the gross. I'm afraid I gulped at this point. That brought on that icy stare again. 'Did you say something?' he asked. 'No, it's just cold in here—we're the only people in this enormous restaurant. That was just a shiver you saw.'"

"'If you shiver in here, you should have seen what it was like being underwater all day,' he said. 'Then you'd shiver.' Cameron's body seemed to swell as he reflected back on his *Titanic* shoot, like a general recalling an immense victory."

"Did you raise the issue of penalties if he goes over budget?" I asked.

The executive looked at me as if I was hallucinating. "I tried, but I think there's a language problem with the word 'overage,'" he said. "Cameron—I mean, King—wants to be rewarded for overages. He argues that when he exceeds the budget, this shows the movie will be that much more commercial. Hence, for every $20 million he goes over, he wants to be rewarded with another five percent of the gross."

Now it was my turn to gulp. "That means that if he doubles his budget as he did last time out, he would end up with over fifty percent of the gross?"

"I don't mean to suggest that he's uncompromising," the executive put in. "I mean, he implied there would be a lid. A silver lining for his financiers to cling to."

"And a completion guarantee? Any thought about that?"

"The King suggested the Fed." He shrugged helplessly, realizing that this was becoming somewhat surreal. "He feels he is a national treasure, that he has single-handedly saved the U.S. film industry, so that in return the Federal Reserve Bank should step up and cover overages."

I started to ask another question, but the executive was clearly becoming nervous. "Look, I can't tell you anything more. I have to report to my four employers, you know. Then I have to get back to the King. I mean, this thing is moving fast."

"I understand completely," I said. "Thanks for the information. I can't wait to see the movie."

"I'm sure the Federal Reserve Bank feels the same way," he said.

—*Variety,* March 30, 1998

.   .   .

Despite the huge success of Titanic, *some of the other special-effects epics of 1998 failed to live up to expectations. The most prominent under-achiever was* Godzilla, *a misbegotten movie I discussed in the June 1, 1998,* Variety.

LESSONS FROM THE LIZARD

MEMO TO: Roland Emmerich and Dean Devlin

You've certainly earned a niche in the history books this week, guys. You're the first filmmakers ever to experience a $74-million opening week and still be called losers. "*Godzilla* isn't so huge after all," leered the *Wall Street Journal.* "Limpin' Lizards!" exclaimed *Daily Variety.* One theater chain, Carmike, is already forecasting lower earnings, blaming it on the *Godzilla* blahs.

You must both be reeling after all this, guys, so I hope you'll take the time to shut off the phones and reflect on whether there's a message here.

When all this started, you cleverly positioned yourselves as a couple of genial underdogs. You'd taken your lumps in the B-picture business and been given the cold shoulder by the studios, yet you

still managed to shock the town with *Independence Day*. The press
ate up Dean's "aw-shucks" style as well as Roland's inverse snobbery—he's the only German film-school student who'd ever aspired
to become George Lucas rather than Wim Wenders.

But look what a few months has wrought. No longer the underdogs, you've become the fat cats—multimillionaires with a huge
studio deal. And, if you're not careful, you could easily become a
symbol of Hollywood greed.

To many, *Godzilla* has become the ultimate example of a marketing campaign in search of a movie. The movie was seemingly
made not to entertain audiences but to help sell tacos and T-shirts.

That's why a nasty undercurrent developed in the opening
week, guys. Every major popcorn movie has its share of detractors,
but critics of *Godzilla* were downright shrill.

Sure, the movie itself, with all its action, was disappointing
in several areas. The creatures seemed like dropouts from *Jurassic
Park,* minus the personality. The actors looked like they realized
they had second-billing to the retro reptiles. There seemed to be
too much of everything—too much noise, too many creatures,
too many plot twists, and, most urgently, too much rain, as
though the elements were needed to wash away shortcomings in
the special effects.

While we all know that summer movies are exercises in hype,
the *Godzilla* campaign seemed so over-the-top as to become self-
parody. For the first time, marketing men throughout the industry
were asking, How much is too much? At what point does the hype
reach such a high decibel-level that it turns the public against the
very movie it's supposed to promote?

So many articles were written about the "genius" of selling
Godzilla that the studio took on the aura of smugness, as though
Sony were counting its money even before the movie was released.
"How Sony Created a Monster!" screamed a headline in *Fortune,* of
all places, even quoting John Calley, of all people, trumpeting that
"the film isn't so much an end in itself as it is a way for the company

to get into the *Godzilla* business." The magazine went on to quote Calley as saying, "Of course, we're all artists here."

At least Calley hasn't lost his talent for self-mockery, fellas. How about you? After all the grandiloquence, perhaps a little levity would be called for rather than pronouncements about sequels and new tie-ins.

Any road-weary magician can detect the problem here. You can't spend hours explaining your tricks and still keep your audience interested. Further, if you have the balls to announce yourself as the greatest show in town, you sure as hell better deliver.

Last weekend I dropped by a toy store and tried to get the attention of a sales clerk. They were all in the back, ripping open cartons of *Godzilla* toys and trying to assemble them. And they were not in a good mood.

"Look at these damn things," one saleswoman said. "They arrive after the movie opened. They're hard to assemble. And they look like leftovers from an old Spielberg epic." OK, salesclerks are notoriously grumpy, but she still had a point.

Despite the naysayers, *Godzilla* is going to do huge business around the world. Your career at Sony will soar. I'd only suggest you reconsider the meaning of your own slogan. Size isn't everything, fellas. Taste is a useful component. So is self-restraint.

It's not *all* about tacos and T-shirts, guys.

—*Variety*, June 1, 1998

.   .   .

Among the effects movies of '98, none stirred more vehement argument than the film version of The X-Files, *which inspired this column in* Variety *on June 22, 1998.*

THE PEDDLING OF PARANOIA

The most interesting aspect of *The X-Files* movie is that it isn't a movie. Chris Carter, renowned as the most arrogant writer-producer in television, has lived up to his reputation by blowing up a TV episode and calling it a movie—one that only his cult-like TV

following could either understand or appreciate. If his curious exercise succeeds, the mind boggles where it will lead. Next summer our
multiplexes will be showing expanded episodes of *Touched by an
Angel, Xena,* and *Dawson's Creek.* Maybe Jerry Springer will become
a movie star after all.

In view of the fact that *X-Files* apparently was designed specifically for its TV audience—a strange stratagem considering its $65-
million budget and $25-million marketing tab—I have asked Jenny
Hontz, *Variety*'s assiduous TV writer, to share this column with me
so that, together, we might present a balanced view.

HONTZ: While viewers who have never seen *The X-Files* TV show
will probably be a bit confused by the movie, fans of the series
will love it. It's a chance to see two of their favorite characters,
Mulder and Scully, on the big screen, like one supersized episode
with more action and better effects.

Because the film is dropped in the middle of a continuing
story line linking last season's finale and this fall's opener, it
doesn't stand alone like most films. The result is similar to
that of the second *Star Wars* movie, where Han Solo is frozen
and you have to watch the sequel to find out what happens.
Fox is hoping this cliffhanger will force *X-Files* novices to
tune in to the series, but it could backfire by frustrating some
moviegoers.

BART: Well, it backfired as far as I'm concerned. The very elements
that allegedly lend the TV show its noirish character don't work
on the big screen—the flat dialogue, the TV-style closeups, the
incessant clangorous music. And, most of all, the cast. I realize
that *X-Files* fans accept the fact that Scully and Mulder, the two
leads, never change either their facial expressions or their tone
of voice, but on the big screen they tend to disappear altogether. It's little wonder that Janet Maslin, the *New York Times*'
meticulous film critic, starts referring to Gillian Anderson, who
plays Scully, as "Ms. Armstrong."

HONTZ: At the center of the film is the platonic love between Mulder and Scully that stems from sharing intense experiences that no one else believes or understands. The chemistry is palpable, but, as usual, you leave wanting more than you get.

That's the case in many aspects of the film, and it's a deliberate attempt to keep us coming back. The aliens in the film, for instance, are never completely visible, which is in keeping with creator Chris Carter's view that showing too much isn't as terrifying.

The film answers many of the puzzling questions posed by the series, but it raises new ones too. And while much is revealed, "X-Philes" know that the show always has a way of taking things you thought you knew and turning them completely upside down a week later. If you want all the answers, you'll go nuts. But if you sit back and enjoy the ride, you won't be disappointed.

BART: Well, I was disappointed. Also perplexed. I realize that *X-Files* is designed to appease conspiracy theorists and government-haters. What other show would depict, as its ultimate heavy, the Federal Emergency Management Agency—those "dangerous" folk who turn up in times of disaster? With his customary modesty, Chris Carter declares, "The show's original spirit has become kind of the spirit of the country, if not the world." Sure. What this really means is that the show fosters paranoia by sowing confusion. It weaves a plot that is essentially unintelligible and therefore encourages unintelligible analysis. Charles McGrath, editor of the *New York Times Book Review*, no less, concluded his essay on *X-Files* last week with the following pithy analysis: "*The X-Files* has taught us that it's more entertaining, and probably more epistemologically sound, to believe in everything and in nothing at all."

I knew I could count on the *Times* to clear things up.

HONTZ: The thing to remember is the movie carries little risk for Fox because *The X-Files* has twenty million fans who tune in to the show each week. Even if half of those viewers see the film, Fox will likely recoup its investment.

Some people are, no doubt, questioning whether viewers will pay to see something they can get for free each week. But *The X-Files* has a cult following, and its fans are extremely devoted. Much like *Star Trek*, fans often pay $25 to attend *X-Files* conventions, so eight bucks and some popcorn won't be much of a deterrent.

For TV executives at Fox, the film provides the kind of free publicity they could never afford. While Fox lost some ad dollars by trimming the number of episodes produced last season to accommodate the film's production schedule, exposure from the movie could give it a real shot in the arm going into its sixth season.

The film remained completely true to the series, which is necessary because the show is still on the air and will pick up where the movie left off. The film had the trademark sardonic humor of the series, combined with a dark look and eerie tension that taps into apocalyptic paranoia surrounding the end of the millennium.

BART: I'll take your word for it, Jenny, but frankly I'm more inclined to subscribe to Joe Morgenstern's observation in the *Wall Street Journal*. He writes: "The most intriguing conspiracy here is the one cooked up by Twentieth Century Fox and Fox TV."

It's all about hyping a TV series. Nothing wrong with that, but why pretend you're making a movie as part of the exercise?

—*Variety*, June 22, 1998

.   .   .

While Godzilla *and* Armageddon, *among others, seemed to fall under the spell of the special-effects wizards, several other major movies retreated from the techies, as I related in* Variety *on June 20, 1998.*

ARE MOVIEGOERS GOING "RETRO"?

Notice something awry about the reception to this year's fusillade of summer pictures? Each of the vaunted, effects-laden megapics has arrived amid a buzz of controversy among critics and "civilians" alike. *Godzilla,* many felt, was overhyped and underwritten; *Deep Impact* lacked empathetic protagonists; *Armageddon* was edited like the world's longest music video.

Consider, on the other hand, the summer's "retro slate." The stunts in *Lethal Weapon 4* appear to have been sliced from a Warner Bros. gangster film, circa 1939—you could almost visualize the tows and pulleys. The swordplay in *The Mask of Zorro* seemed like a throwback to Douglas Fairbanks in the '20s. The physical gags in *There's Something About Mary* looked like they were created for the Three Stooges—for that matter, the entire movie represents a continuity nightmare.

Similarly, the word went forth weeks ago that the CGI work in *Dr. Dolittle* would represent a formidable advance, but frankly I thought that computer-embellished animals "talked" more persuasively in several TV commercials, not to mention in *Babe.*

Yet *Doolittle* is a big hit; despite Eddie Murphy's disappearance from the promo circuit, the movie seems destined to top his previous "comeback" smash, *The Nutty Professor.*

Indeed, all the movies on the "retro slate" have been received warmly by critics and audiences alike. It's almost as if moviegoers want to end the "tyranny of the techies."

And all this is in advance of *Saving Private Ryan,* which seems destined for acclaim. Not only has Steven Spielberg stepped back from special effects, but he also shot his combat scenes in a hand-held, in-your-face, semi-documentary style reminiscent of low-budget "indie" filmmaking. To compound this impression, he's cast "indie" actors, not Hollywood bit-players.

So what's going on here? Has Hollywood finally got the message that audiences want more from movies than theme-park rides, à la *Speed 2*?

If moviegoers are a bit exasperated with effects movies, their impatience is shared with some top-ranking studio executives who feel they've been sold a bill of goods by the techmeisters. The effects business has finally reached a level of maturity, they'd been told. Complex as it may be, the work could be delivered on time and on budget. The troubled days of the computer-graphics suppliers were behind us.

Sure.

The hard facts are these: Effects budgets, by and large, skyrocketed for summer '98 projects. Equally upsetting, the techies weren't able to meet their schedules. Or perhaps the directors overseeing their work saw to it that they missed delivery dates.

In some cases, such as Polygram's $85-million Robin Williams project, *What Dreams May Come,* the effects houses ran into a range of problems, technical and financial, and the movies missed their summer dates completely. In others, however, studio executives suspect that directors manipulated effects scheduling to minimize studio input.

No one will talk about it on the record, but senior executives at one studio in particular, who never got to see the final cut of their major summer movie until the eleventh hour, are furious that other motives were involved. "There were a lot of improvements that could have been made had we seen it at the scheduled time," one top production executive confides. The director and producer, however, kept assuring the studio that the final effects simply couldn't be ready in time.

The bottom line: On their most expensive projects, studios run the risks of not being able to test or preview. For that matter, they can't even show their movies to long-range reviewers or key exhibitors. "Block-booking" laws in many states forbid exhibitors from closing deals on new movies until they actually get to see them.

None of this is to suggest that the era of "effects movies" is behind us. Quite the contrary. This much is apparent, however:

Audiences are in a mood to demand more than seeing New York get stomped by a reptile, blasted by an asteroid, or swamped by a tidal wave. They want story and character.

Studios will be reluctant to commit to big-budget CGI epics unless vastly more time is built into the schedule for previews and testing.

There probably will be fewer $100-million-plus effects movies made in the future than over the last two or three years.

Apparently, this summer's "retro slate" may have had a deep impact after all.

—*Variety*, July 20, 1998

.   .   .

Gross-out movies became a recognized genre in 1998, albeit with mixed results. There's Something About Mary *ended up grossing an astonishing $340 million around the world, but many other entries in this category failed miserably. The ins and outs of gross-outs were scrutinized in a* Variety *column appearing on August 10, 1998.*

NO GROSSES FOR GROSS-OUTS

A glimpse at the box-office charts often raises intriguing questions about our pop culture. For example: Do the meager openings of *BASEketball* and *Jane Austen's Mafia* suggest that the market for gross-out movies is less substantial than anticipated? Has the moviegoing public's appetite for jokes about semen, onanism, and mental retardation been satiated by *There's Something About Mary*?

This question is causing considerable angst among distributors whose gross-out movies are lined up on the runway, and there are a good number of them. They include *Wrongfully Accused* from Warner Bros., *Dead Man on Campus* from Paramount, *Stiff Upper Lips* from Miramax, not to mention *Orgazmo* from October.

Several theories have been advanced to explain the meager reception for the latest crop of gross-out movies.

The reality of our political life is so gross that no one needs to go to the movies for more of the same. When the press, not to mention late-night comics, obsess over semen stains, filmmakers find it all but impossible to be more outrageous.

How could even the Farrelly brothers top Monica Lewinsky's decision to save her famous dress and send it home to mommy for safekeeping? The fields of politics and entertainment started converging back in the Kennedy era, and today that amalgamation, for better or worse, seems complete.

The latest cluster of gross-out movies relies too heavily on male-oriented locker-room misogyny, which turns off the female movie-goer. The women in these films, like Cameron Diaz in *There's Something About Mary*, are always gullible airheads who are suckers for every ploy.

Consider the possibilities if filmmakers moved beyond their farts-and-phalluses fixation and dealt humorously with male frailties—impotence, premature ejaculation, mommy fixations, et cetera. The women might stream to the theaters if guys were the airheads for a change.

The new gross-out movies just aren't funny enough. Ever since the Zucker brothers got *Airplane!* aloft in 1980, the machine-gun school of humor has been predominant—keep firing off the jokes until one or two of them hits.

The formula worked for the Zuckers for two reasons. Their jokes were funny, and they also had a genius for casting the right straight men, such as Lloyd Bridges, Robert Stack, Peter Graves, and, of course, Leslie Nielsen, the Charlie Chaplin of the gross-out genre. The same cannot be said for movies like *Jane Austen's Mafia* or *BASEketball*.

There's another issue too. The great old-time comics never used a joke in a movie until they'd tried it before a live audience. Most either grew up in the final days of vaudeville or emerged from the comedy-club circuit. Today's gross-out filmmakers think that testing their material for research mavens like Joe Farrell will suffice. Get real, guys.

So where does this leave us? The gross-out purveyors may be facing the same dilemma that confronts more conventional genres of movies. Grossiosity per se is simply not enough. Prosaic elements like character, story, and, yes, even laughs must be part of the equation.

If that can be accomplished, then the handwriting is on the wall. For the remainder of the '90s and beyond, gross-out will be as ubiquitous as takeout. Now that's a prospect even more daunting than having to read Kenneth Starr's final report.

—*Variety*, August 10, 1998

.　　.　　.

By the end of '98, while many comedy directors, including those of the "gross-out" school, were reassessing their audience, the Farrelly brothers were going their merry way, far removed from Hollywood and its box-office obsessions. In a column appearing in Variety *on January 18, 1999, I described what it's like to have lunch with the bountiful brothers.*

THE FARRELLYS STRIKE PAY DIRT

An aura of tension customarily surrounds filmmakers when they're in the final throes of putting together their next movie as they zero in on cast, budget, and location.

Not so with two directors I encountered last week, who were about as tense as beachcombers in Maui. They dawdled over their lunch, tossed off a few jokes, and reminisced about growing up in small-town New England, where they still live.

Peter and Bob Farrelly, on the face of it, would have reason to savor the moment. Their surprise hit of last summer, *There's Something About Mary*, is about to pass $340 million worldwide, which is almost $340 million more than their previous film. The brothers' personal take from the sleeper hit could ultimately approach $15 million, according to studio suits.

But the Farrellys, both in their early forties, clearly aren't bowled over by this largess. "We're not exactly overnight successes," notes Bob Farrelly. "Not that we would have minded that fate as against being overnight failures."

Flaky and idiosyncratic to the extreme, the Farrellys are determined to keep their feet on the ground, provided it's not Hollywood ground. "It's not some big reverse snobbery thing," Peter Farrelly explains. "We prefer our friends back home. We like the blue-collar camaraderie. They're our audience. We relax with them."

The brothers drift into town periodically, and their visits have been fruitful. A week after *Mary* opened, they were at a small dinner party in Santa Monica hosted by their producer. Bill Mechanic and Tom Sherak from Fox showed up and handed each of the brothers a check for $1 million, intended as a "good will" advance against profits. "It's gestures like that that can really warm up a dinner party," Peter Farrelly observed wryly.

The brothers were in town last week to try to advance their next directing effort, *Stuck on You,* which focuses on semi-Siamese twins who share the same liver but otherwise have quite different dispositions. They would like Jim Carrey and Woody Allen to play the twins, realizing that this pairing will require some surreal deal-making maneuvers. They gladly leave all that to the studio and to Richard Lovett, their longtime agent at CAA.

Since they figure on writing and directing only one film every two years, they're also putting together some producing ventures. One is a love triangle called *Me, Myself and Irene,* about a man with a split personality. Another is *Basketcase,* starring Denis Leary as a sports nut who takes one of those million-dollar shots during a televised game.

Upon completing their Hollywood meetings, the brothers head back to the Providence area where they settle in with friends and family. Bob, admittedly the more conservative of the two, is married with two kids and could pass for a small-town lawyer in his blue blazer and tan slacks. Peter, clad in T-shirt and jeans and with a wisp of facial hair, is more boisterous and admits to being "a bleeding-heart liberal." Both would come across as easygoing, small-town guys, except for the glint of go-for-it, hell-raising nihilism in their eyes.

"We like to push the envelope," Peter acknowledges. "We like to test how far we can go without embarrassing ourselves and everyone else."

To that end, the Farrellys cling to the same crew and, shooting away from Hollywood, try to create a completely relaxed set. Even when ordering up the next shot, they tend to ask their sidekicks, "How do you think we should set this up?"

"We know our actors go way out on a limb in many of these scenes," Peter Farrelly says. "Our crew is like an extended family. No one is going to look down their nose at anything. It's all very supportive." Indeed, they want their assistant director, 32-year-old J. B. Rogers, to direct their next project, which the Farrellys will produce.

Turning out their films for under $25 million, the Farrellys effectively function as an in-house independent at Fox. Not surprisingly, they prefer to test their films locally in small college theaters in New England, where they can learn which jokes are working and which are bombing.

"It's amazing how much you can find out without all the official studio testing apparatus all around you," Bob Farrelly says. To be sure, they got burned on one "sneak" preview last year when one of the self-appointed Internet critics sent out a ten-page review. Fortunately, it was favorable.

The brothers' movies, even going back to *Dumb and Dumber*, their first effort, are more leisurely and more character-driven than the Zucker brothers' school of machine-gun gross-out humor, though it was the Zuckers who gave them their first gig.

"We want to give the audience a chance to like our characters," Peter Farrelly explains. "Unless you like our people, you won't go along with the craziness that happens to them." A case in point was Cameron Diaz, who won over her audience in *Mary* in addition to getting the big laughs.

Peter, 42, who has written two novels, recently got married and is expecting his first child, much to the approval of his conservative brother, Bob. Peter's also planning on building a home on Martha's Vineyard, but, other than that, has no cosmic plans to spend his sudden wealth.

"I thought of myself as an entrepreneur once," Bob says. "I invented and marketed a round beach towel so that people wouldn't have to get up and move the towel around whenever the sun shifted. For some reason the product didn't sell."

Movies have worked better for them than towels, the Farrellys concede, provided they do them on their own terms. And that means staying away from the center of the action and, as Peter puts it, "hangin' with the real folks."

Their success would seem to underscore the argument that more and more filmmakers are propounding these days: Namely, that the studios might do well to loosen the reins, to hold back the flood of script notes and editing suggestions and give their filmmakers some more breathing room.

They may come up with more surprises like those supplied by the Farrellys.

—Variety, January 18, 1999

. . .

Aside from Steven Spielberg, only a very few members of the directing fraternity managed to sustain a consistent success record during the decade of the '90s. The hit-and-miss trend in filmmaking was reviewed in this memo to Tony Scott, published August 26, 1996, in Variety. *Since then, Scott, a man known for his fecundity, directed a successful thriller entitled* Enemy of the State *for Disney, which grossed well over $100 million.*

MEGAHITS AND MEGAFLOPS

MEMO TO: Tony Scott

You must be feeling a bit like a dartboard these days, Tony, reading the ferocious reviews of your latest film, *The Fan.* Of the thirty-five critics whose opinions are sampled each week in *Variety*'s Crix' Picks section, only seven could muster kind words for the film; worse yet, audiences are not exactly lining up outside theaters.

Of course, you've been there before, Tony—many times. In your fifteen-year career, you've repeatedly ricocheted back and forth between hits and flops, getting pilloried, then praised. Indeed, your career has come to epitomize the erratic paths being plied by a whole school of contemporary filmmakers who seem to bounce between extremes of success and failure. Never before have directors commanded such big bucks and delivered such an unpredictable parade of product.

Now, you're a thoughtful man, Tony, and also a very independent one. To assure your future autonomy, you and your brother, Ridley, have founded a company to help finance your films, plunked down $19 million to buy Shepperton Studios, and also invested in an English rival to George Lucas's Industrial Light & Magic.

Which brings us to an interesting anomaly: If autonomy is that important to you, why is it that all four of your most successful movies were made not only under studio auspices but also in concert with one of Hollywood's most hands-on production teams, Jerry Bruckheimer and the late Don Simpson? That association yielded films grossing almost $900 million worldwide—movies like *Top Gun* and *Crimson Tide*. Away from that protective cocoon, Tony, you proceeded to make movies like *The Hunger, True Romance, Revenge,* and, of course, your latest bête noir, *The Fan*.

Given this record, I wonder if you've reflected on the whys and wherefores. Why are so many present-day directors registering such inconsistent performances?

Now, I already hear you protesting that these are fatuous questions, that directors are artists who have always been entitled to their successes and failures.

Well, yes and no. Examine the filmographies of some of the more prominent craftsmen who labored during the heyday of the studio system, and you find some rather remarkable batting averages. Howard Hawks from the late '30s to the early '50s managed to deliver eleven hits in a row, including *Sergeant York* and *Red River,* according to his biographer, *Variety* chief film critic Todd McCarthy. Others of that era, like William Wyler and Alfred Hitchcock, also seemed models of consistency.

The difference was that these directors were nurtured by the studios. Today's filmmakers operate in a far more chaotic environment, wherein it's often the top stars and their coteries who determine which movies get made.

I can also hear you railing about costs, Tony, and with some justification. When the budgets of big commercial pictures spiral off in the direction of $100 million, a certain craziness seems to infiltrate the process.

There's simply too much at stake to take artistic risks, and there are also too many voices in the mix. As a result, some of these megapix develop a built-in self-destruct mechanism.

From what I hear about *The Fan,* Tony, you were determined to ignore this cacophony. Your producers and studio executives say they tried to warn you about some of the excesses, but you turned a deaf ear. You were even warned about the weird mistakes and incongruities of your baseball footage, but you chose not to listen.

Now, I guess that's why directors receive the big bucks, Tony, but in the case of this film it apparently worked against you. In the end, *The Fan* was more than disappointing—to many it was downright depressing.

I gather your next film, Tony, is entitled "Where the Money Is"—apt title for your present dilemma. You and your brother have proved astonishingly adept at turning up the big money, both for yourselves, through features and commercials, and for the studio.

Not long ago you told a reporter for *Variety* that "darkness was always something that intrigued me." You added that Don Simpson, himself the Prince of Darkness, had admonished you that "there's a life outside darkness. There's life in redemption."

Well, it's your call now, Tony: darkness or redemption. Good luck with that one.

—*Variety,* August 26, 1996

.   .   .

Few filmmakers "work" Hollywood as shrewdly as director Ron Howard, of Opie TV fame, and his partner, Brian Grazer, while maintaining a laid-back, "aw-shucks" veneer. In the May 1999 GQ, I talked about my concerted effort to try to understand these men and their success.

OPIE THE CONGLOMERATE

In the interest of full disclosure, I must confess I don't "get" Ron Howard and Brian Grazer. I think readers should know this, since my task supposedly is to explain the reasons for their success and to summon up insights into what makes them tick. After all, the two partners in Imagine Entertainment are probably Hollywood's hottest creators of movies and TV shows. With their existing studio deals running out, there's a veritable feeding frenzy among rival companies to sign them up.

Except I can't really deliver. Mind you, I've tried. I have talked at length with Grazer, a spike-haired onetime TV–comedy writer (not an especially gifted one) who has emerged as a megaproducer in late-'90s Hollywood. I've also chatted with Howard, a good-natured, aw-shucks sort of character who, in shedding his child-actor persona to become a top director, has managed to defy F. Scott Fitzgerald's dictum "There are no second acts in American lives." I've fired suitably tough questions their way, to which they have responded with apparent candor. Having done all this, I should be able to set forth the reasons why they've moved to the head of their class, right?

Wrong. In fact, I haven't a clue—which is all the more frustrating, since I've always thought myself skilled in analyzing the components of showbusiness success, the key element being persuasiveness. Take Steven Spielberg. He can mobilize a mesmerizing, childlike exuberance when describing a new project that can melt the resistance of any superstar or studio czar. Or Joe Roth, the Disney chairman, who brandishes a laid-back, I've-seen-it-all savvy in selling an idea to a filmmaker or a Wall Street pooh-bah. His cool is downright contagious.

Then there's Mel Gibson, who summons up an edgy, twitchy, from-one-superstar-to-another conviction in advancing his plans as a celebrity filmmaker. The same star who jauntily ad-libbed his way through a programmer like *Lethal Weapon 4* communicates his passion superbly in hopes of raising the artistic bar on films he's proposing to direct.

And how about Grazer and Howard? Sure, they're industrious and conscientious, but they exude as much charisma as Wal-Mart managers. Over the past thirteen years, they've built up a formidable body of work. Who can argue with a producer-director team that has given us *Splash, Parenthood, Cocoon, Far and Away, Backdraft, Ransom, Apollo 13, Liar Liar,* and last month's *EDtv,* not to mention such TV fare as *Felicity, Sports Night,* and the HBO miniseries *From the Earth to the Moon*? No other private production entity (with the exception of Spielberg's high-powered company, misleadingly called Amblin) in Hollywood has accumulated as sturdy a record.

Indeed, with Spielberg's departure from Universal to start his ambitious new venture, DreamWorks SKG, Imagine has become the backbone of that studio's motion-picture program. At the same time, Imagine's TV efforts have become pivotal to Disney. Yet their deal with Disney will expire a year from now, and their Universal deal will end in two years, opening things up to the highest bidder.

Ask Grazer or Howard about this delicious development and they take cover in their aw-shucks mode. "Brian and I have spent lots of time talking it over," Howard says. "Maybe there's a play to be made, but we both feel we've had enough success without having to reinvent ourselves. It's making the films that carries me along. I want to avoid a situation where I have to force growth, as in a publicly owned company." The reason they want to avoid it is that they've been there before. In fact, six years ago Grazer and Howard found themselves in dire straits. A group of Wall Street heavyweights led by financier Herbert Allen had levitated Imagine into a public company. There was grandiose talk of creating a diversified entertainment conglomerate that would finance its own films and TV ventures, ultimately expanding into other arenas. There was a stock offering, annual reports were issued, and soon Imagine had built up its own mini bureaucracy.

It was a great scheme, but it never went anywhere. Grazer and Howard increasingly resented the pressure and the public scrutiny, especially since they seemed unable to conjure up the sort of *Titanic*-size megahits that would satisfy their investors. Indeed, though Howard continued to pursue his successful directing career, he and Grazer produced flops such as *Cry-Baby, Sgt. Bilko,* and *The Chamber.* "The whole public-company thing made Brian goofy," recalls one longtime friend. "Both Ron and Brian seemed to be pressing. The work just wasn't as good as it should have been, and there was a sort of frantic neurosis within the company."

After seven years, in 1993, the partners opted for a $23.4-million buyout. Having gone public at $8 a share in 1986, Howard and Grazer took the company private at $9 a share, triggering a wave of indignation among a number of investors. Universal helped fund the buyout in exchange for a semi-exclusive deal with Imagine. "It amounted to a lifestyle decision," reflects Howard. "The cost of making movies had risen drastically. We were badly undercapitalized. Our business plan no longer made sense. To make Imagine work as a public company, we would have had to become hardware people, not filmmakers. We would have had to start buying radio stations, for example. It didn't make sense anymore."

Relieved of the pressures of moguldom, the partners began to do fine work once again and to get their priorities back in order. Howard, a confirmed family man, and his wife (his high school sweetheart, naturally) wanted to bring up their four kids in the non-showbusiness confines of Greenwich, Connecticut. Meanwhile, Grazer remarried and was able to spend more time surfing in Malibu. Not only did the movie hits start rolling in again but so did the TV shows too. While similar companies that started at roughly the same time, like Rob Reiner's Castle Rock, were stumbling, the reconstituted Imagine became hot.

So now Grazer and Howard find themselves at a crossroads yet again, only this time the situation is even more complicated. For one thing, there are the studio offers to consider. Some studios are dangling proposals for Imagine to take up residence as an internal production powerhouse. A couple have also talked to Grazer about becoming their production boss, presiding over not only Imagine but also the entire studio.

And the normally wary Grazer admits he's tempted. "Sure, it's something that interests me," he says matter-of-factly, as though he were talking about managing a bookstore. The Hollywood studios have been suffering through a severe profit squeeze, he acknowledges, and there might be an opportunity to impose new thinking. "Still, when you get right down to it, what it would mean is hanging out with investment bankers and becoming a suit," Grazer says. It might even mean combing down his hair, which at present he wears porcupine-style, as if to emphasize he's his own man.

Modest by nature, Grazer remembers his early days in town, when he felt like an awkward outsider. "When I finally managed to get myself invited to a couple of chic parties, I noticed the hot producers making all the right moves, saying all the right things, and there I was, putting my foot in it, getting it wrong." Still, Grazer persevered, and before long he found people heeding his movie ideas, starting with *Splash*. He also found himself comfortable in the presence of Howard, an equally diffident, low-key individual who was the product of a totally different world. Grazer was interested in being the dealmaker, the producer who assembles the elements; Howard, the white-bread onetime child actor, aspired to be a director. "We found it easy to talk," Grazer says. "We never argued or yelled at each other. That's not our style. We just talked things through. It was always very easygoing."

There was nothing in Ron Howard's background to suggest he would emerge as a thoroughly sensible, down-to-earth adult. Born in Oklahoma, he made his stage debut at age two in a production of *The Seven Year Itch* directed by his father, a confirmed theater-lover. In time, the family gravitated west and Ron Howard became

Hollywood's perfect middle-American child star, cast at age six as Opie on *The Andy Griffith Show* and, eight years after that show ended, moving on to *Happy Days*. He kept working throughout his childhood and cannot remember a time when someone wasn't stopping him for his autograph. Yet his parents kept him enrolled in public schools, intent on preserving some normalcy in an otherwise aberrant life.

Howard's fascination with directing intensified during his teen years, which seemed at odds with his persona as the freckle-faced icon of small-town America. He won second prize in a Kodak-sponsored movie contest and dabbled briefly at film school at the University of Southern California. Though stereotyped as a TV actor, he stalwartly sought out movie roles, never making an impact until the amazing sleeper hit *American Graffiti*.

Nothing about the film seemed to hold any promise: It was desperately underbudgeted. The company got tossed from its initial location after the first night and had to forage for another place to shoot. Its inexperienced young director, George Lucas, was chronically uncommunicative and seemed intimidated by his executive producer, a garrulous young wheeler-dealer named Francis Ford Coppola.

When Universal executives saw the first cut of the film, the production chief said it wasn't even good enough to be a TV movie. But it became a huge hit, all of which made a considerable impression on its gawky costar, Ron Howard. While TV seemed like a cozy, sure thing to him, movies were obviously an adventure, a new frontier, and he longed to pursue them.

Like so many other aspiring young filmmakers, Howard found his angel in Roger Corman, the B-picture maker who cranked out films on a dime. It was a typical sell-your-soul Corman deal: Howard could direct a little movie called *Grand Theft Auto* provided he starred in a dreadful Corman movie called *Eat My Dust*. To Howard's astonishment, *Eat My Dust* was a hit by Corman standards, and so was Howard's first directing effort. His career was launched.

I first encountered Howard in the early 1980s, and he struck me as an unlikely auteur—a seemingly bland young man who could perhaps carve out a career directing action movies but who didn't reveal much in the way of passion or intellect. When I was a senior vice president for production at MGM, he and Grazer came to see me to pitch a movie called "Bad Penny." It was a rather downbeat script about divorce, not the sort of material I thought would interest them. At the meeting, Howard spoke earnestly about the project, but even as he analyzed the characters, his still-cracking, post-adolescent Opie voice worked against him. "I want to create a character-driven movie," Howard said, but I decided not to get behind "Bad Penny," and neither did any other studio in town.

Today Howard displays no bitterness about his early rejections. It's all part of show business, he reasons, and he is, after all, a creature of the business. "In all my work over the years, I have tried to stretch my boundaries," he explains, and usually the effort has paid off. *Cocoon* brought him heightened respect for mastering the difficult genre of fantasy comedy. *Willow* was visually striking, and *Backdraft* showed a tougher attack on his material—a toughness that came to fruition with *Ransom*, which became a major hit. More and more, the major stars came to accept him: Tom Cruise in *Far and Away*, Tom Hanks in *Apollo 13*, and Mel Gibson in *Ransom*. It was 1995's *Apollo 13* that brought Howard the most accolades, but though the film received nine Oscar nominations, including one for Best Picture, Howard came up empty. Indeed, at age 45, having directed fourteen movies, Howard has seen the major awards elude him; Hollywood, while respecting his professionalism, seems perplexed about what to make of him.

Howard seems aware of this conundrum but, typically, he manages to put a positive spin on it. "My objective is to reach the point where no script written in town has my name crossed off as a potential director," he says, framing his aspirations within the context of business realities.

Howard understands that some of his films were unrealized. *The Paper,* for example, was a curiously shallow, TV-ish glimpse at big-city newspapering. The only failure that seems to stick in his craw, however, is *Far and Away,* a rather florid, romanticized period piece in which Tom Cruise, like Howard's grandparents, flees Ireland for the more bountiful opportunities of the New World. Embarking on the project, Howard knew Grazer didn't like it—a rare dissent in the partnership. "I honestly thought I'd brought it off," Howard says. "The previews were wonderful, the test scores great, but the critics beat us up something awful."

With *EDtv*, Howard took yet another major chance: making a film he knew would be compared with Peter Weir's remarkable *Truman Show*. *EDtv* was based on a little Canadian French-language movie dealing with a man who volunteers to have his entire life broadcast on live TV. In *The Truman Show*, of course, the Jim Carrey character was unaware of his oddly "public" life. In the Canadian movie, the protagonist understands what's happening but doesn't realize his life is being manipulated by his handlers. In *EDtv*, which is much funnier than both these films, though arguably lighter than air, the hero, played by Matthew McConaughey, is hip to the setup and even starts to relish his celebrity, until it all turns sour.

Howard, who was famous practically before he could walk, acknowledges *EDtv* became a personal film for him. "The yearning to become a celebrity has become the ultimate American dream, even more so than wealth," he says. "As a kid, I had to learn to deal with fame or go nuts. My character in *EDtv* thinks he can deal with it, until he almost goes nuts."

Howard knows his partner is weighing offers to head a studio. While reluctant to surrender what has been a solid working relationship, he declines to push Grazer in one direction or another. "Grazer has been important to Ron," says one studio executive who has worked with them. "There are many occasions when Brian plays the bad guy when it comes to budgets or ad campaigns or editing decisions, a role he's willing to accept so that Ron can remain Mr. Nice Guy, which seems very important to him. It's like a part of Ron is still the kid actor who doesn't want to offend anybody for fear of losing a gig."

It may well be that Ron Howard is what he seems, the executive concedes. This is a suspicion he'd prefer to nurture, but he admits he doesn't really have a fix on Howard, all of which makes me feel better, because, as I stated at the outset, neither do I. Few directors could be described as Mr. Nice Guy. Most have a nightmare temper (like Robert Altman) or a monumental ego (Michael Mann) or are neurotically obsessive (the late Stanley Kubrick) or fiercely monomaniacal (Francis Coppola) or are simply so rich and mythologized (George Lucas) that no one professes to be able to interact with them on a normal human level.

On the other hand, you can sit down and talk with Ron Howard. You can also have a civil conversation with Brian Grazer, who actually expresses interest in those he's conversing with—a trait totally alien to most Hollywood producers.

All of which underscores why I don't really get either one of them. For all I know, both might be Mr. Nice Guys. And about to become enormously rich ones, at that.

—*GQ*, May 1999

. . .

Despite a filmmaking career that's been spotty at best, Mike Nichols has achieved semi-mythic status—at least in New York—and remains the celebrity's celebrity. I talked about this seeming contradiction in a May 1999 column in Variety.

THE MIKE NICHOLS ANOMALY

New York: In unveiling plans last week to build a substantial new studio in Gotham and expand another, the longstanding hope of creating a separate and distinct New York film subculture received a much-needed boost. After all, why should serious filmmakers have to pay homage to Hollywood in order to get their movies financed or gain access to state-of-the-art facilities?

The new soundstages, some hope, might encourage a school of filmmaking that would be idiosyncratically New York—a school dominated by directors like, well, Mike Nichols, who last week received a Lifetime Achievement Award from the Film Society of Lincoln Center.

The darling of the New York press for three decades, Nichols always manages to say appropriately disdainful things about Hollywood and to vow that he never even touches "the trades." Ask Nichols why, and he reminds you that Hollywood directors are afflicted by "a virus," causing them to fret endlessly about how they're perceived and whether they're making as much money as the next guy.

There's a paradox in Nichols' presentation as "Mr. New York," to be sure. The arc of his career closely resembles that of the proto-typical Hollywood director from whom he's so eager to separate himself. He started out propitiously with *Who's Afraid of Virginia Woolf* and *The Graduate* and then got bogged down in a series of high-budget disappointments. In terms of subject matter, Nichols' more recent films have tended to be vacuous (witness *Wolf*) or emotionally frigid *(Primary Colors)*.

Though his price long has been right up there with the most expensive Hollywood directors, he's turned out more than his share of ordinary studio movies like *Day of the Dolphin* and *The Fortune*.

The early Nichols seemed perfectly tuned in to the Zeitgeist with *The Graduate* and *Carnal Knowledge*. The later Nichols seemed most comfortable with glossy farce like *The Birdcage*, which grossed over $100 million.

That doesn't keep Nichols from retaining his status as a New York folk hero, but he never really remained a New York filmmaker.

Nichols' origins in show biz were mythic. When he and his partner in comedy, Elaine May, were still in their twenties, they owned New York. Their skits could ricochet from two teenagers making out to a deft parody of William Faulkner, but they all worked. The team was everywhere, from the *Perry Como Show* to the legendary birthday party for John F. Kennedy at Madison Square Garden at which Marilyn Monroe sang.

Who but Nichols could get away with a spoof of Tennessee Williams in which the "playwright" thus described a character in one of his works: "Raul has committed suicide on being unjustly accused of not being homosexual."

When Nichols and May broke up, a whole generation of fans was grief-stricken, but Nichols could do no wrong as a director, either onstage or onscreen.

The first sign of trouble occurred on the much ballyhooed *Catch-22* when he intellectualized the material and also managed to go way over budget. Suddenly the man who could do no wrong was doing a lot of things wrong.

The late producer Joe Levine made him the highest-paid director in the business, but through much of the '80s and '90s the work was prosaic—*Heartburn, Postcards from the Edge, Regarding Henry, The Remains of the Day.*

Oddly, with all of Nichols' fondness for New York, his movies rarely depicted the city lovingly, as did, say, Woody Allen's. And, unlike Allen, Nichols avoided venturing into the category of "art" films, telling associates that he considered filmmaking "a popular medium"—that meant big budgets and glitzy casts.

Yet even when he stumbled, Nichols' work consistently reflected a keen professionalism. Though his movies were cold, he had a genius for coaxing a stellar performance from an actor. *Primary Colors* was wrong-headed, but the acting was brilliant.

I remember encountering Nichols and his wife, Diane Sawyer, at a noisy party following the Westwood premiere of *Birdcage* and he looked like someone being led into surgery. Never one to project personal warmth, Nichols shook a few hands, but his body language made it clear that this was not his scene.

Yet it's hard to imagine Nichols ever working in the projected Tribeca/Miramax facility at the Brooklyn Navy Yard or in the expanded Silvercup Studios in Long Island City. After all, why should Nichols assume the role of a New York director when he's got a better gig—New York folk hero?

—*Variety*, May 10, 1999

PART VII

OSCARS

Though the Academy Awards figure so importantly in the economics of Hollywood, its arcane rules and prissy regulations can also be a source of frustration. I addressed these issues on November 27, 1995.

OSCAR COULD USE A FEW RADICAL IDEAS

MEMO TO: Arthur Hiller

Everyone's eyes instantly glaze over at the mention of Oscar rules, so let me get straight to the point: The Academy Award ritual has become ossified, Arthur. It's time for a change.

I can already hear the rustle of readers turning the page, so here is Suggestion 1: Why not "open up" the process a bit by revealing the actual voting results? It would be instructive, for example, to know the margin by which *Gandhi*, that 1982 classic of soporific cinema, beat out *ET: The Extraterrestrial* and *Tootsie*—two films that live in everyone's memory. How many members of the Academy voted for the chintzy adaptation of *My Fair Lady* over the mythic *Dr. Strangelove*?

The whole notion of secret votes is kind of old, Arthur. After all, the Academy is a vital organization of professionals; it's not the Knights of Malta.

And that's just the start. In your role as president of the Academy, you've personally put in many long hours to overhaul the loathsome documentary voting process. Now it's time to take the next step by banishing the documentary and short-subject Oscar presentations from the TV show. According to a *Variety* survey, the acceptance speeches of people who make shorts have been consistently longer than the running-time of the shorts themselves. Let them list their family members offcamera!

With Quincy Jones coming aboard as producer, it seems only fair to give him a fighting chance to enliven the proceedings. Last year's groaner came in at three hours and twenty-five minutes, with millions of viewers tuning out toward the end of the show at a time when interest should be peaking. While eighty-one-million people in the U.S. sampled some portion of the ceremony, the audience averaged out at about forty-eight million. Indeed, the show has never achieved the rating it elicited exactly forty years ago when everyone tuned in to find out whether "Marty" would finally find a date.

Whenever a change in Oscar procedures is proposed, Arthur, one can hear the " harrumphs" emanating from Academy directors, who regard themselves as the guardians of tradition. All of us want to keep the dignity of the Awards intact, but I'd still like to ask, what tradition?

We're talking about the Academy, not the Vatican. It was not that long ago that the Oscar ceremony consisted of a combination roast and cocktail party, with the alcohol consumption matching that of a present-day Golden Globes event. Legend has it that Mary Pickford campaigned for an Oscar for *The Taming of the Shrew* by inviting the so-called Board of Judges to tea at her mansion. (The only memorable element in Pickford's *Shrew* was the screenplay credit, which read "Written by William Shakespeare with additional dialogue by Sam Taylor.")

In that era, the event was such a family affair that the first art-direction award went to the man who'd designed the statuette. At the 1931 ceremony, members of the audience were openly sipping from flasks as one nominee delivered a ferocious attack on Prohibition— the only speech that kept everyone awake.

Traditions are made to be broken, and the Academy should start breaking a few that have outlived their time. The Oscar establishment, for example, is fiercely opposed to the serving of cocktails or hors d'oeuvres before or after Oscar screenings.

Come off it, fellas. During the height of Academy season, members should be encouraged to get out of their homes and avoid those seductive videos that the studios send out. Trouble is, there are a lot of movies to see and the electorate is not exactly buoyantly youthful. Hence what's wrong with rewarding voters for coming out of their homes by doling out a few refreshments—how does that "vulgarize" the proceedings?

The Academy this year is again discouraging companies from sending books, soundtrack CDs, music videos, or other items to the membership, on the grounds that a fusillade of "junk mail" is counterproductive. I see the point in all this, but, again, there's also an educational value to some of this material. Recently the music branch insisted film scores and songs be sent to the voters, despite the objections of the Academy directors. As a longtime Academy member myself, I confess to playing the CDs before casting my votes in the music categories.

Spooky Rules

The newly proposed rules governing the ever-fractious foreign-language branch also seem a bit spooky, Arthur. If journalists, representatives of foreign countries, or other sordid individuals are barred from screenings, the process, already viewed with skepticism, takes on an even greater conspiratorial air. Shouldn't we keep our eye on the main objective—namely, to find a way of giving Academy members a chance to vote for what is truly the "best" foreign-lingo picture, not an obscure entry from Outer Mongolia that no one has heard of?

Which brings me back to my first proposal: Tell voters the results of the voting. It was two-time Oscar winner William Goldman who first advanced this notion after last year's show, and his idea was greeted with thunderous silence. His central argument: "We ought to be able to accurately sense the mood of the industry, just as in elections we can sense the mood of the country."

Taking the Fifth

Goldman acknowledged that it could prove embarrassing for someone to finish fifth, but, "After all, it's not fifth out of five, it's fifth out of a choice of hundreds of movies and thousands of actors. What, pray tell, is so terrible about that?"

I think he has a point, Arthur—one that I wish you would discuss with your board. While it might seem insensitive to announce the tallies during the ceremony itself, the results could be discreetly disclosed to Academy members and the press on the following day.

And if one of your fusty board members protests about tradition, ask him a few quick questions. Like, why was the award for best comedy direction abolished? Why were write-in votes banished? Those were once traditions too.

Tell everyone to lighten up a bit, Arthur. This is show biz, after all, isn't it?

—*Variety*, November 27, 1995

.   .   .

Arthur Hiller, a distinguished director and a witty writer, who was president of the Academy at the time, promptly responded with this letter, which ran in Variety *the following week.*

POLITE "NO THANKS" TO OSCAR CHANGES

MEMO TO: Peter Bart

FROM: Arthur Hiller

As the only Academy member in the world with his own paper, you certainly send high-visibility mail, and I read your memo (*Daily Variety*, November 27) with great interest but with some confusion.

This "lighten up" campaign you've been running recently is intriguing. Am I misreading you? It seems to me you're telling us to quit being so damend concerned with ethics, and try to get back to the days when a nominee could stand in the Academy's lobby after screenings and enthusiastically pump hands for votes. Are you saying that Academy members should be no more embarrassed about special-interest blandishments than say, a congressman? Come on, Peter do we really want the vote of those who, as you suggest, would come to the Oscar screenings because we serve cock-tails and hors d'oeuvres as an enticement?

Of course we all realize newspapers might be a little dull, jour-nalistically speaking, if they only wrote articles about how well someone is trying to behave. It's a lot more fun for reporters to write about how the fix is in and the prize is coated in grease. I wish we could be more help with that.

Then I thought: Suppose I wrote you a memo full of advice along the lines of the following:

"Why doesn't *Daily Variety* lighten up on this 'journalistic stan-dards' kick? This is show biz, isn't it, and what's a trade paper doing taking itself so seriously? We're talking about *Daily Variety*, not the *New York Times*.

"Quit mincing around with all this 'two confirmed sources' prissiness and just give us the gossip and innuendo. Take your paper back to the good old days: Issue your reporters a daily ration of rye whiskey and let 'em accept anything up to mid-size sedans from the companies whose movies they're reviewing. Lighten up, Peter."

Does that incline you to relax your standards any? Knowing you, Peter, I'm inclined to doubt it, and I have a hunch that we're not headed down the low road either.

Now, before I take up your primary suggestion, I'll do what I can to respond to some of the other ideas you've volleyed at me.

1. I doubt that we'll be "banishing" any categories of Oscars from the show. We realize that we could boost our ratings by pruning the awards down even further than you suggest, to just five or six categories, but we're not likely to do that either. We like high ratings of course, but the pursuit of them, oddly enough, isn't our highest objective. We're there for Academy purposes on Oscar night. If a category is robust enough to jus-tify its existence (meaning that it's represented in enough the-atrical films), we'll give it an award and we'll give it on the

show. If, like black-and-white cinematography, it essentially disappears from theaters, we'll pull the plug.

2. Hey, which of our "directors" (we call them governors, actually) are the fusty, harrumphing ones? Haskell Wexler, Martha Coolidge, Sid Ganis? Kathy Kennedy, Bob Daly? Which ones? Bob Rehme? Saul Bass? It would help my thinking considerably if you could be more specific in this area of criticism.

I must point out to you that the board doesn't consider itself as the "guardian of tradition"; indeed, as you point out, many traditions have been broken in the past. The purpose of the Academy as you well know is to reward and to nurture excellence. The board is there to guide and enhance that purpose, and most of our Oscar-show producers display a respect for the past and an eagerness to shake things up a bit. (Within limits. I don't expect us to be giving out the Best Picture award first anytime soon.)

3. The Music Branch hasn't "insisted" that scores and songs be sent to our voters. The branch governors made the change, and there was no objection from any other Academy governor.

4. I'm not sure why you think it's "spooky" for us to bar journalists from our Foreign Language voting screenings. The more interesting question is why we ever allowed them into the voting sessions for this category in the first place. We don't do it in other categories, and I don't see many first-person press accounts of jury discussions at Cannes or Venice. Why isn't that spooky?

We're workin' here, and we want to be able to make critical remarks without having them replayed on the eleven o'clock news.

Now then, as for your main proposal, I realize that you're only trying to add some zest to our proceedings, but I honestly think the suggestion of releasing the full results of the Oscar voting is a bad one.

We're not, as you note, the Vatican; on the other hand, we're not a government either. In national and other elections it's useful for the public to know which candidates received how many votes, because one of the candidates is going to end up in charge and it's good for the governing and the governed to know just how strong the mandate is, and how the vote may have been fragmented.

Releasing the vote tallies for the Oscars serves no purpose except as grist for gossip. There already is a regrettable tendency in some quarters to relegate four of the nominees in each category to the status of "losers" after Oscar night, instead of regarding them as recipients of one of the highest honors our industry can bestow. And while I'm sure it wouldn't happen at *Daily Variety*, there's just the teeniest chance that some reporter somewhere would cozy up to a story about how receiving only eighty-nine votes was sure to send a performer's career into a tailspin.

And to what point, really? All of us of course share the curiosity at times about who came in second (especially us nominees), but it's not a curiosity that needs to be slaked. (Following your logic, we could release the full tally of votes at the nominations level too, and then people could see how many of their friends lied about voting for them.) We've always felt that lusting for that information is a little, well, unworthy of us frankly, and in an increasingly vulgar age it's a good feeling, now and again, to do the mannerly thing.

That's just my take on the issue, but I'll do what you suggest and bring the matter before the board. I think I hear someone harrumphing already though.

Looking back over this, I realize that it may seem that I've been less than receptive to most of your well-intentioned suggestions. I'm always honestly glad to receive feedback from members though, and I consider it thoughtfully. Needless to say, I'd welcome further thoughts from you, Peter.

Next time though, a fax would be OK.

Director Arthur Hiller is serving his third term as president of the
Academy of Motion Picture Arts & Sciences.

—*Variety,* December 5, 1995

.   .   .

The victory of The English Patient *and other "art" pictures at the 1997
Academy Awards caused many to wonder whether mainstream studio pictures had become almost irrelevant. That concern spurred the following
hypothetical column, published March 31, 1997.*

BRINGING OSCAR BACK TO LIFE

EDITOR'S NOTE: The following article appeared in *Variety* on
March 25, 2002. It is reprinted here in its entirety.

Network and studio execs alike were exultant over the soaring
ratings and overall public reaction to the Oscar show, which has
staged a remarkable comeback from the doldrums of the past
two years.

Industry leaders attributed this recovery to the decision by
Academy governors in June 2001 to ban in perpetuity the distribution of videos to Oscar voters. This drastic move was made as a
result of the debacle of the 2001 Oscar show, when ratings plunged
an additional thirty percent following the ten-percent dive in 2000,
the lowest in a decade.

A key reason: The five best-picture nominees in 2001 were
all art movies that had a combined world gross of $8 million.
Two of the five had been rejected by Sundance as being too eso-
teric. One was an Albanian coproduction with Sanskrit subtitles
that qualified as an American film because it had been fully
funded by Miramax and shot in the South Bronx, doubling as
war-torn Albania.

Moreover, surveys showed that only two percent of the U.S.
moviegoing public could identify a single nominee for best actor or
actress at the 2001 ceremony. Indeed, three of the ten nominees

were unable to attend the awards show because they couldn't get past security at the Shrine Auditorium.

"The 2001 debacle demonstrated that something drastic had to be done," said Arthur Hiller, who is serving his fourth term as Academy president. "Clearly the videos had to go." The problem was apparent as early as 1997, Hiller said, when a secret study demonstrated that only one percent of Oscar voters had actually seen *Sling Blade* at a theater and only five percent had seen *The English Patient.* Indeed, because of the blizzard of videos, Academy members had essentially stopped going to the movies at all, the study showed.

"The ban on videos is a complete outrage," said Harvey Weinstein, the fiery Miramax boss, after the Academy governors took their action. His indignation was not surprising, since all five of the 1998 nominated pictures were from Miramax.

Weinstein was clearly hedging his bet, however. Nine months ago, Miramax established a new high-end wing to produce expensive, star-driven movies. It's already shooting a $100-million sequel to *The English Patient,* which tells the story of a killer sandstorm in Morocco. Brad Pitt joins Ralph Fiennes and Juliette Binoche in the lead roles (Fiennes' "death" had been misdiagnosed in the first film, it turned out—only his epidermis had died).

Also shooting is *Sling Blade II,* in which Billy Bob Thornton plays a feeble-minded Southern sheriff who blows away a gang of Chinese fundraisers who have taken over the Arkansas statehouse. Robert Redford is cast as Billy Bob's mentor. The projected budget is $150 million.

Miramax's new program of high-end projects theoretically puts the company in competition with its corporate parent, the Disney studio led by Joe Roth. A direct conflict is still a year off, however, because Disney is releasing nothing but animated megapics this year in a clear effort to demolish the new DreamWorks animation slate—a payoff to the well-known feud between Michael Eisner and Jeffrey Katzenberg. The first DreamWorks feature, *The Prince of*

Egypt, grossed only $15 million, opening against a fusillade of four Disney animated pictures with a combined budget of $300 million.

The impact of the video ban was readily apparent at this year's (2002) Oscar show. The winner was an intimate romantic triangle directed by James Cameron, which he did on the rebound from his 1997 disaster picture, *Titanic,* a movie that finally was delivered for $235 million.

Cameron's film had also won at Sundance, making it the first heterosexual love story to win critical approbation there in five years.

All five of the nominated movies at the Academy Awards ceremony this year emanated from major studios—a sharp turnaround from recent trends. Moreover, all five experienced substantial boosts at the box office as a result of their nominations, which seemed to remind studio moguls of the value of making movies that had characters as well as special effects. "For the first time in years, we're looking for pitches with character arcs," said one vice president for development at a major studio. "This is a real change for me. I'm used to looking only for action arcs."

Commenting on the impact of the new rules, Hiller concluded, "Banning the videos seemed like a drastic step, but I am beginning to think it was worthwhile. I actually saw two Academy members paying their way into a multiplex the other day. I hadn't seen that in years."

—*Variety,* March 31, 1997

PART VIII

RANDOM RUMINATIONS

With Hollywood taking a constant beating from the censorship advocates of the far right, publication of the Starr Report, with its R-rated content, prompted the following epistle in Variety *on September 21, 1998.*

FALLOUT FROM THE STARR CHAMBER

A year or so from now, when the various TV and movie versions of the Bill-and-Monica affair start reaching the screen, the same people who are now defending Ken Starr will be condemning Hollywood for vulgarizing our media. The trouble with venal studio chiefs and network heads, they will argue, is that they never consider the plight of the average parent who has to explain things to his kids.

Yet, if you clear away the rhetorical fog, here's the central irony of the Starr Report: It is the righteous right that has now dropped the ultimate pollutants into the nation's media bloodstream. It isn't because of Jerry Springer or Oliver Stone that our children are now educated in the psychosexual uses of cigars or the expansive variations of oral sex. And it isn't because the public demanded to know—polls show that easily two-thirds of the public doesn't want to know the sexual details in Ken Starr's report and doesn't want to see the Clinton videotape that the prosecutor now insists on showing us.

It is because of Ken Starr, not those prurient Hollywood honchos, that the public, against its will, has learned the following weighty details about the presidency:

- Though Monica had oral sex with the president nine times, he never was hospitable enough to reciprocate.

- The president preferred oral sex while leaning against the doorway of his bathroom across from the study because that position eased his sore back.

- Though the president "touched" her on ten occasions, Monica only experienced orgasm twice.

- The couple was so intent on keeping the noise level down that she frequently bit her hand—apparently that's all she bit—in order to remain quiet.

- The president never ejaculated during their encounters, until their last two meetings, because he said he didn't know her well enough.

- Monica kept calling him "handsome," but all she could elicit from him was "sweetie" or "dear."

- Because Monica experienced difficulty with his button fly, the president switched to zippers.

- The president seemed so pleased at receiving a Hugo Boss tie from Monica that he reciprocated by suggesting she insert his cigar into her vagina.

Now, why did Ken Starr, the preacher's son, the Pepperdine paragon, choose to inflict this vital data on the public? To understand his true motivations, perhaps it would be useful to think of Starr not as a prosecutor but as a film director who has come to realize that his movie is in trouble.

To begin with, he has spent four years and $40 million on what is at best a confined, small-canvas story. Not only has he gone over budget, but he's also changed characters and story lines faster than Stanley Kubrick. And despite his overages, he's nonetheless found time during the production to shoot some cigarette commercials. Indeed, his dedication to the tobacco industry is such that one wonders whether this recurrent business with cigars represents an arcane form of product placement.

Finally, panicked that his show won't capture an audience, he's decided to abandon his PG-13 rating and go for the hard stuff. A colleague apparently told him that old director's axiom, "If it ain't good, at least make it graphic."

OK, I can already hear that rustle of dissent among my readers, so let us pause for a moment to let the Starr camp defend its decision. Only by introducing explicit sexual detail, they argue, could they expose the fact that the president perjured himself by indulging in absurd sexual word-games. So intent was the president on hiding these sexual acts that he abused his power in letting aides lie in his defense. It was this cover-up that led the Clinton presidency down the road to what constitutional experts call "high crimes and misdemeanors."

So says the Starr camp, and political orthodoxy decrees that no one disagree with them. It is considered inappropriate to point out that the "cover-up" here involved acts of sex, not acts of treason. As Richard N. Rosenfeld reminds us, the Fathers of our Constitution in 1792–93 decided that Alexander Hamilton, the first secretary of the treasury in George Washington's cabinet, did not commit "high crimes and misdemeanors" when he tried to cover up his own sexual peccadilloes. Hamilton, it seems, not only had a flagrant affair with the wife of a convicted securities swindler, but also helped gain his release from prison provided he kept quiet about the libidinous encounters involving his wife and Hamilton.

But Ken Starr and his followers seemingly are not interested in precedent; they're interested in attention. In the 445 pages of the Starr Report, Whitewater, which started this whole thing, was mentioned only twice while oral sex averaged three or four mentions per page.

And since that document got Starr media attention, he decided to top himself with the Clinton video, whose release is imminent.

The only problem Ken Starr faces is that no one really wants to know. He's like a film director who, having made a movie no one wants to see, now insists on flogging it relentlessly.

Certainly no one can accuse Bill Clinton of bringing much in the way of civility or class to the presidency, but it remained for Ken Starr to force-feed us a media diet of self-degradation.

—*Variety*, September 21, 1998

.   .   .

With an independent-minded electorate voting the issues, not personalities, in the 1998 congressional elections, and remaining stalwart in support of the president despite the noise from the Rush Limbaughs of the media, I took a quick glance at the content of local news shows on November 9, 1998, and asked this rhetorical question: Don't viewers deserve better?

TV NEWS IS A SNOOZE

A local news anchor once confided to me what a jolt it was to cover an election. He was a friendly guy who earned the basic million-plus that seems to be minimum wage for people of his trade and who also regularly enjoyed a few drinks between his 6:00 P.M. and 11:00 P.M. broadcasts.

Elections like last week's were a shock to the system, he said, and it wasn't because of the frenzy of vote-counting or the quick cuts to election headquarters. Suddenly he's not talking about another mugging in the Crenshaw District or a purse-snatching in Venice. There's hard data to review, historic trends to analyze, important newsmakers to interview.

"You don't know what it's like," he told me, "you actually have to think like a newsman!"

I thought of my friend last week as I watched the shell-shocked expressions on some local news anchors as they stumbled through their reportage. Where was the freeway chase to cut to? Where was that weatherman with his idiot smile?

The ratings on local news shows continue to plunge year after year, and it's not hard to figure out why. I kept a list of the so-called "breaking stories" on one 11:00 P.M. news show the other day. A liquor-store robbery was the lead. "A murder is in progress," the anchor said ambiguously before cutting to his man in the field, who didn't seem to know quite what the anchor meant. The next story involved a robbery in downtown L.A., then a piece about the trial of members of an Asian gang, a woman in South Central whose house was rammed by a car, and so forth.

It was the usual menu of mayhem. None of the stories would even make the newspapers the next morning, but for the geniuses who decide what the public is interested in, they were grist for the 11:00 P.M. news.

By any reasonable definition, was any of this news at all? There was one "foreign" story—a piece from Las Vegas (that's overseas to news directors) about an extortion plot. And there was even one story with a business angle: One of the crime victims would have to close his butcher shop as a result of his injuries.

I once had lunch with the news chief of a local TV outlet, and she told me in no uncertain terms, "I give the public what it wants."

Why is it that everyone seems to have twenty-twenty vision when it comes to what the public wants? If there was one thing we learned from last week's election it is that just about every pundit badly misjudged the public.

People aren't obsessed with Monica or impeachment, yet the national news shows OD'd on this story, spouting information, we now learn, that was spoon-fed them by Kenneth Starr's operatives. Not surprisingly, the ratings of the network news shows are dropping even faster than their local counterparts.

In the same vein, the myriad "talk radio" stations popping up all over the country thought they'd found the winning formula by programming a steady diet of Rush Limbaugh wannabes. Only the other day, the clumsy people who run Disney-owned KABC in Los Angeles reinvented their format yet again (they do it about twice a year) with a solid diet of shrill far-right talkmeisters.

But if Limbaugh and his acolytes have had such a sweeping impact as we'd been told, it didn't show up in last week's election returns. The nation is moving to a moderate centrist philosophy in defiance of the radio noise.

If the voting public really cares about health care, education, Social Security, taxes, and other such issues in their community, as the election returns tell us, then why can't local TV news devote at least a modicum of time informing them about these matters? Is it really necessary for every local station to shut down its news coverage every time some poor drunk decides to flee down a freeway? Sure, the O. J. chase was engrossing, but I'm sure even he didn't think he was giving birth to a new TV genre.

The freeway chase has become a metaphor for the extraordinary irresponsibility of local news directors. "We'd love to try something different, but the station managers won't let us," the local TV news chief told me over lunch. Every station has to hold to the same format and cover the same stories or it will catch it from the hierarchy, runs the cry.

That's a pretty poor excuse for news judgment. After reading the election returns, I think the public deserves better.

—*Variety*, November 9, 1998

.   .   .

One of Hollywood's darkest periods occurred during the blacklist days, when careers were jettisoned and many artists literally had to flee town. On May 22, 1995, fifty years after the blacklist made its first appearance, I decided to look back on this wrenching epoch.

DARK DAYS OF THE BLACKLIST

I'm not sure anyone wants to be reminded, but it was just fifty years ago that the era of the blacklist, one of Hollywood's darkest episodes, had its beginnings.

It all got under way rather quietly. A few "fringe" types began knocking on doors at the studios and networks, professing to have lists of writers, directors, and even a few executives who supposedly were Communist Party members. At first they got the cold shoulder. Then, to everyone's surprise, the climate abruptly changed.

Walter Winchell, who in those days had a top-rated radio show, started warning his audience, "Wake up, America, or you and your children will die in your sleep"—a line that sounds like a slogan for today's militia groups. The American Legion began rumbling about a possible boycott of movies that showed a "Soviet bias." Even the *Hollywood Reporter* chimed in with a front-page editorial headlined: "Red Beach-Head!"

Inevitably, publicity-hungry congressmen began sniffing around and a race commenced as to who could start the first hearings about the "Hollywood Reds." The bad times had begun.

In his new book, *The Agency*, Frank Rose relates the sorry saga of the blacklist from an intriguing point of view—that of the taciturn, doggedly nonpolitical William Morris Agency. The prime mission of Rose's book is to trace the ninety-seven-year rise of the agency through the colorful epochs of vaudeville, radio, movies, Broadway, and TV. Throughout its history, the Morris office, as it was always dubbed, proved singularly resilient in accommodating defections or other trauma. It accommodated the incursions of flashier competitors like MCA or CMA. It accommodated the hoods who founded Las Vegas by appointing its own in-house hood who could speak their language. The late Abe Lastfogel, the belligerent bantam who ruled the Morris office for several decades, was convinced he could accommodate the Red-baiters as well. His troops were too busy making deals for pictures and pilots to let this nonsense get in their way.

He was wrong. Indeed, the supremely self-confident Lastfogel was so unaccustomed to being wrong that it threw him into a complete funk. He looked on in utter confusion as industry leaders like Jack Warner and Louis B. Mayer paraded before congressional committees to proclaim their patriotism and denounce the lefties in their midst. "Why doesn't everyone just shut up?" he wondered.

Then events hit close to home. The names of important clients like Judy Holliday, Edward G. Robinson, and screenwriter Ring Lardner Jr. were dragged into the proceedings. The agency's top TV clients, such as Milton Berle, were throwing tantrums because Red channels vetoed potential guests—"You've got to tell these bums to get lost!" Berle told Lastfogel.

In the midst of all this, the unthinkable occurred. Suddenly the self-styled patriots were naming not just clients but employees of the agency, starting with William Morris Jr., the benign, debonair son of the founder who nominally headed the agency. During the war, when Russia and the U.S. had been allies, Morris helped found the National Council of American-Soviet Friendship, and he had retained a strong interest in the Soviet Union as well as a friendship with such prominent left-leaning activists as the late Corliss Lamont. As such, he was clearly grist for the enemies list. So was a man named John Weber, who headed the agency's literary department.

The Morris office was paralyzed. Back in the days of vaudeville, William Morris the First had vigorously fought titans like Albee and Keith when they tried to blacklist clients who refused to play by their rules. But that was business. This was politics—what the hell did the William Morris Agency know about politics?

John Weber made it easy for Abe Lastfogel. He handed in his resignation, packed up his belongings, and left for Paris.

The William Morris Jr. problem was more painful. Lastfogel and Morris had a lengthy meeting in New York. Lastfogel reportedly explained that he hated the blacklist but he hated Communism even more. Morris said he would never do anything to hurt the agency his father had founded and Lastfogel, who had once been the elder Morris's secretary, had built to its present wealth and power.

A terse press release was put out announcing the retirement of William Morris Jr. The newspapers went along with the ploy. *Variety* even added that the move was "in line with a longtime aim to personally lighten his load. . . ." Since Morris had never really worked, there was no load to lighten, but only a few insiders understood the subtext.

Eventually the dark clouds passed. The agency had survived the trauma. Some of its clients had lost their careers and, indeed, some had fled the country, but the agency kept rolling along.

Politics, like MCA, had proved to be just one more temporary interference.

—Variety, May 22, 1995

.   .   .

It is an ancient cliché but, like most, it holds a germ of truth: One of the main lures drawing people to Hollywood is the pursuit of sex. In recent years, arguably, the appetite for money has superseded the desire to get laid, but nonetheless most transactions in Hollywood have a sexual subtext, as I sought to examine in the GQ *of February 1996.*

SEX AS THE ULTIMATE WEAPON

Early last summer, several youngish Beverly Hills socialites decided to throw a surprise birthday party for a friend. They reserved a private room at Jimmy's, a favored haunt for women of their set, then drew up their invitation list of about forty.

This being Beverly Hills, most of the party organizers had ties to the movie industry, so it was with some zeal that they set out to organize the entertainment for their event. After much deliberation, it was decided to invite two of the town's most attractive and expensive call girls to make an appearance. The birthday girl, they knew, liked surprises, so why not give her one?

But what would these women want with two hookers? It was all in the cause of research and information, one later explained. There had been a number of recent mini-scandals of the Hugh Grant variety—the names of several affluent middle-aged men, some from their circle, had turned up in the phone logs of known prostitutes. Since their boyfriends and husbands were straying, why not solicit the theories of trained professionals as to the causes and ramifications?

On the day of the luncheon, several of the guests were taken aback by the "entertainment," but most seemed to settle in with a sort of benumbed fascination. The hookers spoke and answered questions for well over an hour, at the end of which they were accorded generous applause (and a $2,000 stipend) from their audience—women who seemed at once appreciative and apprehensive.

Appreciative of the call girls' candor and self-deprecatory humor, apprehensive because much of the advice they received was as disturbing as it was clinical.

The circumstances of this unusual social event point up the sexual self-scrutiny that has gripped Hollywood as a result of a series of unexpected occurrences. The fallout from the Heidi Fleiss affair is certainly one factor. The arrest of the Beverly Hills madam, with her lists of johns and her telephone logs, had a far more traumatic impact on the Hollywood establishment than most would like to admit. Hugh Grant's encounter with Divine Brown ignited a lot of gossip about several highly placed Hollywood figures whose similar behavior had been quashed in the press. The O. J. media blitz was another factor; a number of notables had not only been golfing buddies of the onetime football star, but had also introduced him to their "party girls."

All this was exacerbated by a manuscript that had been quietly circulating around Hollywood, causing a great deal of nervousness along the way. Called *You'll Never Make Love in This Town Again* (a play on the title of Julia Phillips's *You'll Never Eat Lunch in This Town Again*) and edited by Joanne Parrent, the book was published last month by Dove Books, whose chief is the well-connected Michael Viner, husband of actress Deborah Raffin. It purports to relate the confessions of three hyperactive prostitutes and one party girl who are well-traveled around Hollywood and Beverly Hills. The book names names and also rates clients in terms of endowment, appetite, generosity, and, perish the thought, courtesy. More important, it presents a vivid picture of Hollywood manners and mores from the working girl's point of view.

The net effect of this onslaught is that the showbiz community has been indulging in some serious introspection, as evidenced by the ladies' luncheon at Jimmy's. On one level, the questions are those of simple survival: Why are people doing these things? What can be done about it?

But beyond all this, there clearly are more complex forces at play. The protective structure that existed during the heyday of the studio system has long since been shattered and so have the rules of the "boys' club" that it fostered. The Hollywood of the '90s is more of a corporate state, a toy of the multinational conglomerates who've imposed a new set of rules and standards. It's a whole new playing field. Insofar as the sexes are concerned, however, is it a level one?

Before dealing with this question, I should point out that Hollywood is not so much a microcosm of a typical American community as a gross distortion of one; it is fueled by narcissism and primal appetites.

Men are drawn to Hollywood because they crave money, power, and sex. Similarly, Hollywood tends to attract ambitious women who've been told since childhood that they're beautiful and talented and should use those gifts to good advantage. Bring together men and women with these propensities in an atmosphere of high expectations and you get an environment rife with sexual tension.

Back when the studios ruled Hollywood, its important players were protected by phalanxes of security men and press agents who were astonishingly efficient at suppressing news of peccadilloes. Even when the notoriously indiscreet Errol Flynn spent two days in a state of nonstop sexual congress with an underage girl on his yacht (anchored within swimming distance of Santa Monica), the ring of protection held firm. When Flynn was ultimately arrested for his transgressions, his attorneys got him acquitted and his press agents spread the word that the star had been taken advantage of. The implication seemed to be that behavior of this sort was acceptable from a superstar as a byproduct of his mythic persona.

Denizens of the "studio town" of pre–World War II days would be shocked by Hollywood, the corporate town. In place of the wall of security sycophants, mandates have been imposed—mandates that are alternately defied or deferred to, depending on the circumstances.

Take sexual harassment. Despite all the stern rules and memos, Hollywood studios are experiencing a record number of sexual-harassment complaints, which, on the surface, would suggest that the boys are not behaving themselves. Talk to the human resources executives whose job it is to handle these tricky situations, however, and you realize it isn't that simple. "The bulk of our complaints," confides one woman studio executive, "come either from young men who are being hit on by other men or from secretaries who've been fired because of incompetence and are bent on revenge."

Does this mean the days of the casting couch are over? Hardly. Many women in Hollywood are regularly hit on by men. Many men are also regularly hit on by women or by other men. In my own eighteen years as a studio executive at three different companies, I noticed that tactful "approaches" were made toward me not just by wannabe actresses but by women with scripts to sell, pictures to produce, or projects to package. When I headed a studio that released a war movie called *The Big Red One* (a Samuel Fuller picture that I inherited from the previous regime), three different women sent me packages of bikini underwear bearing the inscription "Home of the Big Red One."

I wasn't morally outraged by this—it's just the way things are in Hollywood, which is full of aggressive men and equally aggressive women. The notion that women are somehow victims of the system is mind-bendingly out-of-date. Men and women alike are all "victims" to the extent that they allow themselves to play out the victim scenario.

To be sure, there are many high-achievers in Hollywood who are simply too obsessed with their work to be either victim or victimizer. "I was at a party a couple of weeks ago," said one bright thirtysomething filmmaker, "and the place was full of hot young agents and studio types—people in their late twenties or early thirties, probably making $500,000 to $1.5 million a year—and they're all hanging out, guys with the guys, girls with the girls, like in high school, most of them fighting to stay awake after another eighteen-hour workday. I couldn't help think, like, these are boring, asexual people, blabbing about their projects or their clients or their goddamn scripts."

One young woman who dates an agent at Creative Artists Agency acknowledged that "my biggest challenge is to try to keep the guy awake when he isn't reading scripts or taking phone calls."

The somnolent libidos of many of Hollywood's young movers and shakers have made it considerably more difficult for people to "fuck their way to the top." Many men who are consumed by their work tend to prefer anonymous sex, even if they have to pay for it— a financial payoff is easier than an emotional one. And this, of course, helps account for the considerable success of Heidi Fleiss, who, as the daughter of an affluent Los Angeles pediatrician, understood the psyches of Hollywood's upwardly mobile. Though her client list included the usual Arab potentates and high-living Eurotrash, she catered to a formidable number of bright young men from the entertainment industry who, one would think, wouldn't need to summon "professional" help.

The women whose diaries make up *You'll Never Make Love in This Town Again* (which is blurbed on the jacket by Gloria Steinem) also grasp these nuances. "It's all about having good sex and not owing anything to anybody," writes one woman. "In the end, like Cher said in her song, 'We all sleep alone.'" While the women's journals reveal a certain tough-minded understanding of Hollywood mores, they also suggest that this understanding was acquired at considerable emotional cost. These women first set foot in this town with an almost simpleminded naïveté that their looks would take them wherever they wanted to go. Two of the girls acknowledge that they were "always drawn to rich and powerful men," as though this were a unique trait, and one contributor, identified only as Liza, admits to succumbing to "the false sense of importance and acceptance" one feels by being around famous people. Yet Liza also expresses her indignation over the time a rock star, upon receiving "some of the best oral sex" available in Beverly Hills, simply zipped up and stalked away without even saying thank you, as though rock stars brushed up on their Emily Post before receiving sexual favors.

All four girls, despite their affinity for the rich and famous, disapprove of most of their johns. One superstar draws bad marks on the grounds of premature ejaculation (no, he didn't get a discount), another because he preferred simply to watch two girls make love (no discount for him either), still another for beating up girls, and another for enjoying "water sports." Most of the wealthy customers are criticized for being cheap, the exception being everyone's favorite, Charlie Sheen, who, the girls state, always paid "$2,000 a pop," plus a generous tip.

All of the contributors to the book seem genuinely surprised, if not outraged, that they ended up alone rather than as wives to the rich men they serviced. As Robin concludes, "Any girl who thinks she can sleep around to get ahead in Hollywood can just plan on getting fucked." Or, as Linda puts it, "In Hollywood people want you when you're young and beautiful. But as the looks fade, so do the good times." No kidding.

Though these girls ended up disappointed, there are instances of women in Hollywood who played their hands more shrewdly. A couple of major stars are married to onetime party girls who proved adept at making their shady pasts disappear.

Similarly, several powerful women in Hollywood—major winners in the game—had affairs with important executives at pivotal moments in their careers and in return received important, well-timed help. These women, to be sure, were by no means hookers; they were already well launched on their career paths and knew exactly what they wanted and how to get it. When I was an executive at one studio, it was an open secret that one of the senior officers of the company—a delightful, if rather homely, little fellow—had a regular Wednesday "nooner" with an attractive young woman whose career he helped foster. That woman went on to a position of considerable importance and affluence.

As Tiffany, one of the contributors, puts it, "Hollywood is the most exciting place in the world if you can keep your wits about you and play the game from a position of control over your mind, body, spirit, and destiny."

Which brings us back to the two prostitutes who lectured the Beverly Hills socialites. They too had a great deal to say about the Hollywood power game—indeed, their level of understanding was far more sophisticated than their audience had anticipated. The speakers also reinforced their listeners' worst fears. Yes, they said, many of their customers were "respectable" married men who regularly looked elsewhere for an evening's recreation.

Why did the men solicit the favors of professionals? For several reasons, the women responded. Some simply wanted good sex. "How many of you women really know what your men want?" one admonished. "How many of you know the tricks of the trade, like how to hold a vibrator against your chin when you're giving head so the guys get an added sensation?"

Some of the johns were also searching for something "different"— most frequently, the chance to make it with two women at the same time, or at least watch. Good sex is really about mind games, the hookers advised. It's about creating a sense of adventure, whether real or imagined. Powerful men feel drawn to adventure—witness Hugh Grant. To showbiz men, the hookers said, the best sex is dangerous sex.

The women listened, attentive and guarded. These were, after all, only call girls—what right did they have to lecture them about making love? Especially in a town like Hollywood, where money is power and the women in the audience had money. But the doubt lingered. Indeed, maybe Cher had Hollywood in mind when she sang, "We all sleep alone."

—*GQ*, February 1996

.   .   .

During the so-called Golden Era, the major studios effectively "managed" the news emanating from Hollywood thanks to their extraordinary control over the news media. In the corporate Hollywood of the '90s, however, the studio PR types often reacted with singular ineptitude to the mini-crises that

confronted them, all of which only further encouraged the attack-dog men-
tality of the press. I tried to analyze the growing tension between the studios
and the press in the May 1995 GQ.

A WALL OF SILENCE

Regrettably, I never got to meet Howard Strickling or Whitey
Hendry, but I've heard a lot about them. Howard and Whitey both
worked at MGM during the banner years of the studio system and,
while they were hardly Thalberg and Mayer, they had an important
role to play in keeping the system on track back in the '30s and '40s.
Strickling controlled MGM's publicity machine while Whitey ran
its private police force, and both operated with a swagger befitting
their epoch.

When a major star from the MGM stable committed an "indis-
cretion"—cross-dressing, smoking dope, or even getting involved in
an occasional murder—Howard and Whitey would spring into
action. Whitey's boys invariably were first on the crime scene to
"tidy things up." By the time the cops and reporters were allowed
access, the official version of what happened had been well-
rehearsed. The transgression had been transformed into a "household incident" or "simple misunderstanding" (on one occasion, a
murder victim magically became a suicide). There would be no
arrest and rarely a story in the paper.

Howard and Whitey would recoil in horror if they witnessed
the way Hollywood handles things today. There are no "fixers"
around anymore to help a celebrity in distress or a movie that has
run aground. Whenever the suits try to intervene, they usually
manage to ignite a firestorm. Where the studios once shrewdly
"managed" the press, today they are engaged in an ongoing battle
with the small army of reporters and editors assigned to cover the
entertainment industry. If Hollywood once functioned with a sort
of clubby conviviality, now there is pervasive fear and loathing.

All of which is astonishing, given that each side is so dependent
on the other. Showbiz companies need the media to publicize their

product and stars in the global marketplace. The publicity is vital because the cost of paid advertising keeps spiraling. The media, meanwhile, need the studios to fuel their articles and TV shows and thus feed the public's seemingly insatiable appetite for news and gossip about Hollywood.

This would seem to be grounds for some sort of creative collaboration, right? Wrong. What prevails instead is a state of war that is at times bewildering; at others, downright hilarious.

To illustrate, here is an example of Hollywood spinmeisters at work and at play.

The Swamp Called Waterworld

With hundreds of millions of dollars flowing in from Steven Spielberg's incredible recent doubleheader, *Jurassic Park* and *Schindler's List*, Universal may have gotten carried away by a sense of giddy invincibility when it decided to move forward with *Waterworld*, a futuristic epic. Special-effects action movies were dominating the world market, it was reasoned. Even as clumsy an effort as *Stargate*, which no company initially wanted to distribute, was packing them in at theaters. Besides, the star of *Waterworld* was Kevin Costner, and who could argue with his success? (After *Waterworld* got its green light, however, Costner came out with a couple of turkeys.)

There were a few concerns, to be sure. The project's initial $100-million budget was formidable enough, but even that figure was highly speculative because much of the filming had to be done on water and would be subject to the exigencies of nature. In addition, the studio could effectively exercise no direct control over the project. The tough-minded Costner had insisted that his close friend Kevin Reynolds be selected as the director. Hence, if the production started to falter, Universal would have little leverage in negotiating with the creative team.

Two weeks into shooting, it became clear that the worst-case scenario was coming true. The seas were hostile, the weather dreadful, and the preparations inadequate. The crew was barely completing half a day's work daily. The $100-million budget was scuttled.

To make matters worse, the press was already clamoring to visit the set. *Waterworld* was shooting in Hawaii, after all, and a location visit could easily be folded into a quick vacation. Moreover, Costner had become embroiled in a nasty divorce, which could spice up a location story.

Faced with this assault, the bureaucrats at Universal went into round-the-clock deliberations. The studio could not afford to let *Waterworld* become a replay of *Last Action Hero,* Sony's 1993 disaster. That production had been so savagely ridiculed by the press because of its runaway costs that the onslaught tainted its reviews, not to mention the audience reaction. The film was ultimately a box-office disappointment that all but paralyzed the studio for more than a year.

What could be done to save *Waterworld* and avoid a similar PR fate? Absolutely nothing, Universal concluded. Anyone asking about the movie or about the budget was given a gruff "No comment." Requests to visit the location were summarily rejected. Any reporter caught infiltrating the set was ordered off by security guards. Here was stonewalling on a cosmic scale.

To be sure, this policy flew in the face of one cardinal principle: When confronted with a wall of silence, the press always creates its own noise. Gossip items soon proliferated. *Waterworld* would end up costing $150 million, per one story, or $175 million, according to another. It would be the most expensive movie in the history of Hollywood, the press chorused. And the script, having already survived six writers and thirty drafts, was still so lame that it was being rewritten day by day by, of all people, Kevin Costner.

The rumors were quickly made respectable by long stories in the *Los Angeles Times* and the *Wall Street Journal.* An informal contest emerged among the media to coin the best epithet for the project. "Kevin's Gate" was one, after director Kevin Reynolds and the famous disaster *Heaven's Gate.* Another was "Fishtar," after the legendary flop *Ishtar,* starring Dustin Hoffman and Warren Beatty.

In my role as editor of *Variety,* I decided to contact Universal with a simple proposal. To fight the rumors, I would dispatch a reporter whose mission it would be to describe the situation objectively and dispassionately. There would be no innuendo, just the facts. Since, after the initial difficult weeks, the production seemed to be proceeding in an orderly fashion, *Variety* would describe how things stood.

The offer was curtly dismissed.

One of my reporters, Beth Laski, a petite, mild-mannered young woman with a disarming smile, decided on more direct action. Vacationing in Hawaii, she checked into the hotel where the *Waterworld* company was housed and introduced herself around. Her hopes of being an ambassador of goodwill were quickly dashed. One crew member tried to push her into the hotel pool. People in the production office instructed hotel switchboard operators not to put through any of her calls. The unit publicist warned her that any effort to visit the set would be dealt with sternly. As for a chance to talk with Reynolds or Costner—forget it.

Waterworld, Laski concluded, had consigned itself to a state of siege. The studio was circling the wagons, hoping that everyone would simply go away.

The old gonifs of Hollywood's vintage years surely were turning in their graves. These self-styled showmen—the Mike Todds and Jerry Walds—took fierce pride in their profligacy. Big budgets were synonymous with spectacle, which, in turn, was synonymous with showmanship.

In the corporate culture of the 1990s, however, the instinctive response is to hide rather than to strut. Universal, after all, is owned by MCA, which is owned by Matsushita, the giant Japanese company. Trapped in this corporate cocoon, *Waterworld* was simply a product that had gone over budget and had thus become an embarrassment.

Next case.

—GQ, May 1995

.   .   .

Whether battling with studios or with the ratings board, Scott Rudin, more than any other contemporary producer, has found a way to get his movies and plays made according to his rules. I attempted to ask him about this prior to a July 1999 column in Variety.

RUCKUS OVER RATINGS GIVES RUDIN A RUSH

I put in a call to Scott Rudin the other day to find out how the producer of *South Park*, among myriad other projects, felt about the ratings wars. Rudin's movie had ricocheted back and forth six times between the ratings gurus and the studio before being blessed with an R rating instead of a dreaded NC-17, thus becoming one of several "hard R" pictures appealing to young audiences during this sensitive post-Columbine period.

Detailed notes of the *South Park* ratings negotiations, the specifics of which would embarrass a longshoreman, have started circulating around town, further fueling the controversy. (Where else would one encounter a debate over the etymological nuances of "rim job"?)

I realized reaching the bear-like, 40-year-old producer would not be easy. When Rudin sits down for a chat he can be great company, since he's an intelligent man with a churlish sense of humor, but no one has actually observed Rudin sitting down for years. In fact, best I can tell, few have actually seen him at all. It's not that he's unfriendly; he just has a lot on his plate.

"Between now and the end of the year, I figure Rudin will be responsible for about six movies and five plays," says one Paramount executive who actually managed to get him on the phone recently. "I don't think even he keeps count." I decided to check that out with Rudin and, sure enough, I got a message the next day that he'd returned my call at 7:00 A.M., which was two hours before either my assistant or I ever get to the office.

My curiosity about *South Park* had heightened after reading notes of the meetings with the ratings board. Exchanges over the so-called "code" are often vivid, if laborious, but in this case the word "fuck" was the mildest expletive cited. The board was clearly alarmed over scatological dialogue covering everything from anal entry to a sex act involving God. The only thing they didn't object to was the double-entendre subtitle: "Bigger, Longer and Uncut," the meaning of which apparently had eluded them.

In view of all this, it's been no surprise that *South Park* has become a hot button at this moment in time. The plot of the animated film concerns young kids who sneak into an R-rated movie and become so caught up in its four-letter lexicon that they can't stop using their new vocabulary. To exacerbate the problem, the co-creators of the film, Matt Stone and Trey Parker, are on record as saying that the reactions of the ratings board were "stupid," revealing "an absence of true standards."

So how in the world was the movie awarded an R? Rudin called me again the next day, presumably to explain. Since he'd placed his call at 6:00 A.M., however, we didn't connect.

"Scott's on a plane to London," an aide later explained. "He knows you'll understand." I did understand. Sort of. I knew he was nursing along at least two new plays: a Stephen Sondheim show called *Wise Guys* and a musical to be directed by George Wolfe called *The Wild Party*. In postproduction were movies directed by Martin Scorsese, Tim Burton, and Curtis Hanson.

"He likes to stay below the radar, but Scott's more prolific than any studio," says one producer who's working with him. "I'd call him a force of nature, except I don't think he likes nature that much."

A studio executive who occasionally deals with Rudin has a slightly different story. "Scott is getting impatient with producing movies," he confides. "Like most producers, he has to come up with at least half the financing for his films, which means he's constantly dealing with subdistributors all over the world."

According to one source, Rudin told a studio chief that, since the studio was putting up only one-third of the financing, he intended to listen to only one-third of its comments.

Did that mean that Rudin, who switched his base to New York five years ago, intended to back away from the movie business? I placed a new call to verify this and, sure enough, the next morning at 5:15 he dutifully returned it. Alas, no one was in.

Rudin's reputed frustration with the process was relevant, of course, given his remarkable track record. In the last decade, he'd had his stamp on about twenty-six movies, ranging from *The Truman Show* to *Ransom*, from *A Civil Action* to *Clueless*. He'd had his hits, like *The First Wives Club*, and also an occasional flop, like the remake of *Sabrina*. On Broadway he'd been a producer of *Indiscretions*, *Hamlet*, *Skylight*, and the Sondheim musical *Passion*.

"Scott loves the opera, ballet, and the theater," explains one associate. "He's become the ultimate New York prince, with a giant apartment at the San Remo on Central Park West."

The prince has his occasional tantrums, to be sure. His tempestuous relations with his assistants are legendary, and last year he became so angered with the handling of a movie premiere that he dispatched a note to a Paramount executive warning: "The only thing separating my hands from your neck is the fact that there are three thousand miles between us."

"Scott's tired of reading about his tirades and even about his success," says someone close to him. "He really only cares about the work. He still gets a rush when he finds a great piece of material. You may not believe this, but he has actually mellowed."

Was Scott Rudin really mellowing? I decided to put in another call to check this out and, sure enough, he returned it—at 4:00 A.M. I hadn't reached my office yet, so I have no idea what he intended to say.

—*Variety*, July 12, 1999

.   .   .

The industry's self-imposed ratings code may have started as a means of liberating filmmakers from the tyranny of local censorship groups, but arguably it's set in place yet another repressive brand of censorship, as I discussed in the October 1999 GQ.

THE RATINGS DON'T RATE

For most filmmakers, the act of running a movie past the industry's censors is akin to that moment in a physical exam when the doctor says "Bend over." Having your film chopped and critiqued seems like a personal assault. Some anonymous outsider with dubious credentials is suddenly empowered to decree which scenes are acceptable and which cross the line, and, most remarkably, no one can explain the ground rules.

The movie industry spends a lot of money each year to persuade people that its ratings are prudent and responsible, but in actuality they're weird and dopey. For instance, if a character says "fuck you," a movie merits a PG-13, but if he says "I want to fuck you," that gets it an R. The mutilated bodies and dripping intestines in *Saving Private Ryan* yielded an R, while coarse language alone brought Martin Lawrence's *You So Crazy* the dreaded NC-17, which is similar to the old X.

The world outside the United States saw the orgy scene in *Eyes Wide Shut* as the director, Stanley Kubrick, shot it. But in this country the actors were partially concealed behind digitally created figures, caped and hooded, who were strategically imposed in front of the action. The "digital adjustment" was mandated to conform to the ratings gurus' crotchety rule that partial nudity and pretend sex are OK, but visible thrusting sends a movie into NC-17 country, even if no genitals are visible and no penetration is portrayed.

Amid the post-Columbine paranoia, ratings have become a hot-button issue across America as new pressure for censorship has emerged from Congress. The self-styled "culture warriors" found it easier to attack Hollywood and speechify about V-chips than to take on the gun lobby. And self-proclaimed moral guardians such as Representative Henry Hyde and Senators Joe Lieberman and John McCain were eager to pin the blame for the undermining of societal values on creators of movies and TV shows.

Of course, Hollywood has seen all this before. As early as 1930, the movie industry signed on to the Hays Code, which mandated, among other things, that husbands and wives sleep in separate beds. Risqué vulgarisms such as "chippy" and "fairy" were banned. Thirty years ago, the code was transmogrified into a new and supposedly more enlightened ratings system.

Replacing the moralistic tyrants of the Hays era was a twelve-member board suggested by PTAs and similar bodies, most of them middle-aged, middle-class parents from California's San Fernando Valley. All that's known about the board members is that they represent a Noah's ark–type cross section—a hairdresser, a cabinetmaker, a repairman, and, of course, the inevitable postal worker, presumably to add some equanimity to the deliberations. The raters serve an average of four years and during that time often evaluate as many as three movies a day. Unbound by the rigid rules of the Hays Code ("promiscuous sex . . . is forbidden"), the raters are by and large free to set their own criteria, however pedestrian.

Whatever its limitations, the present-day code has been successful in achieving its prime objective: It has discouraged the formation of local censorship bodies that would have imposed Bible Belt values on their communities. Proponents of the code, like that ubiquitous lobbyist Jack Valenti, head of the Motion Picture Association of America, would also suggest that the ratings have provided a vital guide to parents and have curbed the excesses of edgy filmmakers by forcing them to play by the ground rules.

All this sounds plausible enough, but in fact it's pure baloney. True, the code has kept local censors off the backs of filmmakers, which is no small achievement, but that represents the sum total of its achievement. Having dealt with the ratings board as both an executive and a filmmaker, I think the whole self-censorship process is egregiously flawed.

A visit to the nerve center of the ratings office provides a vivid metaphor for the innate absurdity of the entire process. It was a few years ago that I made my pilgrimage, but I remember a rather austere building, with offices housing the somber raters who reminded me of school principals waiting to chastise errant pupils. In front of their offices were rows of conservative-looking, if not dowdy, women pounding away on computers. A look over their shoulders revealed that they were hammering out letters to producers, directors, and studio executives listing the changes that would have to be made in their movies to qualify for their desired ratings.

I often wondered what these women told their families over dinner. "I typed cocksucker twenty-four times today, dear," one might say. "And I told those nasty people from *South Park* that it just wouldn't do to have a character say he fucked God in the ass."

Framed communiqués from these ladies and their bosses adorn the offices of filmmakers all over town, representing at once a standing joke and a vivid reminder of the absurdity of the system. By bringing down the number of four-letter expletives from, say, twelve to four, a film may elevate itself from an R to a PG-13 and thus theoretically be opened to a wider audience or satisfy a contractual mandate with a studio. Again, the ground rules are never precise, nor is the playing field even. Independent filmmakers have long protested that the studios have more negotiating clout with the ratings board, a fact that Jack Valenti and his colleagues vehemently deny. Time and again, tough, gritty studio films have landed favorable ratings while independents have been socked with an NC-17. Hence the serious independent movie *Bent* ended up with an NC-17, but the producers of *Boogie Nights,* from New Line Cinema (owned by Time Warner), managed to negotiate an R despite explicit language and the unveiling of the protagonist's penis (albeit a prosthetic version).

The casual moviegoer might well ask, "Who cares?" Do the whims of the ratings board really make any difference to the typical adult buying a ticket at the neighborhood multiplex?

Unfortunately, it makes more of a difference to adults than to the kids, who supposedly are the most affected. Despite the admonitions of the president and Congress, most enterprising kids who wanted to see last summer's hot R pictures—*South Park* and *American Pie*—could simply buy a ticket to *Tarzan* and, at the opportune time, scoot over to the theater playing the restricted movie. Theater owners may refuse to sell R tickets to thirteen-year-olds, but there are rarely security guards in the multiplexes to enforce the strictures. Recognizing this, *Variety* last summer published a facetious box-office chart, comparing the "real" and "surreal" grosses on a particular weekend. One chart listed the announced returns, revealing, for example, that *Tarzan* grossed twice as much as the R-rated *American Pie*. The second counted bottoms in the seats, not tickets sold. The result was that *American Pie* grossed twice as much as *Tarzan*.

"I was in a movie theater last summer when the stampede took place," reports the distribution chief of a major studio. "I'd bought a ticket to *American Pie*, and the theater was almost empty. When the lights went down and the movie started, within two minutes my theater was packed. All these kids had migrated over from *Tarzan*. I checked it out, because that theater was suddenly empty." Most kids will go to great lengths to avoid a G movie, and since two-thirds of all movies are tabbed with an R, they hold the most allure.

Ratings are merely nuisances to the kids, but they can be serious obstacles to adults wanting to see more-serious movies. If a movie is slapped with an NC-17, for example, some of the larger theater circuits won't book it and many major newspapers won't carry its ads. The huge Blockbuster Video chain also won't stock the movie, thus sharply limiting its aftermarket.

There is an enormous hypocrisy behind this restrictive environment. When the Motion Picture Association introduced the NC-17 rating a decade ago, there were promises that this tag would carry a certain respectability. Seminal movies such as *Midnight Cowboy* had once gone out with the X rating and still found wide audiences, but by the mid-'80s the rating had come to be synonymous with porn.

"The advent of the NC-17 was supposed to be a great moment in film history," recalls writer-director Philip Kaufman. "We were getting rid of the old, restrictive code. We were coming up with a new label for adult films that didn't carry the stigma of an X." Kaufman's movie *Henry & June* was the first movie to get an NC-17, and Kaufman soon realized the result. "I was shocked at how quickly everyone backed away and allowed the NC-17 to become the new X," he says.

After Kaufman's debacle, director Todd Solondz elected to release *Happiness* without a rating rather than submit to the indignities of the ratings board. In doing so, he was insisting that the ratings system essentially vulgarized the filmmaking process by mandating that a gesture or a fragment of dialogue in a serious art movie conveyed the same meaning as it did in a big action epic. It seems ridiculously literal-minded to suggest that the appearance of a breast in an arty French-language love story should be judged in the same way as a scene showing bare-breasted bimbos in *Showgirls*. Why should a fleeting shot of a penis in a sensuous romantic movie carry the same weight as if one appeared in *Godzilla*? That's why film critic Roger Ebert proposes the establishment of yet another rating—an A, for adult—that would apply to serious art movies to distinguish them from the more exploitative NC-17s.

In fact, most of the standards supposedly used by the ratings gurus continue to buckle under pressure. *There's Something About Mary* in 1998 ended the semen ban: Suddenly, not only was dialogue steeped in semen jokes but the substance even made its physical appearance as a hair gel. In 1999 a couple of movies, including *American Pie,* erased the stricture against erections. It was now permissible for a character to have a blatant hard-on, albeit well clothed, without incurring an NC-17.

Many filmmakers insist the prohibitions on sexual content are still more stringently enforced than are those on violence, but Jack Valenti disagrees. Last year, says Valenti, 174 movies were given provisional NC-17s for reasons of violence compared with 154 for "sensuality" and language. In virtually every case, to be sure, the violence offenders made their nips and tucks to qualify for an R rating. They eliminated a beheading here, a maiming there, and in some cases simply lowered the body count. The sexual offenders had greater difficulty since, in many cases, the sexual contact was more intrinsic to the story line.

Still, some shrewd accommodations had to be negotiated. On James Toback's upcoming movie, *Black and White*, the excision of an offending elbow turned an NC-17 into an R. When one actress moved her hand into the panties of another, the camera focused on a few strokes of the elbow. Toback tried to appease the board by reducing the number of elbow movements, but he still couldn't elicit his required two-thirds majority. "They indicated the movie would always be an NC-17 as long as the elbow moved," says Hooman Majd, one of the film's producers. Given the fact that the board at no point would explain firm guidelines, he says, "it was a huge waste of time and money." It isn't clear whether Stanley Kubrick volunteered to insert the digitized figures into *Eyes Wide Shut* or whether it was mandated by the studio after his death (he died soon after completing his cut), but a few critics who saw both versions were appalled by the artifice.

The arguments over foul language in *South Park* seemed especially surreal, because they cut to the very point of the movie. The animated movie revolves around several kids who become intoxicated with dirty words after infiltrating an R movie. During one scene, a character advises his friends, "Remember what the MPAA says: 'Horrific, deplorable violence is OK as long as people don't say any naughty words.'" Given this attitude, the movie, without its lexicon of expletives, would be pointless. According to notes from the deliberations of the ratings board, *South Park* spurred some spirited, if bizarre, debates over the meaning and propriety of expressions like "rim job," "fisting," and "cum sucking." Not surprisingly, the board seemed alarmed over a kid's asking, "Mom, if you went down on a horse, you'd let me know, right?"

Interestingly, the original title of the movie was *South Park: All Hell Breaks Loose,* but presumably bending to suggestions of the board, the filmmakers changed the title to *South Park: Bigger, Longer and Uncut.* One of the film's executive producers, Scott Rudin, believes the raters simply didn't get the new subtitle's penile implications, though there's always the possibility they got it but assumed the public would not.

In denouncing the raters as "stupid," Trey Parker and Matt Stone, the creators of *South Park,* followed the lead of Miramax's Harvey and Bob Weinstein and others in gleaning some free publicity from these encounters. The Weinsteins brilliantly capitalized on run-ins with the censors to create a buzz for movies like *Tie Me Up! Tie Me Down!* and *The Cook, the Thief, His Wife & Her Lover.* They even hired a civil-rights lawyer, the late William M. Kunstler, to defend their movie *The Advocate* when it was smacked with an NC-17. "Some ingenious producers have learned that if you bash the ratings system you gain a million dollars in free publicity," says Valenti. He cites LBJ's epigram that "any jackass can kick a barn down, but it takes a damn good carpenter to build one," and clearly sees himself as that carpenter. He points out that despite the criticism, his system has rated more than 15,200 movies and it endures. Research data shows that seventy-four percent of parents with children under thirteen find the ratings system either "very useful" or "fairly useful" in guiding their kids' filmgoing behavior.

Well, perhaps, but at what price? Today's crop of movies has arguably reached an unprecedented level of blandness. The studios, under unrelenting pressure from their multinational parents (Rupert Murdoch and his ilk), are gearing much of their product to teenagers who can be reached through the most cost-efficient media buys. It is left to the independent sector to create and market edgy, character-driven movies—films that all too often seem to get crowded out of the multiplex.

In a new book called *Pre-Code Hollywood,* Thomas Doherty reminds us of the sudden outpouring of daring films with titles like

Merrily We Go to Hell that emerged between 1930 and 1934, at the start of the Depression years—a movement that was brought to a crashing halt when the industry caved before the Legion of Decency's crusade to clean up, as the legion put it, "the pest hole that infects the entire country with its obscene and lascivious motion pictures." Hollywood instantly became spick-and-span, and the anarchic, antiauthoritarian, wisecracking genre faded into the night.

In the post-Columbine hysteria, the House voted on a bizarre amendment that would have authorized the Federal Trade Commission to create a system requiring the labeling of violent movies, video games, and CDs, replete with criminal fines for nonenforcement—a development that Valenti uses to defend his existing system. (The amendment was defeated.) But Valenti knows full well that Congress will always have its culture warriors, whose initiatives will prove both futile and unconstitutional. Fear of these yahoos should not become a weapon that is wielded to promote "voluntary" censorship.

Hence this might be as appropriate a time as any to go cold turkey and abolish the ratings system with all its political artifices. Given the obviousness of movie ads, trailers, and Internet campaigns, it's no mystery for parents to figure out which movies are appropriate for their kids—those few parents who take an interest, that is. And the kids, like the characters in *South Park*, will continue to sneak into whichever movie they wish, or at least buy the video or DVD.

If filmmakers and studios stopped fretting about the impact of nasty little designations such as PG-13, R, and NC-17, all sorts of felicitous things might occur. Kids could file in to see kid pictures once again without being embarrassed over a G rating. There might even be a resurgence of the sort of serious adult movies that marked the decade between 1967 and 1977. It would be gratifying to see another X-rated *Midnight Cowboy* infiltrate the multiplex. I would even go for a rerun of *Merrily We Go to Hell*.

—*GQ*, October 1999

.   .   .

Self-styled culture warriors find Hollywood a much easier target than the gun lobby, but none of their initiatives have a chance in the congress of the courts. I looked at this issue in a June 1999 column in Variety.

THE RHETORIC ON VIOLENCE

The rhetoric on violence in Washington and Hollywood may seem in conflict, but actually there's a shared agenda at work: namely, to lull the public into believing that problems are being addressed when, in reality, they're being ducked.

Indeed, times like this bring out the worst in everyone.

President Clinton says he's gratified that the nation's theater owners will scrutinize kids' I.D.s at the multiplexes, but surely no one believes this will stop a kid from buying a *Tarzan* ticket, only to dart into an R-rated movie like *The Matrix*.

That white-maned oracle, Henry Hyde, is fast-tracking his Children's Defense Act, aimed at banning entertainment for children under seventeen that may contain "gratuitous" or "morbid" violence. That's like waving a red flag in front of a First Amendment lawyer.

While the rhetoric heats up in Washington, Hollywood proceeds as quietly as possible to make its cosmetic nips and tucks. TV episodes are canceled or shuffled around. Scenes in movies are snipped. Development deals are stalled. Titles are softened. Everyone knows that this storm, like those before it, will blow over.

But will it? There's a certain messianic zeal behind the post-Columbine pronouncements that's distressing to those who keep their ears to the ground. In part, it stems from a frenzied desire among politicians to sidestep gun control. But it also taps into the "culture war" that always festers just beneath the surface of our political life.

It's no accident that the Henry Hydes and Joseph Liebermans keep inserting the language of sexual censorship into the violence issue. Representative Hyde (R–Ill.), who has emerged phoenix-like from his impeachment meltdown, wants to ban entertainment containing "the kind of violence that appeals to the prurient, morbid, or shameful interest of children without redeeming social value."

What he's done is substitute the word "violence" for "sex." Senator Lieberman (D–Conn.), too, keeps asserting that Hollywood "doesn't understand piety," as though this were some sort of brand name by which pop culture could be reassessed.

The Bible Belt notion that sex and violence are equally dirty is embedded in the motion picture ratings system, which is much more exclusionary about sexual content than about violence, in contrast to Europe's censorship codes. In the U.S., a movie exhibiting timid sexuality can be relegated to NC-17 hell, while extravagantly violent films escape that fate.

The Hydes and Liebermans want to embrace the same "redeeming social value" measures used on sex, but who is supposed to assess whether *Natural Born Killers* is as "redeeming" as *Saving Private Ryan*? Is Henry Hyde going to be the arbiter of what is or is not "gratuitous"?

The only encouraging element in all this is that, rhetoric notwithstanding, consciences have been stirred. With all the quick-fix changes being applied in Hollywood, a number of executives and filmmakers on the firing line are doing some serious reassessing of marketing materials and are revisiting projects sitting on the assembly line.

Paradoxically, Hollywood, much more than Washington, has become a town of relatively young people raising families and worrying about the influences on their children. "I should be embarrassed to admit this, but in recent weeks for the first time I've begun to think of how my own kids would be affected by the material that passes through my hands," one ad executive told me. "I'm asking myself, do I want to entice them to see this particular show?"

One filmmaker took the time to survey his son's collection of video games for the first time, embracing such cheering titles as "Revenge," "Vigilante," and "Army Men." Inevitably, a serious family conference ensued.

It's this sort of intervention, of course, that carries a lot more weight than the speechifying. In Hollywood, as elsewhere, parents have to get involved. Interest has to be taken.

When a parent stares at his kids and asks himself, "Do I really want to shoot this scene?" that, in the end, is the only workable standard worth embracing. It will have to come from the heart, not from the Bible Belt.

—*Variety*, June 14, 1999

. . .

Even as the rest of the economy continues to boom, Hollywood fights off the impact of its own mini-recession—an economic setback the community seems ashamed to openly acknowledge. I talked about the situation in a May 17, 1999, Variety *column.*

THE SILENT RECESSION

Sometimes Hollywood is too creative for its own good. When price levels were on an even keel throughout the rest of the economy, Hollywood managed to create its own private inflationary cycle with production costs spiraling upward. And now, as economic indicators across the nation continue their resolute surge, Hollywood, ever creative, has manufactured its own private mini-recession.

In some respects, the economic downturn in Tinseltown is following a predictable course. Big companies are downsizing, small ones are merging or going out of business, and cost-cutting is rife.

In its specifics, however, the mini-recession, as with everything else in Hollywood, has veered away from classic economic models.

For one thing, this mini-recession is oddly surreptitious, as though people feel it will go away if no one talks about it. "I can't recall a time when so many of my clients were secretly putting their homes on the market and cutting back on their spending," observes one of the town's top attorneys.

One below-the-line artisan, who has always worked steadily and earns a sturdy six-figure income, told me, "I get calls from guys I've worked with who chat it up for a few minutes, then finally get around to asking if I know of any jobs around town. They don't want to admit they're hurting, but it usually turns out they haven't had an offer for months."

If the mini-recession is oddly secretive, it also is producing some seemingly contradictory policies that could cause damage long-term.

For example: Studios are fiercely cutting below-the-line expenses, paying less to crews while working them harder. At the same time they're lavishing ever-greater sums of money on superstars, top composers, writers, and the rest of the favored few. The result is an increasing Great Divide between the elite and the working stiffs.

They're also virtually eradicating an entire spectrum of producer and filmmaker studio deals, implicitly relying on squadrons of executives to identify new material and come up with creative ideas for developing and packaging it. "We're redefining the producer as the guy who can produce half the money," says a senior executive at a major studio.

In the midst of the new cost-consciousness, the power struggle between agents and managers seems an unwelcome intrusion. "In the present economy, if a manager demands a big paycheck as a packager or executive producer, it's going to come out of his client's fee," says one senior business-affairs executive. "It becomes the talent's problem."

Faced with the silent realities of the mini-recession, Hollywood denizens are hurting, but they're also adapting. *Variety* has been running an ongoing series of articles about the process of adaptation that reveals some shrewd maneuvers.

For example: Some grips and other below-the-line stalwarts are launching entrepreneurial sidelines, renting equipment to producers at discount prices, thus undercutting the studios while boosting their incomes.

Cinematographers are immersing themselves increasingly in TV, videos, and commercials, mindful of the shrinking opportunities in features.

Producers have stepped up their efforts to come up with matching dollars from everyone from Internet companies to insurance entities in an effort to get their films started and also meet their overheads. The infusion of fresh capital from Europe also has spurred hopes.

Nonetheless, talent agencies and management firms are slicing overhead and shedding marginally productive employees. And a few grizzled veterans are taking early retirement.

All this is being done amid a discreet silence, to be sure. After all, the Hollywood recession is the only one taking place at the moment. Perhaps if everyone will just be quiet about it, maybe the goddamn thing will simply go away.

That's the way things happen in Tinseltown.

—*Variety*, May 17, 1999

.　.　.

Dealings in Hollywood seem to be taking on an increasingly nasty tone, which is either a great psychological release or merely serves to underscore the fear and loathing. I solicited the opinions of a prominent psychiatrist for this May 3, 1999, column in Variety.

RAGE UNLIMITED

The acrimonious Eisner-Katzenberg proceedings are stirring criticism in management circles. It is indecorous, if not downright unprofessional, for CEO types to be battling publicly about pay, perks, and parachutes, it is argued.

However, I was talking the other day with Dr. Ernst Weberschmitt, a noted psychiatrist whose patients include members of the corporate elite, and Weberschmitt sees a hidden benefit in the Disney clash. Senior executives, he points out, live in a state of suppressed rage as a result of the extraordinary pressures of their jobs. It is a healthy exercise, therefore, for two moguls like Michael Eisner and Jeffrey Katzenberg to confront each other and express pent-up hostilities. In short, it's cool to grouse, even in the Mouse House.

Hostility has certainly been on display during week one of the trial as Eisner charged, through his attorney, that Katzenberg hogged credit in the press even though his live-action movies lost money, and was dismissive of Walt Disney's billionaire nephew, Roy. Katzenberg in turn declared, through his lawyer, that Eisner's "personal animus" was behind the entire controversy.

A petulant confrontation between two egotistical hierarchs? Perhaps. But in the view of Weberschmitt, it's also a healthy exercise in blowing off steam.

Indeed, the good doctor suggests that these proceedings could be a model for other prospective face-offs. Under this model, the ever-contentious Bert Fields, who is Katzenberg's attorney, might be repositioned as a sort of Judge Judy, weighing the charges and countercharges as various industry figures confront one another.

Hence Edgar Bronfman Jr. would be able to go head-to-head with Chris McGurk, who defected from Universal last week for the stormy shores of MGM. Under this scenario, Edgar Jr. might call McGurk an "ungrateful cad," adding, "You wanted Polygram International, and I gave it to you. You wanted Working Title, and I got it for you. And now you bail on me?"

To which McGurk might respond, "It's been thirty years since Kirk Kerkorian first bought MGM, and he has yet to have a profitable year, so I figure there's no place to go but up. Besides, you have to take your best shot if you weren't born with a billion bucks in your trust fund."

Yet another set of proceedings could bring Michael Ovitz and CAA's Richard Lovett together for a heart-to-heart. "How could you set out to dismantle the very institution you created?" the earnest Lovett might inquire. "Who's dismantling?" Ovitz would reply. "All through my life, wherever I go, I turn around and find people following me. I even had Michael Eisner following me for a while, until he lost his sense of direction."

Even more valuable would be an encounter involving Garry Shandling and his former manager, Brad Grey, whose trial will commence in a few weeks. According to Weberschmitt, it would be extremely therapeutic for Shandling to quietly tell his onetime friend, "I've always valued you as my manager, but must you also produce all of my shows, collect a packaging fee, own my company, receive a percentage of everything including my dry-cleaning bill, and bill me for dental care?"

Grey, a soft-spoken and eminently reasonable man who never loses his temper, could respond, "Garry, you are an ungrateful piece of shit." That's healthy stuff, according to Weberschmitt.

The problem with Hollywood, the good doctor asserts, is that an excess of suppressed fear and loathing has been allowed to build up. This is what accounts for the increasing number of pitched battles between studios, between networks and station groups, and even between colleagues within individual companies.

Given this phenomenon, Michael Eisner and Jeffrey Katzenberg should be held up as role models—men who are honest about their emotions and healthy enough to vent them in public. "Neither of them will ever need therapy," Weberschmitt says, with a certain regret.

—*Variety*, May 3, 1999

. . .

Though it's easy to target movies and TV shows as contributors to the atmosphere of violence, youths increasingly trawl for inspiration in many other arenas, as the Columbine tragedy underscored. Among the most inscrutable: the Internet. My April 1999 column in Variety *looked at the potential opportunities this new venue may have provided.*

RUNNING THE GOTH GAUNTLET
There was something downright eerie last week about the interplay between the media and the blank-eyed kids in Littleton, Colorado. Eager to escape the grim repetitiveness of Kosovo, the avid anchors streamed to the suburbs of Denver in search of fresh angles and facile explanations for the high school carnage.

On the surface, the results were bountiful. Even MSNBC's puny audience sustained a major jolt as the all-news cable format

again demonstrated its vitality in crisis situations. Second-day ratings bumps also aided *20/20* and *Dateline NBC.*

The overriding problem with last week's saturation media coverage, however, was that it overwhelmed the events. The poignance of
watching teenagers clutched together in prayer was compromised by
the ubiquitous cameras surrounding the scene and the megamillion-
dollar anchors standing by to interrogate the bereaved. The viewer
expected to hear someone shout "cut" at any moment, as the kids
peeled off to deal with prospective agents.

It was the culture clash, however, that rendered the Denver
spectacle particularly surreal. Newsgatherers are most secure when
they can identify a killer who watches *Natural Born Killers* twenty-
four/seven, or at least *The Basketball Diaries,* broken only by a quick
hit of Rammstein. We all know what that portends—another mind
subverted by the nasty detritus of Hollywood.

The nihilistic musings of the two alleged gunmen, Eric Harris and
Dylan Klebold, had more abstruse origins, however. Katie Couric and
her colleagues seemed somewhat disoriented by random references to
Goths or to industrial bands with catchy names like Christian Death
or My Bloody Valentine.

As far as the anchors were concerned, the last Goth newsmakers
attacked the Roman Empire in the third century, and the CNN of
that era called them barbarians.

Well, welcome to the '90s: The "new" Goths represent a rancid
residue of the punk movement of the late '70s that apparently was
late in reaching Denver. For edification, visit such Los Angeles
establishments as Retail Slut. Or, for that matter, scrutinize the black
wardrobe of the Trenchcoat Mafia, the band of retro misfits to which
Harris and Klebold belonged.

As the media celebrities sprinted through their interviews, it
became clear that the usual cliché explanations were no longer relevant. Violent behavior can't be cozily explained away by pointing
to Oliver Stone or TV violence. Not when there are also digital
footprints to scrutinize.

After all, Eric Harris had his own Web page on America Online, where he deposited curious drawings of horned beasts, obscure references to Hitler's birthday, and a recipe for pipe bombs.

He and his pals couldn't pay a visit to Melrose Avenue's Retail Slut, but they nonetheless fostered their own associations in the great no-man's-land of cyberspace, where they extrapolated from the wisdom of Marilyn Manson and drew their own nuances from the lulling sounds of KMFDM—a group whose first performance in Paris reportedly featured the sound of Polish coal miners banging their shovels.

None of this dampened the ardor of Katie Couric, Dan Rather, Peter Jennings, or the other media celebrities assembled in the suburbs of Denver last week. Couric even pushed back her live interview with Monica Lewinsky in New York to languish another day on the Goth scene.

And if honest emotions seemed to wilt in the heat of the TV cameras, no one seemed to be especially embarrassed by it. Not even Charlton Heston, that paragon of the gun lobby, who assured everyone that the National Rifle Association would go right ahead with its annual convention, appropriately set in Denver, but would see to it that the partying was scaled back.

Now, that's sensitivity for you.

—*Variety*, April 26, 1999

·   ·   ·

When it comes to down-and-dirty rudeness, Los Angeles increasingly is emulating the example of New York, as recent encounters illustrated in this April 5, 1999, column in Variety.

THE RUDE MOOD

The other day a producer friend told me about an especially abrasive encounter he'd had with an agent. "Here was this kid in Calvin Klein black who made me wait for half an hour, then kept taking phone calls when I was into my pitch," the producer complained. "His manners were so bad I thought I was back in New York."

Showbiz practitioners, who've long compared the two coasts in terms of manners, or lack of them, seem to agree that agents and studio executives in Los Angeles are fast becoming as rudely dismissive as their eastern counterparts.

The archetype of New York Rude, of course, has long been Sam Cohn, the veteran ICM agent who recently made his exit from that agency's ruling directorate. A stubby man who fancies tattered sweaters, Cohn has always rejoiced in his reputation for not returning phone calls, among other random incivilities.

I once made the mistake of doing Cohn a big favor, for which he thanked me warmly, promising to reciprocate. I'm sure he would have done so, except I could never again get him on the phone.

Brilliant, well-read, and deemed even by friends to be an intellectual snob, the 70-year-old, Princeton-educated Cohn in his heyday represented the likes of Mike Nichols, Meryl Streep, and Woody Allen, plus an assortment of novelists and playwrights, but he suffered fools badly, to put it mildly.

Cohn's macho style was widely emulated in New York and then spread like a virus to Hollywood studios, networks, and talent agencies. "I hear my colleagues talking to people, and I'm shocked," observes one veteran agent. "I remind them that we're in the service business, but they think I'm old-fashioned."

New York Rude has long since become a way of life in that city, to be sure. The current holder of the Sam Cohn trophy is a top literary agent named Esther Newberg who routinely scolds clients, snaps at buyers, and begins many of her sentences with "how dare you."

"Esther returns phone calls, but then she often hangs up on me," says one star client.

Newberg, nicknamed "Lobster" by client Don Imus, presumably because of her tendency to snap at everyone, routinely controls much of the bestseller list with clients like Patricia Cornwell, Carl Hiassen, Leslie Stahl, and Peter Jennings.

"I like her because she never patronizes me," Imus declares, recalling on the other hand that he once introduced "Lobster" to

Donald Trump at a mutual friend's wedding and she promptly unraveled "the Donald" by correcting his bad grammar.

"People who don't know her just see the toughness, but she's a good kid underneath," Leslie Stahl assures us.

But at least one important publisher says simply, "Newberg scares me. If I make an offer she doesn't like, she takes it as a personal affront."

Though abrasive, Newberg has not adopted all of Cohn's traits. Once when I was trying to close a deal with Cohn in his office, he got upset with one proposal and nervously started eating the paper on which he'd scribbled his notes. Newberg doesn't eat paper but gives great snarl nonetheless.

Some associates say Newberg's crusty style stems in part from her involvement in the infamous Chappaquiddick incident that enmeshed Senator Edward Kennedy in scandal. Newberg was one of the five women partying at the compound the night that Mary Jo Kopechne drowned—an experience Newberg later told a reporter had left her "with more lines on my face than you can count." Others dismiss all that, stating simply that Newberg doesn't really intend to be discourteous—"She just doesn't know the difference," as one client put it.

What troubles some denizens of the business is that this style has become standard. Even mid-level studio executives aren't returning phone calls anymore. "There's a nastiness in the air," says one producer with solid credits. "It's like everyone is getting over a really bad night."

One senior agent recalls a time in years past when no one would leave for the night until every phone call was returned. "Now even clients don't get call-backs," he says ruefully.

I tried to ask both Cohn and Newberg whether they agreed with his observation. Neither returned my call.

—*Variety*, April 5, 1999

INDEX

ABOUT THE AUTHOR

Peter Bart is the editor-in-chief of weekly *Variety, Daily Variety,* and its sister publication, *Daily Variety–Gotham Edition.* He spent ten years as a reporter for the *Wall Street Journal* and the *New York Times* before entering the motion-picture industry. He was also a studio executive at Paramount, Lorimar, and MGM/UA, overseeing such influential films as *The Godfather, Harold and Maude, Rosemary's Baby*, and *Being There*. He lives in Los Angeles.